MODERN LANGUAGES IN PRACTICE 7
Series Editor: Michael Grenfell

The Elements of Foreign Language Teaching

Walter Grauberg

MULTILINGUAL MATTERS LTD
Clevedon • Philadelphia • Toronto • Sydney • Johannesburg

Library of Congress Cataloging in Publication Data

Grauberg, Walter
The Elements of Foreign Language Teaching/Walter Grauberg
Modern Languages in Practice: 7
Includes bibliographical references and index
1. Language and languages–Study and teaching.
I. Title. II. Series
P51.G69   1997
418'.007–dc21   97-5030

British Library Cataloguing in Publication Data

A CIP catalogue record for this book is available from the British Library.

ISBN 1-85359-387-7 (hbk)
ISBN 1-85359-386-9 (pbk)

Multilingual Matters Ltd

UK: Frankfurt Lodge, Clevedon Hall, Victoria Road, Clevedon BS21 7HH.
USA: 1900 Frost Road, Suite 101, Bristol, PA 19007, USA.
Canada: OISE, 712 Gordon Baker Road, Toronto, Ontario, Canada M2H 3R7.
Australia: P.O. Box 586, Artamon, NSW, Australia.
South Africa: PO Box 1080, Northcliffe 2115, Johannesburg, South Africa.

Typeset by Archetype IT Ltd, http://www.archetype-it.com
Printed and bound in Great Britain by WBC Book Manufacturers Ltd

Contents

PART I: THE SUBSTANCE OR STRUCTURE OF LANGUAGE:
VOCABULARY, GRAMMAR, PRONUNCIATION

Section 1: Vocabulary

Section 2: Grammar

Section 3: Pronunciation

Preface

I have been concerned with the teaching of foreign languages throughout my professional life — as a teacher, teacher trainer, university lecturer in applied linguistics and examiner. During this time I have read scores of books on the subject and noted that they seem to fall into two distinct categories. Some, though nominally about language teaching, concentrate on an analysis of language and discuss language learning and teaching in very general terms, without taking account of differences between languages and learning situations and without examples from the classroom. Others emphasise pedagogic issues, such as the selection and presentation of material, ways of ensuring pupils' motivation and participation, and how to cater for different abilities, without relating these practical concerns to the nature of language and to the specific features of language learning.

In the present book I have tried to bring the linguistic and the pedagogic aspect together, and to present an integrated description of what is involved in learning and teaching foreign languages in general, and French and German in particular. I examine the features of each of the components or levels of language — vocabulary, grammar, pronunciation, and the characteristics of each of the four skills of communication — listening, reading, speaking and writing. On the basis of this analysis I make detailed suggestions for teaching at different stages of a course, with a large number of examples from classroom practice.

In trying to satisfy the interests of both linguists and teachers it is easy to please neither. Linguists might have welcomed a fuller treatment of the vast research literature on Second Language Acquisition; teachers might have wished for closer attention to the general topics of lesson planning or learner characteristics, or to more specific aspects of method, such as the use of the target language or information technology. In the end I decided that an analysis of what is to be learnt and of what this involves for learners and teachers was fundamental and therefore deserved priority. An educational perspective, which is sometimes ignored by linguists, has also been included.

The book is aimed at teachers, teacher trainers and applied linguists — in that order. To teachers at the beginning of their career it offers a comprehensive introduction to the main aspects of foreign language learning and teaching, an insight into why certain features are easy or difficult to learn, and many practical suggestions. Experienced teachers may appreciate the distinction between different kinds of grammar rules and the different modes of learning that ensue, the analysis of skills, the range of vocabulary teaching activities and the stress on personal involvement. The connection between linguistic description, research on learning and the practice of teaching could form the basis for discussions during initial and in-service teacher training, and the attempt to bring concepts from linguistics into the classroom could appeal to applied linguists.

I have concentrated on French and German, and on the problems which their study poses for English-speaking learners. There is both a theoretical and a practical reason for limiting my focus in this way. I believe that in any discussion of language learning one needs to take account of the specific characteristics of the learners' language and of the target language. More practically, French and German are the two modern foreign languages principally taught in British schools. As a teacher of these languages, I can also feel more confident about my examples than if I had written about foreign languages in general. However I believe that my analysis of language learning and of the language skills would underlie the teaching of other languages too.

Teachers and those who write about teaching are often influenced by the practices of their own country and times. A British perspective may be noticeable in the assumption that pupils start the study of a foreign language aged 11–12, with its implications for classroom activities, and that visits or exchanges across the Channel can be arranged. The communicative approach, widely followed in Britain since the late 1980s and early 1990s, with its topic-based syllabuses, performance objectives and much pupil interaction, forms the background to several suggestions for teaching.

However the book is not tied to a particular approach and quotes several practices from other countries and from other approaches. Teachers still retain considerable freedom in many classroom decisions — what to emphasise, how much or how little to explain or correct, how to respond to the specific needs of a class. This book aims to strengthen their autonomy in a field where methods are often subject to swings of fashion, and to help them make their decisions *en connaissance de cause*.

I wish to express my thanks to several people who have helped me at various times. I owe a particular debt of gratitude to my wife for her constructive criticisms and for overseeing the presentation of the manuscript. I am also grateful to Michael Stubbs for his support over a long period and to Andrew Crompton for checking the accuracy of the pronunciation section. Do Coyle, Derek Green, Paul Meara and Karsten Stephan read major parts of the book in draft form and offered valuable comments. Philippe Lanoë, Ursula and Siegfried Wirth, Marianne Joerg-Keller and her family collected classroom expressions to be used in the Appendix.

Notes on abbreviations

Readers unfamiliar with the British, or more accurately, the English educational scene, may wish to consult the following short glossary of abbreviations used in the text.

APU   Assessment of Performance Unit, operating 1975–90 within the Depart-
             ment of Education and Science. Its remit was to develop methods of
             assessing and monitoring the achievement of pupils at school in several
             fields, including foreign languages.

A-level   Advanced Level Examination, taken at the age of 18+ after a two-year
             course in a small number of subjects, and following good performance
             at GCSE. Schools can choose between slightly different syllabuses drawn
             up and examined by separate Examination Boards.

DES   Department of Education and Science, the Ministry responsible for
             education in England and Wales. Renamed DfE (Department for
             Education) in 1992 and DEE (Department for Education and Employ-
             ment) in 1995.

GCSE   General Certificate of Secondary Examination, taken at the age of 16+ at
             the end of compulsory schooling and after five years of secondary
             education. Schools can choose between slightly different syllabuses
             drawn up and examined by separate Examination Boards.

MFL Report   The Report on *Modern Foreign Languages for Ages 11 to 16* (1990). It made
             recommendations on attaiment targets and programmes of study in the
             National Curriculum established under the Education Reform Act of
             1988.

Acknowledgements

The author and the publishers wish to thank the following for permission to reproduce copyright material:

Mr E.A.L. Bird: a drawing (Box 9.11) and a poem by a pupil (Box 9.9), distributed at a conference in Leicester, 1993.

Cambridge University Press: an extract from Tranel, 1987: *The Sounds of French* (Box 11.1).

Centre for Information on Language Teaching and Research (CILT): three extracts, from (a) Kavanagh and Upton, 1994: *Creative Use of Texts* (Box 17.1); (b) King and Boaks, 1994: *Grammar! A Conference Report* (Box 4.1); (c) Swarbrick, 1990: *Reading for Pleasure in a Foreign Language* (Box 19.2).

Verlag Moritz Diesterweg GmbH: an extract from Häussermann *et al.*, 1994: *Sprachkurs Deutsch* (Neufassung) 1 (Box 18.2).

Editions Gallimard: an extract from Camus: *La Peste*, in *Théâtre, Récits, Nouvelles*, 1962 (c) (Box 5.1).

Le Français dans le monde: an extract from Blas *et al.*: *Combien ça coûte?* in No. 235, août/septembre 1990 (c) (Box 3.3).

Friedrich Verlag: three extracts from *Der Fremdsprachliche Unterricht*, 1991/3: (a) two poems by pupils in Minuth: 'Freie Texte im Anfangsunterricht Französisch' (Box 18.5); (b) a poem by a pupil in Mummert: 'Kreatives Schreiben im Fremdsprachenunterricht' (Box 18.6).

Her Majesty's Stationery Office (HMSO): two extracts from APU, 1987: *Foreign* Language Performance in Schools (Boxes 8.4 and 8.6) 'Crown copyright is reproduced with the permission of the Controller of HMSO'.

Mr B. Jones: two poems by pupils quoted in a talk in Nottingham, 1991 (Box 19.1).

Verlag Kiepenheuer & Witsch: an extract from Böll in *Und sagte kein einziges Wort, Haus ohne Hüter, Das Brot der frühen Jahre*, 1973 (Box 6.3). 'Abdruck mit Genehmigung des Verlages Kiepenheuer & Witsch Köln'.

Ernst Klett Verlag GmbH: (a) two extracts from Grunwald *et al.*: *Echanges*, Edition longue, Bd 1 (1981) (Box 9.5) and Bd 3 (1984) (Box 9.8); (b) three extracts from Mebus *et al.*, 1987: *Sprachbrücke* 1 (Boxes 6.2, 9.3 and 19.5).

Langenscheidt Verlag: three extracts from Neuner *et al.*, 1983: *Deutsch Konkret* as adapted in Neuner *et al.*, 1988/9: *Deutsch mit Spaß* 4e and 3e seconde langue, Belin (Boxes 9.11, 18.3 and 19.7).

Dr H. Maas: a drawing, published first in *Wörter erzählen Geschichten*, Deutscher Taschenbuch Verlag, and later in Mebus *et al.*, 1987: *Sprachbrücke*, 1, Ernst Klett Verlag GmbH (Box 19.3).

Dr C. Morgan and the editor of *Language Learning Journal* No.10, 1994: a poem by a pupil in 'Creative Writing in Foreign Language Teaching' (Box 18.6). The poem is also printed in Millward and Thompson (eds) 1996: *The Teaching of Poetry: European Perspectives*, Cassell.

National Foundation for Educational Research (NFER): three extracts from APU, 1987: *Foreign Languages Writing* (Boxes 8.5, 8.7 and 8.8).

Norddeutsche Landesbank: a publicity picture reproduced in Mebus *et al.*, 1987: *Sprachbrücke* 1, Ernst Klett Verlag GmbH (Box 19.4).

Professor Dr. G. Neuner: two extracts from 'Spielend schreiben lernen' in *Fremdsprache Deutsch*1/89, Ernst Klett Verlag GmbH (Boxes 18.1 and 18.4).

Oxford University Press: three extracts from: (a) Lightbown and Spada, 1993: *How Languages are Learned* (pp. 86–87); (b) Martineau and McGivey, 1973: *French Prounciation* (Box 11.3); (c) Rivers, 1975: *A Practical Guide to the Teaching of French* (Box 18.7). (All by permission of Oxford University Press.)

Pan Books: a graph from Maddox: *How to study*, as reproduced in Child, 1993: *Psychology and the Teacher* (5th edn), Cassell (Box 2.3).

Mr A.J. Peck: two extracts from Sanderson, 1982: *Modern Language Teachers in Action*, Language Materials Development Unit of the University of York (Boxes 2.1 and 5.3).

Penguin UK: an extract from Crystal, 1986: *Listen to Your Child* (pp. 1–2). Reproduced by permission of Penguin Books Ltd.

Quelle & Meyer Verlag (c): three extracts from Piepho, 1980: *Deutsch als Fremdsprache in Unterrichtsskizzen* (Boxes 3.1, 3.2, 9.4).

Stuttgarter Zeitung: an extract from an article (4.8.1984), reproduced in Mebus *et al.*, 1987: *Sprachbrücke*1, Ernst Klett Verlag GmbH (Box 19.5).

Suhrkamp Verlag: (a) two extracts from Brecht: *Gedichte*, 1964 *Ich will mit dem gehen, den ich liebe* (Band 5: 195) and *Liedchen aus alter Zeit* (Band 7: 51) (p. 21); (b) an extract from Frisch, 1961: *Andorra* (Box 6.3)

Dr R. Weinert: an extract from her unpublished PhD Thesis, 1990: '*A Study of Classroom Second Language Development*' (Box 8.2).

List of Boxes

Introduction

When people say that they are learning about British agriculture or learning to drive, we can estimate what they have to learn by looking to the intended goal. In one case they will be expected to know about climate, soil, crops, the system of land tenure, the place of agriculture in the British economy, etc. In the other they will be expected to control their car when starting, turning, reversing and braking, and to drive with due regard to the safety of themselves and other road users. Learning about agriculture requires the learning of a number of facts and how they interrelate, learning to drive involves the acquisition of a skill.

If one wants to look to the intended goal for foreign language learning and how to reach it, the following excerpt from a book about language development (*Listen to Your Child* by D. Crystal, 1986: 7–9) provides a useful starting point:

Consider Susie.

Susie is 0 years, 0 months, 0 days, and 1 minute old. Life has been quite fraught recently, and there's been a lot of noise about — mainly hers. But now it's time to settle down and take in something of the world around. There is a lot to feel, to smell, to taste, to see and, above all, to hear.

Susie saw nothing of what was going on, in fact, for her eyes were tightly shut for the first few minutes of her birth day. But during that time she had the chance of hearing around her:

- over a hundred utterances, containing in total
- over 500 words, containing in total
- over 2000 vowels and consonants.

They were utterances such as these:

(1) It's a girl, Mrs. Smith!
(2) Oh, isn't she gorgeous!
(3) OK, I've got her.
(4) Put that on there, will you?
(5) You're lovely, you know that?
(6) Another one, please, nurse.

Once she had stopped crying, there was no way she could shut these sounds out — apart from falling asleep (which came half an hour later) or putting her fingers in her ears (which came two years later). That is the peculiar power of sound, compared with vision. You cannot 'shut your ears', as you can 'shut your eyes'.

Susie has evidently been born into an English-speaking community, so, if she stays within it, she will have to learn the grammar, vocabulary and pronunciation of many utterances of this kind. To be precise, if she is going to end up speaking the same language as her parents, she needs to learn the following:

- the 20 vowels and 24 consonants of the spoken language, and over 300 ways of combining these sounds into sequences (e.g. *s + p + r* can be combined in such words as *spring*);
- an adult-speaking vocabulary of around 50,000 words, and an ability to understand the vocabulary of others that may be twice as great;
- around 1000 rules of grammar, which will tell her how to string words together to make acceptable sentences.

If she had been born into any other language community, things would not have been very different.

What has Susie to learn before she can understand and produce utterances like the six that are quoted? Crystal answers by referring in traditional terms to the three components, or levels, that make up language. 'She will have to learn the grammar, vocabulary and pronunciation of many utterances of this kind.' The three components constantly interact with each other. Words are sequenced through the rules of grammar and often conveyed through the medium of speech sounds. Yet each component has its own organisation: different kinds of analysis can be undertaken of the speech sounds and intonation patterns, the vocabulary, grammatical forms and syntactic patterns of English found in the six utterances.

What is noteworthy is that Crystal can follow up his general statement with a quantified specification for each of the three levels. The rules of grammar and the patterns of pronunciation are relatively few and the total is finite, with minor, fairly regular variations, influenced by regional or educational factors. The third level, vocabulary, is open, containing a large number of words for productive use, another large number for receptive use and a further number which varies with the interests and occupation of individual speakers.

To talk about language in terms of pronunciation, vocabulary and grammar means viewing it in terms of *structure*, or *substance*. But there is a second important aspect of language: what it is used for, its *function*.

Most people would say that the function of language is to communicate. This implies that a message is transmitted from a sender to a receiver. Sometimes we use language to give vent to our feelings or to think aloud; neither the poet nor the diarist is overtly addressing anyone. Yet if communication is understood in its widest sense as expressing ideas, emotions, intentions, requests, in speech or in writing, in short as *conveying meaning*, the term will serve.

Even such a small sample as the six utterances illustrates some functions of language: (1) is a statement of fact, (2) expresses admiration; (3) conveys reassurance; (4) is a request or polite command; (5) is as much a way of making social contact; probably accompanied by a smile or gesture, as an expression of opinion; (6) is again a polite but firm request.

The utterances also illustrate some of the subtle and flexible ways in which the structural patterns of language can be used and the various levels can combine to express a particular function. For example, the inversion of subject is commonly found in questions, yet in (2) the negative yes–no question with a falling instead of a rising intonation acts as as an exclamation. In (4) the verb is in the imperative, but the addition of the question form *will you?* softens it into a request. In (5) the second clause *you know that* is formally a statement, but the intonation turns into a rhetorical question. It is clear that there is no one-to-one relationship between form and function.

A further feature of language use is apparent in this excerpt. Even though the snatches of speech are uttered by different people, there is a common context, a situation in which they all participate. This ensures that references to elements in that situation will be readily understood by all, even though they are not fully explicit. People, objects and places are simply referred to by pronouns or adverbs: *Isn't she gorgeous! Put that on there. Another one please.* Here it is the common context that provides thematic unity, but it is a general feature of our use of language that we feel the need to connect the different parts of what we say or write, to produce something which *hangs together*, a coherent piece of discourse or text.

There is a third important aspect of language. The two kinds of knowledge mentioned so far, knowledge of structure and knowledge of how structure is used, are displayed and made operational through the *skills* of speaking, listening, reading and writing. In other words learning a language, whether it be that of the language community into which one is born or that of another, requires both knowledge and the skilled application of knowledge, 'knowing' and 'knowing how'. It is not by accident that in German *kennen* (to know a person) and *können* (to be able) are historically related. Significantly, it is *können* that is used when talking about language: *können Sie Deutsch?* (from now on quotations from French or German will not normally be translated into English).

Those who were present at Susie's birth were probably *speaking* at a rate of 250–300 syllables per minute (Crystal, 1987: 125), and the nurse to whom (6) and perhaps (4) were addressed had to give almost instantaneous proof of her *listening* proficiency. *Writing* is normally not under a time constraint, but *reading* needs to be swift to be efficient. Native readers of English probably took under two minutes to read the Crystal excerpt, normal reading speed being about 250 words per minute (Crystal, 1987: 210).

To sum up: to know a language means to know its structure or system, with its three interrelated levels, to know how this system is used to convey meaning, and apply this knowledge for efficient comprehension and production of spoken and written language. Learning a foreign language means becoming competent in all three aspects.

For a first impression of what this means in practice for English learners one can look at some versions of the six utterances that have served as examples of language use. A small number of native speakers in France and Germany were asked to say what they might expect to hear under similar circumstances:

French

(1) *C'est une fille/(jolie) petite fille/Madame Dupont.*
(2) *Oh, (regardez) comme elle est mignonne/adorable! Qu'est-ce qu'elle est mignonne! Elle est vraiment mignonne/ravissante!*
(3) *(C'est) bon, je la tiens (bien).*
(4) *Mettez/posez ça/cela là/là bas, voulez-vous (bien)/si vous voulez bien/s'il vous plaît.*
(5) *Tu es ravissante/belle, tu sais? Tu sais que tu es belle/jolie, toi?*
    Quelle jolie frimousse que tu as!
(6) *Encore un(e), s'il vous plaît, Madame Durant/prénom de l'infirmière.*

German

(1) *Es ist ein Mädchen, Frau Schmidt.*
(2) *Ach, ist die niedlich! Guck mal! Ist sie nicht süß! Wie ist sie süß! Ach, wie niedlich!*
(3) *Gut, ich hab' sie (im Griff). Alles klar, ich halte sie.*
(4) *Stellen/legen Sie das bitte dorthin.*
(5) *Bist du aber süß!*
(6) *Schwester, noch einen/eine/eins/bitte.*

Although these precise utterances might never be called for from English learners, the kind of language used might easily occur elsewhere. It requires learning the following:

- about 20 words, including terms typically used to describe a baby, the actions of holding and placing, and the concept of an additional entity (*encore, noch*);
- some key features of French and German grammar: gender, agreement of adjectives and pronouns, two separate personal pronouns for the addressee;
- a number of sounds not present in English, for example [y] as in *une*, [j] as in *fille*, [ã] as in *encore*, [ç] as in *Mädchen*, [x] as in *noch*;
- ways of expressing admiration and the conventions for addressing a nurse.

Part 1 of the book thus deals with the substance or structure of language: vocabulary, grammar and pronunciation. Each is treated under three aspects: analysis of what is to be learnt, the learning process, teaching approaches.

Part 2 deals with language as modes of communication and a set of skills: listening, reading, speaking and writing.

Part 3 considers more briefly the contribution of foreign language study to education at school.

1 Linguistic Perspectives

The Importance of Vocabulary

In this chapter I look at vocabulary with a focus on language, in the next two chapters I shall focus on the learning process and on teaching approaches.

'The fact is, that without grammar very little can be conveyed, without vocabulary *nothing* at all can be conveyed' (Wilkins, 1972: 111). Many language learners would support this statement. It is meanings we wish to communicate, and meaning is expressed above all through vocabulary. When we hear an unfamiliar foreign language being spoken, it seems to be a continuous stream of sound, with just a few breaks. It is partly our syntactical but primarily our lexical knowledge that enables us to break down the continuous signal into separate stretches and to make sense of them. We use the words we recognise as islands of knowledge, and try to build bridges from one to the other. When it is our turn to communicate, the search for the right word to express our meaning can be intensely frustrating.

The experience of the average learner is confirmed by research evidence. A large-scale study in the UK of the performance of pupils after two years of learning a foreign language identified lexical knowledge 'as the most important factor in a successful performance on all of the assessment tasks' (Assessment of Performance Unit, 1987a: 71). At more advanced levels too, though the grammatical foundations may have been secured, lexical choices continue to present difficulties (Grauberg, 1971).

Criteria for selection

Some selection of vocabulary is clearly necessary. *Frequency* has long been the most important criterion. A computer survey of spoken and written texts in English, amounting to 20 million words, undertaken to prepare the *Collins COBUILD English Language Dictionary*, produced the following data:

- The most frequent 700 words of English constitute 70% of text.
- The most frequent 1500 words constitute 76% of text.
- The most frequent 2500 words constitute 80% of text.

On the basis of these findings, and on the fact that the most frequent words also express the basic meanings of English and are found in the commonest patterns, it has been claimed that a lexical syllabus, organised round the commonest words and the patterns in which they occur, can provide a better guide to the learning of English than a syllabus based either on grammatical categories or on notions and functions (Willis, 1990).

Some writers have suggested that one can identify a *core* vocabulary (Stubbs, 1986; Carter, 1987). Words in it occur both in speech and writing, are neutral in regard to attitudes or formality and can collocate with a wide range of other words. In practical terms, most of the most frequent lexical words belong to the core vocabulary. Even a casual glance at a dictionary shows that words like *partie, passer, prendre* or *haben, halten, Haus* meet all the criteria for membership of core vocabulary.

On the other hand, because of its generality, the core vocabulary may fail to include essential terms in relation to a particular topic. That is why *availability* was added as a criterion in the preparation of *Le Français Fondamental* (Gougenheim *et al.*, 1956), when teams of school children were asked to name the first 20 words that came into their mind when certain topics, such as food, drink or clothing, were mentioned. The Council of Europe project in the 1970s took as its starting point the needs of the learners, the topics on which they would wish to speak, the ideas they would want to express and the settings and situations in whch this would occur. This approach is reflected in *The Threshold Level for Modern Language Learning in Schools* (van Ek, 1976), in the ensuing *Grundbausteine* in English, French, German, Russian, Spanish and Italian, published by the *Deutscher Volkshochschul-Verband* (1980) and in the *Defined Content* syllabuses, specified by the Examination Boards for the General Certificate in Secondary Education (GCSE) in England and Wales.

It is possible that for languages that are more inflected than English additional information on the frequency of person, tense or case occurrence of words would be needed. Yet even without such information, the frequency lists available so far for French and German mentioned earlier, or the ones issued by English Examination Boards, comprising 1100–1400 words, can serve as a useful basis for selection.

The case therefore for concentrating on the key words of the language in the early and intermediate stages of a general language course is strong. It is based both on the facts about language and on the pedagogic principles of utility and economy of effort. I.P.S. Nation, an acknowledged authority in the field of vocabulary learning and teaching, insists on the great distinction that teachers need to draw between 'the *small* number of high frequency words which deserve a lot of attention and the large number of low frequency words which require the mastery of coping strategies' (Nation, 1990).

Aspects of Lexical Development

The size of learners' vocabulary will depend on the length and efficacy of their learning effort. The content will depend on their needs and interests. In some countries a list of words to be learnt by a certain stage is drawn up by official bodies, in others, only broad topics are indicated, with course writers and teachers free to decide on priorities. In either case vocabulary grows slowly.

When a word is met for the first time, the essential information is its *meaning*, *pronunciation* and *spelling*. As the learners' experience of language widens and deepens, their lexical knowledge grows in several ways:

- by learning the relevant words for a new topic,
- by using familiar words in new contexts and with new meanings,
- by learning different forms of a word and principles of word formation,
- by learning how a word relates to others in L2 and to words in L1,
- by integrating lexical with syntactic knowledge,
- by developing an awareness of probable collocations,
- by discovering how some words are associated with particular aspects of national culture.

Topic vocabulary

Any topic can be broken down into sub-topics. In regard to the topic of *health*, for example, a pupil may learn in a gradual progression how to say in the target language that they are unwell or feel pain in a particular part of the body, make an appointment at the doctor's or dentist's and describe their symptons in greater detail, then describe accidents and their consequences, and finally move on to general issues, such as various dangers to health and national health care. As they progress from one sub-topic to other, wider ones, old vocabulary will have to be re-used together with the new.

Multiple meanings

New meanings of words previously met will have to be learnt. Sometimes the basic concept is still visible, sometimes it has been extended in the course of time, perhaps figuratively, sometimes the range of meanings has become so wide that the learner is puzzled. Yet the connection between them is never arbitrary. In the next three examples the extension of meaning shows different degrees of transparency.

Important

In this French word the extension from the basic concept is easily understood:

(1) *(choses) (a) 'qui importe; qui est de conséquence, de grand intérêt' question importante, rôle important; (b) (dans l'ordre quantitatif) 'qui est grand, dont la mesure est grande' somme importante, retard important* (significant sum, considerable delay)

(2) *(personnes) 'qui a de l'importance par sa situation' d'importants personnages* (important people).

Lassen

When German *lassen* is used as a modal verb it is just possible to accept the link between causation, permission and possibility.

(1) *'machen, daß etwas geschieht'* *Die Nachricht ließ ihn erblassen* (The news made him turn pale) *Ich habe mir die Haare schneiden lassen* (I had a haircut)
(2) *'erlauben'* *Warum ließ die Polizei den Dieb laufen?* (Why did the police let the thief go?)
(3) *'möglich, ausführbar sein'* (with reflexive pronoun) *Das läßt sich leicht ändern* (That can easily be changed).

Cadre

In this French word the extension in meaning from *frame* to *executive*, has been very long, though understandable. (Not all the meanings are given here.)

(1) literal sense *'bordure entourant une glace, un tableau, un panneau'* *cadre en bois*
(2) figurative sense (a) *'ce qui circonscrit, et par ext. entoure un espace, une scène, une action'* *cadre agréable* (pleasant setting); (b) *'arrangement des parties d'un ouvrage'* *cadre étroit* (narrow framework); (c) *'ensemble des officiers et sous-officiers qui dirigent les soldats d'un corps de troupe'*; (d) *'personnel appartenant à la catégorie supérieure des employés d'une entreprise'* *c'est un cadre moyen* (he is in middle management).

Forms

Content words, particularly nouns and verbs, as distinct from function words like prepositions, conjunctions or adverbs, have more than one form. *Joue, jouerai, joué*, etc. are all variants of one underlying unit of meaning, for which the dictionary entry would normally be the infinitive *jouer*. (To make the distinction clear, linguists use the term *'lexeme'* for this unit of meaning. In the present book I use the non-technical term 'word' in the sense of *'lexeme'* and 'forms' for the different variants). French and German are more inflected than English. If one were to take any regular French verb in the *-er* class, conjugated with *avoir*, and count how many separate forms there are in the 14 tenses in the active mood, the total would amount to 51 distinct spoken forms, counting for example *aime, aimes* and *aiment* only once, and to no less than 77 distinct written forms. Yet each verbal form in the two languages and, in German, each case form of nouns and adjectives has the same full range of meanings as the underlying word. Lexical competence must therefore include morphological competence.

Word formation

Many words, though constituting one unit of meaning, are derived from simpler ones by the addition of prefixes or suffixes or by some combination of words. Pupils will probably begin by seeing them as single words, although they will gradually learn to distinguish their constituent parts, develop awareness of the main meanings of affixes and of some general tendencies. Students of French will find their task easier: in compound nouns the two terms remain separate, yet linked by a preposition, so that the whole can be grasped, as in *pomme de terre, machine à vapeur*, and many of the affixes in verbs and adjectives are the same as in English. Learners of German face a harder task because one-word compounds are common in all parts of speech. They are often long, containing two, three or more components which may not be easy to recognise.

Affixes in the body of the word can cause problems, as in *'unzuverlässig'* or *'Weisheitszahn'*, and one can easily fail to spot the separable prefix at the end of a clause.

Cultural associations

A number of words met by learners will refer to aspects of native culture which cannot be understood without direct experience or detailed explanation. They may refer to kinds of food, festivities, institutions and their practices, abbreviations, forms of entertainment, historical events or quotations from literature. Here are just a few such terms *flûte, sixième, SMIC; Aufschnitt, hitzefrei, der alte Fritz*. And even some words which would count as belonging to the core vocabulary of both L1 and L2 and superficially have the same meaning evoke different images in their users. 'Bread', *'Brot'* and *'pain'* have different cultural associations.

Relations between words

So far I have looked at words in isolation. Yet the more words one meets, the more one becomes aware of relationships between them. In fact in modern semantics 'the primary focus is on the way people relate words to each other within the framework of their language' (Crystal, 1987).

One of the major discoveries that pupils make in learning a foreign language is that different languages do not always 'parcel up' the external world conceptually in the same way. Take the words for a natural waterway. In English one has in order of size: brook, stream and river. In French there is *ruisseau*, which might correspond to both 'brook' and 'stream', *rivière* and then *fleuve* for a long river, particularly one which flows into the sea. Here therefore the same entity, a river from source to the sea, is viewed according to different criteria in French and in English. Alternatively one finds that in one language some features are considered distinctive enough to warrant a separate word. The American Indian language Navaho has two separate words for the black of darkness and the black of objects like coal. French has a special word for car and train doors, *portière*, distinct from the general word *porte*.

Very soon in their study of French and German, English learners meet instances of such new meaning distinctions. In French, for example, there is the distinction between the general term for time *temps* and that for clock time *heure*, between causing a change of state and the change itself *ouvrir, réveiller/s'ouvrir, se réveiller*. In German, pupils must learn that among verbs of movement they must distinguish between going on foot *gehen* and going by vehicle *fahren* and that adverbs of location are expressed differently according to whether state or direction are involved (*wo/wohin, hier/her*). These and many other conceptual distinctions run counter to ingrained habits of thought, and English pupils may need reminding of some distinctions made in English and not in French or German, as between, for example, *house* and *home*, or *umpire* and *referee*, or *shade* and *shadow*.

Semantic fields and nuclear constellations

The distinctions previously discussed have been treated in terms of binary contrasts, but they can also be considered within larger sets of words dealing with, say, movement or time or location.

An attempt has been made in modern linguistics to devise a theoretical framework for these word sets. *Semantic field theory* starts from the premise that the vocabulary of a language consists not of a long random list of words, but rather of many interrelated networks between words. These networks are called semantic fields. For example, the semantic field in English of 'seeing' includes: *see, perceive, discern, notice, observe, glimpse, catch sight of, spot.* But 'see' is also a member of another field to do with understanding and including *see, understand, follow, realise, get the hang of, catch on.* And individual members of these fields could be members of other fields. It is in this sense that the vocabulary of a language can be seen as a set of *interrelating* networks.

Many semantic fields take the form of a general word, embodying the basic concept, followed by more specific terms. One might call them *nuclear constellations* round what Stubbs (1986) calls a *nuclear* word from the core vocabulary of the language. An example in French might be the set of related words round the concept of 'cutting' (see Box 1.1).

Box 1.1 The semantic field of 'couper'

couper	cut (general word)
découper	cut into slices (meat), into shapes, cut out (cloth, paper)
hacher	cut into small pieces, chop (meat), mince (vegetables)
sectionner	sever (artery)
tailler	cut to a particular shape, carve (wood), engrave (stone), trim (hedge)
trancher	cut off sharply, sever (head), also fig. discussion
tronçonner	cut into sections, saw (tree trunk, metal bar)

Whether learners meet meaning related words one by one in the course of their experience of the language, or whether they are presented with a set as a whole, they need to develop an awareness of which feature(s) of the basic concept are emphasised in a particular word. These can relate to manner, attitude, level of formality or some other detail. Understanding in what context(s) the word can be used appropriately is a necessary part of that awareness.

Other meaning relations need a brief mention. There is that of oppositeness, of converseness (lend/borrow) and gradability, where terms can be placed on a scale, by size, speed or, perhaps most usefully, by value judgements from very positive to very negative.

Words also occur in larger *lexical sets*. The relationship within a set may be between a whole and its component parts, or between a specific and a general, superordinate term, so that one can say 'X is a kind of Y', a cart is a (kind of) vehicle. With some of these sets, the term for the whole and for a few of the parts may be sufficient, as with the terms relating to a car, with others it may be more useful to know a few common specific terms than the superordinate: 'boat' and 'ship' rather than 'vessel'. On the other hand some cyclical sets, like the days of the week, or the months of the year, are part of the basic vocabulary, and all the members need to be known.

Contexts and collocations

A distinction needs to be made between these two terms. *Context* refers to the situation in which the word occurs, *collocation* to the habitual co-occurrence of two or more words. *Auspicious* is likely to collocate with *event* or *occasion*, but not with many others. On the other hand core words like *have, find, great* not only occur in almost any context, but have a very wide collocational range. The same applies to their counterparts in French and German, and it is for this reason that it is so important to learn them. Yet another discovery that learners have to make is that even words of similar meaning across languages do not necessarily collocate in the same way. The French *repas* corresponds in meaning to the English *meal*, yet the idea expressed in *repas froid* or *repas à prix fixe* would not be rendered in English by a phrase using *meal* but by *cold buffet* and *set lunch*. It is therefore important that pupils should learn the common collocations for the words they need. In French, for instance, *faire* can be used both with the general word for sport and for individual sports (*faire du sport, faire du tennis*); in German one would use *treiben* for the general word and *spielen* for many individual sports (*Sport treiben, Tennis spielen*). The more fixed a collocation is, the more we think of it as an 'idiom', a pattern to be learnt as a whole and not as the 'sum of its parts'. Idioms can differ, sometimes amusingly, between languages.

Meaning relations between propositions

From good intermediate and advanced students one can expect three further aspects of lexical knowledge. The first involves knowledge of discourse markers, the ability to refer backward or forward and to establish different kinds of logical relations between sentences, of cause and effect, concession, opposition, etc.

The second is based on the fact that in many languages two or more words, formed from the same root, belong to different word classes, but express a related meaning. For example there is an obvious derivational relationship between *kalt, Kälte* and *sich erkälten*, between *hésiter* and *hésitation* or *méchant* and *méchanceté*, even though some sounds or letters may have changed. Knowing the different members of a lexical family greatly enhances one's linguistic flexibility, so that one can say not only *Kaviar schmeckt wunderbar* but also *Der Geschmack von Kaviar ist wunderbar*.

The third involves the use of a metalanguage, by which speakers interpret rather than report what someone else has said or written. It means being able to use verbs like 'criticise, regret, refuse, admit, deny, praise, support'. Thus instead of saying *L'avocat a dit que le témoin avait menti* a student could say more succinctly: *L'avocat a accusé le témoin d'avoir menti* or *d'un mensonge*.

Relations across languages

The relation between the foreign and the native language is probably more important to the learner than any other. Learning a language from a different language family, perhaps with a different sound and writing system and different ways of combining elements within a word, like one of the Arabic or Far Eastern languages, is notoriously difficult. French and German are much nearer to English: 50% of English words are of Romance origin, and over 30% of Germanic origin.

The similarity to French is particularly close. Many core English words, like *hour*, *arrive*, *large* were taken over from French before the end of the 14th century. Many words in French and English in law, literature, science, politics are derived from the same Latin root or have the same Greek prefix, like *auto-* or *poly-*. There is thus a sizeable number of *cognates*, where the similarity of form and generally of meaning facilitates reading comprehension and writing. However, although the existence of these cognates is undoubtedly helpful, their importance must not be overstated. Because of the difference in phonological systems, similarity of form can be a snare in speaking, as the mispronunciation of *Europe* constantly testifies; there are notorious 'false friends', like *actuel* or *librairie*, and words where there is only partial equivalence of meaning, like *important* or *expérience*.

German is, like English, a West Germanic language. One does not need to know the details of the sound shifts that took place in the past to recognise words like *zehn*. *Wasser, haben*. With these cognates, which include some very common words, there are no pronunciation problems, and they are easy to learn. However the reservations made above about deceptive or partial correspondence apply also to German, as, for example, in *bekommen, selbstbewußt, Fleisch*. The difficulty in breaking down a long compound noun has already been mentioned.

In what I have written so far under this heading I have singled out French and German cognates as relatively easy words to understand and learn. However they are in no way as common as those between German and Dutch or between French and Italian. One has to consider the larger number of words in French and German which are not cognates and deal with the assumption that lies behind the question so familiar to teachers: 'What is the French/German for . . . ?' or 'How do you say . . . in French/German?' The learner's assumption is that every word in English is matched by a corresponding word in another language.

There is actually some truth in that belief. As I write these lines and look around me, I can think of a French or German word for every item of furniture in the room. The point that 'chair' has other meanings related to professorships or meetings is not relevant when we talk about furniture: 'chair' is translated by 'chaise' or 'Stuhl' and vice versa. There are also equivalents from the world of emotions or intellectual operations. In some specialised fields, like the sciences, the equivalents are particularly numerous.

Yet side by side with such instances where a word expresses one specific concept only or where the number of meanings and hence the possibility of ambiguity is small, there are also the many instances where, because of the features of language described earlier, the possibility of direct correspondence is limited.

For example, many of the most common words in all languages have multiple meanings, or, put differently, express different concepts. The instances where all the concepts expressed by one word, i.e. its semantic range, are paralleled in the foreign language are rare. English *leave* and French *partir* both express the concepts 'go away, go away from'. But each of them also expresses six or seven other concepts, where there is no correspondence. The different semantic range of *leave* and *partir* is shown in Box 1.2, with correspondence between the two verbs occurring in one instance only, exemplified in *The train is leaving* and *Le train part*. (The data have been taken from the *Collins–Robert English–French Dictionary*.)

Thus, when a learner asks: 'What is the French for "leave"?', one must find out what concept he or she wishes to express.

Box 1.2 The meanings of English *leave* and French *partir* compared

LEAVE	PARTIR
Transitive meanings	*No transitive meanings*
— put, deposit e.g. my keys here (*laisser*)	
— forget e.g. my umbrella (*laisser, oublier*)	
— bequeath e.g. money (*laisser, léguer*)	
— allow to remain open e.g. door (*laisser*)	
— what remains e.g. nothing (*rester*)	
— go away from e.g. town (*quitter, partir de*)	
Intransitive meanings	*Intransitive meanings*
— go away e.g. train =	— *s'en aller, s'éloigner* e.g. train (leave)
	— *aller* e.g. *faire des courses* (go)
	— *disparaître* e.g. *la tache* (go, come off)
	— *provenir* e.g. *du coeur* (come from)
	— *être lancé* e.g. *fusée* (go off)
	— *démarrer* e.g. *moteur* (start)
	— *commencer* e.g. *d'un principe* (start)
	— *être engagé* e.g. *bien* (start off)

Mention was made earlier, through the examples of the waterway, *gehen/fahren* or *porte/portière*, that different languages can make different semantic distinctions. Hawkins (1986) makes the point that semantic distinctions are often explicit in German, but left unspecified in English. He quotes among his many examples *put on* and *take off*, for which German requires more specialised verbs, according to the article of clothing, *anziehen, aufsetzen, anlegen, umbinden, umlegen, anstecken*. By contrast, French often uses general terms where English is more specific: *Où voulez-vous que je me mette?* as against *Where shall I stand?* (Vinay & Darbelnet, 1958).

Thus learners will have to modify their initial assumptions about vocabulary learning. From classifying second language meanings according to the conceptual framework of English, they will have to move towards being able to express their meanings within the semantic network of French or German. It is a process which not only leads to personal satisfaction as communicative powers increase, but also reveals fascinating insights into the nature of words, the way they refer to the world and their relation to each other.

2 Learning Vocabulary: Implications for Teaching

In this chapter I look at vocabulary learning from a psychological angle. I analyse the stages of the learning process, consider some of the factors that seem to facilitate or impede learning and draw some broad implications for teaching, to be worked out in the next chapter.

The process of learning vocabulary involves four stages:

(1) discrimination
(2) understanding meaning
(3) remembering
(4) consolidation and extension of meaning

Discrimination

This is the basic first step. It involves the ability to distinguish sounds and letters from those next to them, and from the sounds and letters of similar words when listening and reading; and to keep them distinct when speaking and writing. As will be seen later, failure to discriminate is a frequent source of error.

Understanding Meaning

This means understanding the concept of the foreign word or phrase. Often this is straightforward because the word can be related to its referent by direct association or because there is an equivalent word in English. Sometimes, as was shown earlier, the concept is unfamiliar.

There are two issues relating to these early stages of the learning process. The first is: *what makes words easy or difficult to learn?*

The factors facilitating learning can be summed up in the word *salience*, those detrimental to it in the word *confusion*. The characteristics of the word and the actions of the teacher can both determine which factor prevails.

One aspect of salience is *clarity of sound*. Beginners tend to store words in their memory according to the sound. Words that are difficult to pronounce are also difficult to remember, and words that sound alike may be confused.

15

Box 2.1 Excerpt I from the tapescript of a French lesson (Sanderson, 1982: 29)

Pupil:	*Il a pensé: Quand le Père Noël entre . . . entrer . . . a . . .*
Teacher:	*Entrera, oui.*
Pupil	*Les livres tombera . . . tomberont.*
Teacher:	*Les livres tomberont . . . oui.*
Pupil:	*et je reverrai . . . je me reverrai*
Teacher:	*Je me . . .* not *reverrai*. Sounds like see again. You know, *je, je verrai*. What can we have? What's the verb: to wake up. *Se . . .*
Pupil:	. . .
Teacher:	*Se réveiller.* So what should she say? *Je . . . ré . . . ré . . . veillerai.*

A second aspect of salience is *clarity of visual shape*. An indistinct visual and auditory shape often go together. In an excerpt from a lesson transcript, reproduced in Box. 2.1, both factors may be contributing to the confusion of a pupil, as she tries, helped by the teacher, to retell a story (Sanderson, 1982: 29):

To the proficient French speaker *reverrai* and *réveillerai* are clearly different, but to a learner they are not!

Faulty discrimination can still cause errors at a fairly advanced stage. In German, with its many prefixes, learners frequently confuse one prefix with another of similar appearance. Among the 102 lexical errors made in an essay by first-year university students of German, 21 were due to similarity with other words, and 16 of these concerned prefixes (Grauberg, 1971). Examples are: *ich hatte mich *beirrt, ich kann nicht absteigen, ich entgegnete eine alte Dame* for *geirrt, aussteigen, begegnete*.

A third form of salience is *stability and regularity of form*. Verbs are more difficult to learn than nouns and adjectives because they occur in so many forms. Regular verbs are easier to learn than irregular ones.

A fourth aspect of salience is *clarity of meaning*. If some vagueness remains about the concept of the word, pupils will be less ready to use it. One reason why cognates are easily learnt is that they can be associated both in meaning and form with a known word in the mother tongue.

Finally a word may gain salience through a personal *association* for the learner. The word may appear funny or striking, or be linked with a certain passage in a text or an event in one's life. One class of beginners remembered *prestidigitateur* for its link with 'hey presto'; for me the word *madeleine* still conjures up Proust's little pastry, dipped in a cup of tea.

The *implications for teaching* are that one should try to promote salience and clarity, and prevent vagueness and confusion. (1) Given the stress on oral work in the first years of a language course, good pronunciation and sharp auditory discrimination become important not only for their role in communication, but also because they aid remembering. (2) If a word is going to be used in writing, special attention may need to be given to its visual shape, the sequence of letters and prefixes. An inexperienced teacher is sometimes surprised to find that varied oral practice does not by itself lead to correct written work. (3) Meaning must be established clearly. With words that have multiple meanings, only a partial explanation may be appropriate at a particular time, but the way should be left open to future extensions. (4) Personal associations should be promoted.

Conversely it is prudent to prevent associations that can blur the semantic identity of a word and lead to confusion in the learner's mind. The use of the same visual aid to teach two different items, the introduction in the same lesson of opposites or two exponents of the same function inadequately linked to examples, or of two verb forms similar in sound yet different in meaning, like *ont* and *sont*, are well known sources of error.

There are two further questions relating specifically to the understanding of meaning. The first one is: *how is new vocabulary to be introduced?*

We do not speak or write through unconnected words. New vocabulary, like new grammar, is presented in textbooks within sentences that make up a coherent, meaningful text. The text often serves as a model for a task that the pupils will be expected to perform themselves later. It constitutes what Willis (1990) calls 'the learner's corpus'. Since the emphasis in school courses at the elementary level is on oral tasks, the text has often been recorded by native speakers to make the model authentic.

The practice of starting a new text by playing the recording is fairly widespread, but it can have disadvantages. It seems appropriate when the meaning can be conveyed at once and unambiguously, perhaps through pictures, but not all words can be represented pictorially, and in any case learners often differ in their interpretation of what they see. At an elementary level they may not yet possess sufficient linguistic knowledge to discriminate accurately or to use contextual clues to guess meaning successfully. That is why a number of writers active in the teaching of German or English as a foreign language (Piepho, 1980, Gairns & Redman, 1986, Nunan, 1989, Nation, 1990) suggest *Vorentlastung* or *pre-teaching* of vocabulary, either in the earlier stages of language learning or when some important words are not easily understood from the context. Pre-teaching means that the teacher selects key items of vocabulary and introduces them through examples, questions and answers or simplified sequences that take account of the abilities, knowledge and interests of the class. Thus prepared, the pupils are better able to understand the recorded text, and *can move faster to model themselves on it.*

There are times too, when silent reading of a text before it is heard allows preliminary recognition of cognates and some grasp of the overall context. When this is followed by selective explanation of key words, pupils are well on their way to understand the recording.

Nothing in what has been written previously should be interpreted as disputing the importance of listening to native speakers, or of developing the skill of gist understanding. My point is simply that in the early stages teachers may sometimes wish to wait before using the recorded text until the ground has been prepared.

At intermediate and higher levels different approaches to the introduction of a text are possible. Sometimes one may wish the text to make an immediate impact and to rely on the pupils' lexical knowledge to recognise which words are important, sometimes a preliminary discussion of a topic prompts from the pupils themselves the realisation that they need certain terms.

The second question concerns *techniques of explanation*. At beginners level the names of concrete objects can be explained through flashcards, drawings and realia, and actions through mime, gesture and simple blackboard drawings. For more abstract items verbal techniques are needed: definitions, examples, synonyms, opposites, placing a word within a lexical set (a kind of . . .) or on a scale. It is important to ensure that the basic concept or differences between words of similar meaning are made clear. For that it is often useful to use more than one technique, provide several examples and even invite learners to suggest their own examples of the word's use. This allows possible misunderstandings to be brought into the open and corrected, and the critical features of the concept to be clarified.

When meaning is conveyed in the foreign language, the pupils' normal reaction, overt or covert, is to produce an English translation. Why then not explain through translation? Translation seems justified with a low-frequency word, or when an explanation becomes too time-consuming or meets incomprehension. Asking the pupils themselves for a quick translation can also be a useful check on under- standing. However the effort to explain as much as possible in the target language is doubly justified, in principle and in practice. First it confirms in pupils' eyes that the target language is a vehicle for communication in its own right, second it demands and receives their full attention. As Gairns and Redman (1986) state: 'In our experience students rarely listen so intently than when they are learning new words.'

Some practical implications flow from this. Teachers need to acquire an armoury of techniques: the ability to use and sometimes to make visuals, perhaps some elementary skills in blackboard drawing, but, most importantly, the ability to explain and define words simply in the foreign language. This needs preparation and practice. It means knowing the central concept of a word and being able to explain it within the lexical resources of the class. Pupils too should gradually become familiar with defining vocabulary and some common superordinates. A few are listed in Box 2.2.

Box 2.2 Some useful terms for definitions

une espèce de	*eine Art*
un objet	*ein Gegenstand*
une action	*eine Handlung/Tätigkeit/Vorgang*
un instrument/outil	*ein Instrument/Mittel/Gerät*
qui sert à, avec lequel	*das man zum . . . braucht, mit dem man . . .*
un endroit où	*ein Ort, in dem*
cela ressemble à un(e)	*es sieht wie ein(e) . . . aus*
cela se rapporte à	*das bezieht sich auf*

Remembering

The next step after introducing and explaining new material is to ensure its retention. Once learners have found out the meaning of a word, they have no reason to attend to it any more, and it will be forgotten. The experience described here by a teacher of French and German, as he struggled with Japanese, must have been shared by very many learners. 'At times I genuinely thought that I had never met a word before and I felt for the teacher who quite clearly knew it had been used in a previous lesson' (Pearson, 1992). In a study of indirect vocabulary learning in context (Saragi *et al.*, 1978) it was shown that, when no active effort was made to learn words, most learners had to encounter them on average 10 times before recognising their meaning. Even more interaction with a word is required before it can be recalled at will.

The explanation lies in the distinction between short-time memory (STM) and long-term memory (LTM). Any new information, whether sensory or verbal, first enters STM, a kind of small anteroom to the vast store of LTM. The capacity of STM is extremely limited, both in the amount that it can store and in the length of time that it can retain the information. Miller (1956) suggested that we are unable to retain more than seven unconnected items at any one time, which seems confirmed by the inability of most people to recall a telephone number of six or more digits, unless it is constantly used. New information quickly displaces the old, unrelated material disappearing faster than meaningful material such as a general principle, or material bonded by a mnemonic or rhyme. Whatever the material, the curve of forgetting is steepest in the first five days after the information has been received. Up to 80% may be forgotten in the first 24 or 48 hours. The graph in Box 2.3 illustrates the rapidity with which different kinds of material are forgotten.

How can learners be helped to learn words?

The graph in Box 2.3 is general in its application. In regard to the learning of vocabulary in a foreign language, Nation (1990) lists three reasons why words are forgotten:

Box 2.3 Curves of forgetting for different types of material (Maddox, 1963)

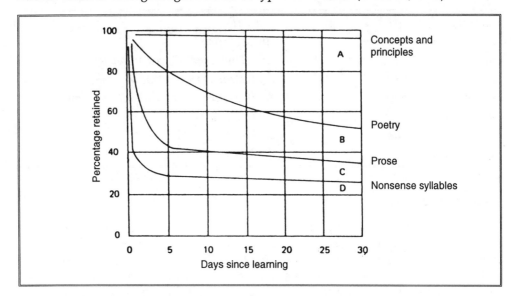

(1) new items are not revised soon enough,

(2) new items are not revised thoroughly enough,

(3) old items are not revised often enough.

There is little doubt that textbook authors and teachers are aware of the need to fix new acquisitions. Peck (1988: 23–63) describes in detail various ways in which teachers observed in different countries set about this task. They may be subsumed under the headings of repetition, by the whole class, groups and individuals, of text reconstitution and, occasionally, of memorization.

One technique about which opinions are divided is the use of *vocabulary lists*. In a review of research on the initial learning of foreign languages, Nation (1982) quotes substantial evidence to show that word pairs can be learnt in large numbers and retained over long periods of time, particularly for recognition. Meara (1980: 225) however issues a warning note:

> Any view of vocabulary acquisition which treats the problem as a simple matter of pairing words with their translation equivalents is an oversimplified one, which cannot adequately account for how semantic networks are built up in the foreign language.

The *Modern Foreign Languages Report for Ages 11 to 16* (Department of Education and Science, 1990), which prepared the ground for the National Curriculum provisions, also criticises the listing together of totally unrelated words. It urges a double strategy: plenty of opportunities to practise and then use vocabulary in realistic situations, where the sheer power of association will aid retention, and, in addition, deliberate learning and re-learning of phrases in a common context (pp. 55–56).

On the other hand it may be argued that a vocabulary list, judiciously compiled, allows concentration on the important words and phrases, and can be followed up by practice in making up sentences in the foreign language, thus building up the necessary semantic networks. A deliberate effort to learn the oral and written forms of a dozen or so words within 24 hours of meeting them can represent the first step towards committing them to LTM. It can also give learners, particularly the younger ones, a sense of achievement, and a feeling that they are in control.

In the end teachers act according to their beliefs and the results of their experience. If they get their pupils to learn from vocabulary lists or, preferably, to make cards with words from L1 and L2 on either side, they know that words learnt in isolation must also be used in appropriate collocations. If they teach words in phrases, they know that words must also become available for use in other contexts.

A brief mention must be made of other techniques to help retention. Visual images, the linking of words to body movements, rhythm and rhyme are well known aids to memorization, but no less powerful for that. Generations of pupils have enjoyed 'comptines' and songs. The two short poems below by Brecht (1964) can appeal to younger and older pupils respectively, and teach language as well.

Eins. Zwei. Drei. Vier.
Vater braucht ein Bier.
Vier. Drei. Zwei. Eins.
Mutter braucht keins.

Ich will mit dem gehen, den ich liebe.
Ich will nicht ausrechnen, was es kostet.
Ich will nicht nachdenken, ob es gut ist.
Ich will nicht wissen, ob er mich liebt.
Ich will mit dem gehen, den ich liebe.

Some learners are helped by the *key-word technique*, whereby a third item, verbal or pictorial, establishes a link between the foreign word and its English equivalent. Pearson (1992: 38) quotes several which he used in order to remember Japanese vocabulary, such as associating the sound of the Japanese word with a familiar English word of quite unrelated meaning *ichi ni* (one two) = itchy knee, or distinguishing related words on an alphabetical basis *asa ban* (morning evening) in that order. He adds however:

Some words defied any of these techniques and were learned only over many regular occurrences. Even where the techniques were applied, many of the words did not remain for more than a few days unless they were encountered, and better still, used.

Echoing the comments of Meara (1980) and of the *Modern Foreign Languages Report*, he continues: 'Ultimately it was seeing the same word in different contexts and making connections with similar words that brought the vocabulary to life and together.'

Finally Stevick (1976: 44) and others urge teachers to bear in mind the importance of personal factors. 'Talking about real objects or events that have nothing to do with long-term needs, either intellectual or practical, esthetic or social, is notoriously unproductive.' What matters is the *depth* of the interaction, the degree of personal involvement in the learning task.

Stevick's remarks are supported by a number of experiments, summarised by Bransford (1979). These show that people recall material more effectively when they have had to restructure or *organise* it themselves, preferably for a purpose of which they approve, than if they have simply had to rehearse or repeat it. Thus pupils asked to rank foods or colours in order of preference, or to draw up a minimum list of clothes to take on a camping holiday, might be expected to achieve better recall than if they had merely to learn a given list of items.

Consolidation and Extension of Meaning

Learning new words is not an instantaneous process — if it were, and if presentation were the only critical variable involved, then words would not be forgotten and need to be relearned. As it is, however, it seems that words are absorbed slowly over time, and that only gradually do they become fully integrated into the learner's personal stock of words, when he can use them with the same sort of fluency that characterizes the words he uses in his native language. (Meara, 1980: 121)

In this quotation, Meara, scholar and researcher, echoes the words quoted earlier of Pearson, teacher turned learner. Achieving lexical command is a slow process. If one tries to analyse this process by relating it to the linguistic description of vocabulary learning of the last chapter, pronunciation and spelling are probably acquired first, after the understanding of meaning, control over morphological forms and syntactic links comes next and full semantic knowledge is last. Here too one can perhaps distinguish three stages, in ascending order of difficulty.

The first is assured grasp of the underlying concept of a word, which is gained by meeting it with unchanged meaning again and again in different contexts, and using it oneself.

The second is growing awareness of the relations into which a word enters with other words. These cover three areas: (1) collocations — the verbs, nouns, adjectives or adverbs one might expect near the word, (2) the variety it belongs to — in regard to medium, formality and attitudes, and (3) its place in a semantic field.

The third is the gradual progress from nebulousness to relative clarity in one's understanding and confident use in regard to words which have a number of meanings, or for which there is no exact correspondent in English. These might include some of the German particles like *doch, ja, freilich* or content words like *préciser, équipements, selbstbewußt, Einsatz.*

Some *implications for teaching* from the sections on remembering and consolidation have already been mentioned. The importance of revision needs to be specially stressed. Nation, as reported earlier, quotes failure to revise old material as one of the main reasons for forgetting vocabulary. Piepho (1980) suggests that in any teaching unit the proportion of old to new material should be two-thirds to one-third. Intervention by the teacher is required in particular when a textbook moves from one topic to another without building on earlier acquisitions or including revision activities.

Revision should offer opportunities to use vocabulary in a context different from the one in which it was first met. Whereas exercises designed for initial learning rightly concentrate on words and phrases relating to a specific topic or function, revision allows acquisitions from different fields to be brought together. The most fruitful material often contains a lot of information, like pictures, contrasting photographs, tables, diagrams, maps. A family tree, for example, offers opportunities to revise family relationships, mini biographies from birth to death, dates and numbers, occupations and locations. The plan of a house can be used to revise not only the vocabulary relating to rooms and furniture, but also spatial and temporal relationships as the visitor is shown round, activities associated with different locations, likes and dislikes, wishes and dreams. It is up to the teacher to decide how to approach the material, which aspects to select, which words and phrases to stress, how much choice to leave to the pupils.

Examples of activities both for initial fixing of new acquisitions and for consolidation will be given in the next chapter.

3 Teaching Vocabulary at Different Stages

In this chapter I describe a number of approaches and activities by which the learning of vocabulary can be stimulated and organised. Drawing on a variety of sources, I shall deal mainly, though not exclusively, with the beginners and intermediate level, with frequent references to the two earlier chapters.

A number of questions arise in connection with the teaching of vocabulary. Some are primarily the business of the textbook writer, although the teacher cannot ignore them. In the early stages of a course, when the foundations have to be laid, grammar, core vocabulary and vocabulary specific to a topic must be taught together. What kinds of situation can provide natural contexts to introduce and practise the particular point of grammar? Once a topic has been chosen, what is the right balance between general and specific vocabulary? The importance of learning core vocabulary has been repeatedly stressed already; on the other hand each topic has its own specific vocabulary. Too little of that reduces the range of what pupils may wish to say, too much increases the learning load unduly. Whatever vocabulary is included by the textbook writer, it will be up to the teacher to decide on the balance between productive, receptive and relatively unimportant vocabulary. Changes will probably be made in that balance between the first encounter with a topic and its subsequent revisions and extensions.

Another question, particularly acute with inflected languages, is how much information to provide when a noun or verb for productive use is introduced for the first time. If the phrase to be used is *je vais au café* or *mit der Linie 5* do pupils also need *le café* and *die Linie* at that stage? The teacher's decision determines how the word is to be introduced and practised.

Having decided what vocabulary to introduce, in what context and what information to give about it, the next question is through what activities the new vocabulary will best be practised. The activities need to be graded so as to build confidence, varied so as to provide repetition, yet maintain attention and interest and, if at all possible, call forth a personal response. As the learners' experience of the language widens, and they can draw on a growing stock of productive and receptive vocabulary, activities can be introduced which begin to throw light on lexical differentiation.

I shall divide vocabulary learning activities into three groups: beginners (the first 2 or 3 years), intermediate and advanced.

Activities at the Beginner Level

These fall into two main groups, clearly related to the stages of the learning process described in the previous chapter. In the first, pupils have to give proof of *discrimination and comprehension*, but are not expected to produce language themselves. Activities in the second group demand *production*, which can be of two kinds: *guided*, when production is steered by pictorial or printed data, or *free*, when pupils make their own choice of what to say. The following is a list of possible activities:

Discrimination and comprehension activities

(1) Repetition

(2) Dictation

(3) Sorting and matching
   Match heard utterance to appropriate picture in set
   Match heard utterance to appropriate written item in a set
   Match pictures and captions from two jumbled sets
   Match questions and answers from two jumbled sets
   Reconstitute words from fragments
   Reconstitute sentences from fragments

(4) Check on understanding without production in L2
   Answer true/false or yes/no questions about the text
   Answer questions on text in English

(5) Transfer of information
   Tick item as it is heard
   Fill in a grid according to information heard or read
   Follow instructions on tape (trace a route, write out an order)
   Fill in gaps on the basis of picture prompts.

Guided production activities

(1) Spoken
   Answer questions on text in L2
   Answer questions in L2 about pictures, photographs, maps
   Role-play on lines laid down by pictorial or printed prompts
   Kim's game (recall objects from memory)

(2) Written
   Fill in crossword
   Write captions under pictures
   Write short texts on given lines and following model.

Free production activities

(1) Speak about oneself, family, hobbies, etc. in answer to questions from partner or from teacher
(2) Ask fellow-pupils about similar subjects
(3) Create dialogue with partner, first spoken then written
(4) Make unprompted statements about pictures or text
(5) Write short texts, with freely created structure.

This list of activities looks schematic and dry, yet it must be borne in mind that the topics change, and it is the interest of the topic and the liveliness of the introductory text(s) that principally determine pupils' motivation. Also, the activities have been analysed and listed in groups, but in any one unit there is normally a progression from discrimination and comprehension tasks to guided and free ones. In fact in many courses a topic is broken down into sub-topics, each of which has a clearly stated objective of what learners should be able to do at the end, and a succession of activities.

Thus in a unit dealing with public transport in a German or French town, there might be separate short sections on how to ask for the best way of getting to a certain destination, what to do about tickets, how to enquire where to get on and off. In each there would be words and expressions to be learnt and practised with different destinations, different means of transport and different boarding and alighting stops.

Topics like using public transport or eating out in a foreign country raise an important question. With such subjects, linguistic knowledge has to incorporate knowledge about the customs of the target country. Gaining this cultural knowledge is an essential part of learning a foreign language, and especially important for learners who are likely to travel to the country. Yet it may be argued that until pupils have had this experience, practice cannot go beyond simulation and cannot engage pupils fully. For that reason in some Eastern European countries, admittedly farther from France or Germany than is the case for Britain, the beginners stage is sometimes set in the home country, with learners talking about familiar surroundings to foreign visitors. One can conceive of a middle way: accept as a main setting the foreign country, for its undisputed motivational and educational interest, but also capitalize on events nearer home or of general interest, if they are likely to stimulate pupils. Thus in a unit on local travel, role-play about journeys in the home area could turn into genuine arguments, with more varied and lively language produced, and opinions about the quickest or cheapest route vigorously contested, because pupils would speak from direct knowledge.

There are other ways by which even beginners with limited vocabulary can be encouraged to produce personal comments about the reality around them. One is through routine notices. Piepho (1980), for example, suggests in Box 3.1 how the well-worn routine of writing the date can be extended, with some pupils writing up the table on the board, and others making up sentences from it.

Box 3.1 Vocabulary extension through routine notices (Piepho, 1980: 130)

Tag	*Freitag*
Datum	*9. Mai 1980*
Wetter	*schlecht, Regen, Sturm*
Geburtstag	*Knuts Vater*
krank/abwesend	*Eva, Henrik*
Hausaufgabe	*siehe 50 : Text umformen*

Possible sentences:
Heute ist Freitag der 9. Mai.
Das Wetter bei uns ist schlecht,
wir haben Regen und Sturm.
Heute hat Knuts Vater Geburtstag.
Es fehlen Eva und Henrik.

Seven pupils can make themselves responsible for preparing something simple about the weather for each day of the preceding week. *War* can thus be used long before it is formally introduced.

Another, widely used device, is to make class surveys and report the results through pie charts or diagrams. The pie chart in Box 3.2 is again suggested by Piepho.

Box 3.2 Vocabulary extension through a pie chart (Piepho, 1980: 129)

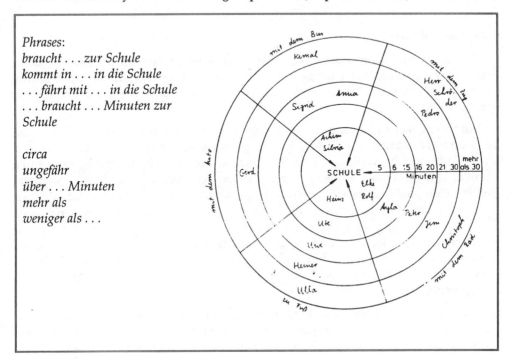

Phrases:
braucht . . . zur Schule
kommt in . . . in die Schule
. . . fährt mit . . . in die Schule
. . . braucht . . . Minuten zur
Schule

circa
ungefähr
über . . . Minuten
mehr als
weniger als . . .

A third, also well-known device, is to invite comments on visual material. This could be one picture or drawing, or two contrasting pictures on the same theme. They may have been drawn expressly to rehearse certain items of vocabulary, while yet allowing scope for an individual perspective, or be authentic photographs, striking enough to provoke a personal reaction.

Another way to tap into pupils' personal semantic network is to put one or two words on the board or on an overhead projector (OHP) and invite pupils to say what they associate with those words. One could imagine interesting responses to the following:

Je pense   *Dans la nuit*

Finally a fruitful, though often underexploited source for communication, is the language of the classroom, expressions used by the pupil when talking with the teacher and with friends (see Appendix).

Activities at the Intermediate Level

After two or three years of a four- or five-year course in school, vocabulary work falls into three categories: revision and consolidation of older acquisitions, addition of new vocabulary and introductory explorations into the way the lexis of the foreign language is structured.

Revision activities

Part of the revision work takes place indirectly. When topics treated rather summarily earlier are taken up again and extended, the older vocabulary is necessarily reworked. If more and/or longer texts are introduced, existing lexical knowledge is strengthened.

But there is need also for direct and systematic revision. Some teachers choose the revision stage to bring together in a list words that have been met over several lessons in connection with a topic or a semantic field, and thus can be related by pupils to a familiar context. Other teachers prefer revision activities with a richer situational content. Composite tables in pictorial or diagrammatic form dealing with, for example, personal details, leisure activities, illnesses with symptoms and remedies, can cover a large amount of language. The different speech acts normally performed in a given situation and a selection of the expressions that realise them can be rehearsed systematically in role play. A role play activity on shopping for clothes can be based on the framework shown in Box 3.3. Under each heading pupils can ring the changes on a number of expressions.

Vocabulary revision can sometimes be made more interesting and increase cultural awareness by comparing data across countries. Personal experiences of pupils who have undertaken an exchange visit or have established contacts with a school abroad

Box 3.3 Example of vocabulary revision (role play on shopping) based on a framework (Blas *et al.*, 1990)

Canevas pour une négociation

1. *Demander un objet précis*
2. *Demander la taille* e.g. *Vous l'avez en 40?*
3. *Demander le prix* e.g. *Il vaut combien ce . . . , c'est en solde?*
4. *Interroger sur la qualité de la matière* e.g. *Et pour l'entretien?*
5. *Comparer la qualité*
6. *Interroger sur les propriétés* e.g. *C'est en laine?*
7. *Appréciation positive/négative*
8. *Demander un autre objet*
9. *Demander son avis*
10. *Demande de conseils liée au choix*
11. *Décision positive/négative (décision d'achat)*
12. *Paiement. Différentes formes de paiement (argent liquide, chèque, carte de crédit)*

---

can provide one source, the many international surveys and statistics published by official bodies and reproduced in newspapers and magazines offer another.

Learning new vocabulary

There is still much new vocabulary to be learnt at this stage, both in extension of topics treated earlier and when opening up new areas. When topics are revisited, the focus may be different. For example the topic of the family may at an early stage introduce only the vocabulary of family relationships, age, perhaps appearance and one or two qualities. For older pupils the emphasis may shift to relations between parents and possible sources of conflict. All this involves new vocabulary.

In some textbooks the presentation remains the same, and the typology of practice activities shows relatively little change, although attention may now be focused on larger stretches of discourse, with events having to be ordered chronologically or different points of view identified.

Sometimes however the topic is treated in a new way and classroom activities alter in consequence. The family, for example, is treated in one German textbook for French schools, *Deutsch mit Spaß* (Neuner *et al.*, 1989), through six different texts: a cartoon strip about a girl missing the last bus, one set of parents' view of their son, one girl's views about her parents, five short texts from different girls about the time by which they must be home, a boy's plea to be allowed to buy a moped, and a song about the appeal of rock music for adolescents. The same themes constantly recur: being granted or denied permission to stay out late, spending time with friends or at the youth club, parents and children getting on or getting cross with each other. By encountering the same vocabulary again and again in different contexts and reading about problems similar to their own, students at the intermediate level are given both the means and the motivation to acquire vocabulary. They can thus bypass mechanical checks on understanding in favour of ones requiring personal interpretation, such as making notes, reporting, comparing and contrasting, as preliminaries to expressing their own personal views.

Lexical explorations

Most of the time at the intermediate stage will still be occupied in consolidating or adding to vocabulary related to specific topic or specific communicative purposes. But there should also be time to let pupils see that there are lexical relations that operate across topics. This is an aspect of study that will become more prominent at the advanced stage, but it has practical relevance as well as intellectual interest even earlier.

Simple exercises in which membership of the same word family is explored can increase pupils' control over the lexical resources of a language. For example, a chapter on winter sports in *Échanges 2* (Grunwald *et al.*, 1981) is followed by a gap-filling exercise which includes sentences like these:

> 7. *Il y a une chose que Claire n'aime pas du tout: presque tous les moniteurs **fument**. Souvent la salle à manger est pleine de* . . . .
> 9. *Gérard aime bien le ski. Il aime tous les **sports**. C'est un garçon très* . . . .

Other exercises practise the relation between words denoting occupations and their place of work or activity (*pâtissier–pâtisserie, vendeur–vendre*), the relation between adjectives and adverbs (*constant–constamment, heureux–heureusement*, or the effect on pronunciation and spelling when the negative prefix *in* is placed before an adjective *une personne connue, inconnue; un résultat attendu, inattendu; une solution possible, impossible.*

While subtle shades of meaning within the same semantic field may not yet be distinguished at this stage, the appreciation of different levels of formality is both possible and directly useful for pupils about to spend some time with French or German families. They will already know about appropriate modes of address or letter writing conventions, but they may need to be alerted to the possibility that expressions which they hear from their friend, such as *elle me tape sur le système* or *das ist echt stark* have more formal equivalents!

This is the stage when the understanding of language specific conceptual distinctions needs to be checked, for example between *an* and *année, savoir* and *pouvoir, legen* and *stellen, entscheiden* and *beschließen*. This is the time too, when the different meanings of some key words, like *mettre, passer, lassen, sollen*, which they will have met in different contexts, can be systematized and revised, with appropriate examples noted and learnt.

As pupils begin to use longer stretches of language, whether in speech or writing, the need to signal the connections between various parts of their text becomes apparent, and the available discourse markers can be reviewed.

Some simple descriptors of speech acts, which extend pupils' lexical resources, can already be introduced. They can, for example, be asked to report on a letter which they have received from their pen friend, and to bring in expressions like *demande, veut savoir, explique, s'excuse, raconte, m'invite*, followed by the right complementation.

Finally, if pupils have not yet started to make their own lists of vocabulary, this is the time when they can take responsibility to organise their own revision, perhaps using information technology. They should be encouraged to write down whole phrases in L2, but still feel free to add an English translation. This is a simple example:

gagner (1) *gagner de l'argent* to earn (money); (2) *gagner un match* to win.

Activities at the Advanced Stage

By advanced stage I am still thinking of students at school rather than at university, albeit students with a declared interest and tested proficiency.

Language study at this stage shows several new features. Much of it is still centred on topics, yet these often deal with social, moral or political issues rather than with interactional situations. Hence the language tends to be more that of exposition and argument. Topic work is still intensive, but one would also expect students to read more extensively and from a greater variety of texts than before. Productive activities too could be more varied, ranging from interviews, speeches, oral presentations and debates to letters, reports and essays, with greater attention paid to the stylistic features of the chosen genre and the appropriacy of the message to its purpose and audience.

What are the implications of this for the kind of vocabulary to be learnt and the possible learning activities?

Clearly new sets of words will have to be learnt that are outside the core, but essential to the treatment of the topic. For example any discussion of economic questions would require a knowledge of the French or German terms for *growth, rise, fall in production, industry* and perhaps *different types of industry, business, trade, exports, imports, (un)employment, redundancies, wages, salaries, profits* and so on, with the appropriate verbs and adjectives.

In addition to this topic-specific vocabulary, terms connected with exposition and argument will be necessary, such as *problems to be dealt with, factors to be considered*, and terms for structuring the argument, indicating *cause, result, emphasis, reservations, conclusions* etc.

There are thus a number of new words and expressions still to be added to the student's productive vocabulary. There should also be an increase in receptive vocabulary, due to more extensive reading. While both of these are still linked in some way to specific topics, now is the time to study meaning relations between L2 and L1. Much independent study and efficient use of dictionaries can also be demanded.

Even at this stage the learning process still involves understanding meaning, now including meaning relations within the same semantic field, fixing the new item and then using it in free production. What is likely to differ are the kinds of activities to be employed.

Preparatory work is now common. Before a text is presented or a topic is introduced, students can be asked to write answers in note form to a set of questions, with the results compared between partners and among the class. Another possibility is to ask each student to write down, in L2 of course, two or three points about the topic which seem worth looking into. This not only starts students thinking about the topic and may already reveal different points of view, but can also bring out what terms will be needed. Yet another approach is for the class to look through two or more texts on the subject and draw up jointly a list of key words and expressions.

Structured practice could first bear on individual words and phrases by gap-filling or giving a definition or synonym for a word in the text, for example: '*Quel mot dans le texte veut dire avantage* (atout)'. In order to learn both the syntactic pattern in which the item occurs and the words with which it collocates, students can be given part of a sentence and asked to complete it. Towards the end of the structured practice a short retranslation exercise can bring out different ways in which ideas are expressed in L2 and L1.

In this approach, which is illustrated in detail by Nott (1988), work on language and work on content are kept separate and alternate. Other teachers prefer to conduct an intensive study of one text, discussing content and the language in which it is expressed at the same time, while using two or three additional texts in a less intensive manner to bring out other aspects of the topic and reinforce important topic vocabulary.

Assimilating the relevant topic vocabulary, by whichever approach, is but a means to an end: the expression of ideas. To do this clearly and logically, students need to learn a further set of words, discourse markers, which serve as connecting links in the development of the argument. This may sometimes appear a purely formal and mechanical exercise, and a succession of well-learnt phrases without any arguments of substance is certainly unconvincing. Yet a comparison of two paragraphs or two texts, one containing ideas presented in a haphazard, repetitive or unclear manner, and the other displaying a logical and clearly marked progression in the argument, should prove convincing. What is important is to show that there is more than one standard procedure.

How, for example, can a problem be introduced? One can start with an event: *Il y a quelques jours, quatre jeunes gens se sont encore tués dans un accident de moto. Ce regrettable événement pose encore une fois le problème de . . .* , or with an assertion: *On entend souvent dire que le niveau des lycéens d'aujourd'hui a baissé. Est-ce bien vrai?* (Vigner, 1975). What other expressions can one use with either approach? What are the linguistic resources available to signal the plan or stages of one's argument, enumerate, recapitulate, concede, exemplify, conclude? A well argued text can serve not only for its ideas but as a model or quarry for how to express them.

Finally, alternating with topic based work, though perhaps sometimes springing from it, there is specifically lexical work to do, in the following areas:

(1) clarifying the different meanings of core words like *lassen, halten, stehen, geben, prendre, faire,* first by studying authentic sentences which illustrate the different meanings in order to clarify the different concepts , then, perhaps as a later revision exercise, asking for reformulations which will involve the use of these words;
(2) clarifying the distinctions between words in the same semantic network like *dire, préciser, observer, constater, remarquer, déclarer, affirmer* by a similar approach;
(3) clarifying possible confusions between words with similar spelling like *parti* and *partie,* or separable German verbs with the same stem but a different prefix, or cases where the same form can either act as an inseparable prefix or as a preposition according to whether it is used figuratively or literally *ich durchschaue den Lügner, ich schaue durch das Fernrohr,* or pairs of apparent synonyms like *pays/campagne; Land/Landschaft;*
(4) learning different ways of expressing certain functions, like indicating cause, result, doubt, opinion or fact;
(5) beginning to understand and use idioms appropriately;
(6) developing a surer feeling for register and collocations.

4 The Grammar Controversy

The role of grammar has become controversial. For centuries both its central position in the teaching of foreign languages and the manner in which it was taught were unchallenged: the systematic learning of language forms and syntactic rules constituted the core of the syllabus at beginner and intermediate level. Since the 1960s different movements have in various ways put in doubt the appropriacy of traditional terms, the usefulness of an analytical and explanatory approach and the importance of grammatical accuracy.

The audio-lingual method, developed in the United States in the 1960s, was based on a view of language in which the large abstract categories like 'tense' or 'case' were rejected in favour of a number of patterns determined by position within a sentence. These were to be assimilated through analogy and drill, and not by explanations of rules. The aim was to form habits, and the following quotation represents, perhaps in an extreme form, the attitude of the time: 'Students eager for *reasons* must be discouraged, as this kind of digression is dangerous, time wasting and will add nothing to the student's assimilation of the language' (McNab, 1969: xx).

British and continental schools were not greatly influenced by the audio-lingual method. Nor have linguists and teachers on the Continent reacted favourably to other theories, put forward in the late 1970s and early 1980s, challenging the role of conscious learning. In Germany a three-phase procedure is normally followed: first a grammatical point is met within a story or a factual account of some important event, such as the first landing on the moon, next it is elicited by pupils and formalized by the teacher, and finally it is practised (Green & Hecht, 1992, Beck, 1993). In the Soviet Union and probably in its successors the *conscious-practical method* involved pupils studying the language theoretically and at the same time learning to use it in practice (Belyaev, 1963). When visiting Soviet schools, a British observer noted both the variety of activities in any one lesson and the fact that grammar figured prominently in all (Muckle, 1981). And in France the Baccalauréat examination in foreign languages still contains one paper specifically testing grammar.

Britain, on the other hand, seems to have taken a different route. The success of the graded objectives movement, the widespread adoption of *notional-functional* syllabuses and the priority given to communication have reduced the attention given to grammar and the importance assigned to grammatical accuracy. Objectives in textbooks are expressed in functional terms, such as *expressing feelings, likes and dislikes,*

Box 4.1 Grammar as pattern (King and Boaks, 1994: 4)

Haben Sie	*einen* Stadtplan?
	einen Prospekt?
Möchten Sie	*eine* Broschüre?

Was gibt es hier zu sehen, bitte?

Es gibt	*den* St Johanner Markt.
Sie haben	*die* Ludwigskirche.
	das Museum.

Meine Lieblingsfilme sind	Krimis
Ich sehe am liebsten	Komödien

Western	kann ich nicht leiden.
Lustige Filme	hasse ich.

how to ask and talk about preferences. Mini-summaries of grammar are still sometimes found at the end of chapters, but 'grammar as rules' has been largely superseded by 'grammar as pattern', at least in the first four or five years of study. The most common way of presenting grammar is through charts such as those in Box 4.1

Two features of the charts deserve comment. The first is that the teaching point is not a grammatical rule or a structure, but different ways of expressing a particular function in a particular context. In the first chart it is requesting and giving information about places of interest in a town, in the second it is expressing likes and dislikes in relation to films. Different grammatical structures are placed together in accordance with a notional-functional syllabus.

The second feature is that what is being presented is a pattern, here made up of two elements, the verb phrase in one box and the noun phrase in the second, with the possibility of permutating any item in one box with any item in the other.

The view of sentences as patterns informs the *Modern Foreign Languages Report* (DES, 1990). In Chapter 9 on 'Sounds, Words and Structures', an article by Widdowson (1989) is quoted in which communicative competence is described as 'a matter of knowing a stock of partially pre-assembled patterns, formulaic frameworks, and a kit of rules, so to speak, and being able to apply the rules to make whatever adjustments are necessary according to contextual demands' (9.2). The *Report* goes on:

> In this view learners make progress in a second language by continually extending their repertoire of chunks of language, but it is knowledge of the underlying rules which enables them to adapt these chunks to cope with the many and various situations in which they need to use them (9.3).

The way in which this essential knowledge is to be acquired is not very clear. 'Once learners have thoroughly absorbed a set of related chunks of language, they need to explore and if necessary be shown how the underlying model works ' (9.4). But being shown must not involve being told (9.4), and in any case not by technical terms, which are at best of very limited value to most pupils (9.14). Altogether 'it is not at all easy to give a clarification of underlying structures appropriate to each pupil' (9.22).

One can applaud the stress on pupils making their own grammatical discoveries, but to deny so categorically the value of any explanations by the teacher or the use of precise terms may hinder rather than further understanding. Nor is the theoretical basis of the report clear when the term 'underlying' is applied interchangeably to rules, models, patterns and structures. After all, a clear distinction is drawn by Widdowson between pre-assembled patterns and the rules with which adjustments in the patterns can be made .

My position will be developed in the following pages, but it may be briefly outlined here:

(1) In the previous chapters the importance of vocabulary for the transmission of meaning was stressed. But grammar too fulfils this function: the communication of meaning can be distorted or fail altogether if the effect of changes in the form or position of words is not appreciated. How, for example, can one express or understand plurality, negation, purpose, a past or hypothetical action without knowing the mechanisms through which these concepts are conveyed? These mechanisms or rules apply right across the language, to any topic and all the four skills.

(2) It is certainly true, as Widdowson states, that learners have to build on and adapt what they already know, but the kit of rules which enables them to do so needs to be quite large. (Crystal (1986) as quoted in the Introduction, writes that Susie, living in an English-speaking community, will need 'around 1,000 rules, which will tell her how to string words together to make acceptable sentences'.) The stress on language as pattern can lead to a reliance on a few fixed phrases or formulas. Yet one of the most important characteristics of language is that very few circumstances require an entirely predictable set of phrases. For the rest, human beings are constantly creating sentences that they have not used in precisely that form before. In order to generate such sentences one needs to know some grammar.

(3) The basic syntactic subdivisions or constituents — the noun phrase, the verb phrase, the clause, have a psycholinguistic as well as a grammatical reality. Listeners organise the interpretation of what they hear, readers process text and speakers plan and execute their utterances around constituents (Clark & Clark, 1977). Knowing how to construct these building blocks accurately and quickly is thus of major importance.

(4) The view, so often expressed, that one can just learn to engage in conversation, 'without bothering about grammar', is fallacious. The following brief conversational exchanges illustrate this:

Ta maman est à la maison, Martine?
Non, elle est allée chez ma grand'mère (nanours) chercher ma petite soeur.

Ist deine Mutter zu Hause, Thomas?
Nein, sie ist zu meiner Grossmutter (zur Oma) gegangen, (gefahren), um meine kleine Schwester abzuholen.

These exchanges are very simple, yet they presuppose grammatical knowledge about forms of verbs and adjectives and rules of concord, about how to express a question and indicate a past action, location and purpose. And most of the grammatical features are specific to a particular language.

(5) The needs and abilities of different learners will determine how extensive and deep their knowledge of grammar has to be. Some parts of grammar, like the gender of nouns or the endings of German adjectives, play only a limited communicative role, but their correct use is esteemed by native speakers, and may thus represent a worthy learning objective.

(6) I believe that the acquisition of grammatical knowledge requires some conscious attention to form as well as practice and meaningful activity. This view is based on my own experience, my visits to many countries to study their language teaching methods, the nature of language learning, the results of research and educational considerations. All these will be reviewed later.

As with the earlier section on vocabulary, the section on grammar will be divided into three parts: linguistic perspectives, the learning process, teaching approaches.

The chapters on linguistic perspectives will consider French and German grammar separately, but with frequent cross-references. Their aim is not to rehearse facts with which readers will be familiar, but to restate them briefly in order to draw out implications for teaching English learners.

The chapters on the learning process will first develop in detail a model of L2 learning viewed as the learning of a cognitive skill. The acquisition of grammatical proficiency in L1 will be compared with the learning of cognitive skills generally, and the results of the comparison applied to the learning of grammar in L2. An important distinction will be made between four types of grammar rule. Other theories, specific to language learning, will then be discussed and data from classroom performance presented. A conclusion will be offered.

The chapter on teaching approaches will be based generally on the description of the learning process, and especially on the distinction between the four kinds of grammar rule.

5 French Grammar: Problems for English Learners and Implications for Teaching

I want to start my analysis of French grammar and the problems that it poses for English learners by quoting an extract from *La Peste*, a novel often recommended for A-level students, by a major 20th century writer, Albert Camus.

I believe that after six or seven years of successful study, most English learners would be able to understand most of this excerpt, and excerpts from many other French 20th century texts of a non-specialist nature, provided they had access to a good dictionary.

The reason is that in several fundamental respects French grammar resembles English grammar. The basic word order of subject–verb–object is the same, with similar inversion in questions. The noun is not inflected, except in the plural, where 's' is the written marker of plurality in both languages. As in English, the object follows a verb directly or after a preposition.

It is these structural similarities that make a French text fairly readable, once the vocabulary is understood. It is they too which allow weak students to convey their meaning when they write in French, even if they make many mistakes of detail. Yet the multiplicity of such mistakes is a sign that there are several features of French grammar that cause difficulties to English learners. I will discuss first those that occur in the noun phrase, next those in the verb phrase. Already at this stage implications for teaching will be drawn, although detailed suggestions for activities and exercises will be postponed until Chapter 9, to take account of the discussion of the learning process in Chapters 7 and 8.

The Noun Phrase

Grammatical gender

The fact that every noun is either masculine or feminine not only increases the learning load but constitutes a psychological hurdle for English learners unused to the concept of purely grammatical gender, not based on a biological foundation. One

Box 5.1 Extract from *La Peste* (Camus, 1962: 140–1)

Il regarda sa mère. Le beau regard marron fit remonter en lui des années de tendresse.

— Est-ce que tu as peur, mère?

— A mon âge, on ne craint plus grand-chose.

— Les journées sont bien longues et je ne suis plus jamais là.

— Cela m'est égal de t'attendre si je sais que tu dois venir. Et quand tu n'es pas là, je pense à ce que tu fais. As-tu des nouvelles?

— Oui, tout va bien, si j'en crois le dernier télégramme. Mais je sais qu'elle dit cela pour me tranquilliser.

La sonnette de la porte retentit. Le docteur sourit à sa mère et alla ouvrir. Dans la pénombre du palier, Tarrou avait l'air d'un grand ours vêtu de gris. Rieux fit asseoir le visiteur devant son bureau. Lui-même restait debout derrière son fauteuil. Ils étaient séparés par la seule lampe allumée dans la pièce, sur le bureau.

— Je sais, dit Tarrou sans préambule, que je puis parler tout droit avec vous.

Rieux approuva en silence.

— Dans quinze jour ou un mois, vous ne serez d'aucune utilité ici, vous êtes dépassé par les événements.

— C'est vrai, dit Rieux.

— L'organisation du service sanitaire est mauvaise. Vous manquez d'hommes et de temps.

Rieux reconnut encore que c'était la vérité.

— J'ai appris que la préfecture envisage une sorte de service civil pour obliger les hommes valides à participer au sauvetage général.

— Vous êtes bien renseigné. Mais le mécontentement est déjà grand et le préfet hésite.

— Pourquoi ne pas demander des volontaires?

— On l'a fait, mais les résultats ont été maigres.

— On l'a fait par la voie officielle, un peu sans y croire. Ce qui leur manque, c'est l'imagination. Ils ne sont jamais à l'échelle des fléaux. Et les remèdes qu'ils imaginent sont à peine à la hauteur d'un rhume de cerveau. Si nous les laissons faire, ils périront, et nous avec eux.

— C'est probable, dit Rieux. Je dois dire qu'ils ont cependant pensé aussi aux prisonniers, pour ce que j'appellerai les gros travaux.

— J'aimerais mieux que ce fût des hommes libres.

— Moi aussi. Mais pourquoi, en somme?

— J'ai horreur des condamnations à mort.

Rieux regarda Tarrou :

might argue that *le sonnette *du porte could replace *la sonnette de la porte* in the Camus text, without causing misunderstanding. Yet French people often resent gender mistakes made by foreigners, mistakes that are as noticeable in speech as in writing and which even the uneducated among them do not make. Furthermore, through the rules of concord or agreement, much else is determined by the gender of the noun: the pronunciation and spelling of many adjectives and the choice of determiners. Learning the gender of nouns is therefore essential.

In *practice* there is more than one way to approach the problem. Starting the course by introducing the names of classroom objects gives pupils visible entities to talk about, but confronts them from the beginning with the need to remember the different articles in *la porte* and *le magnétophone*, *un stylo* and *une gomme*. If one starts by talking about the family and pets, the range of utterances may be limited, but there is an obvious biological foundation for *j'ai un frère, une soeur; ma soeur a . . . ans; mon chien s'appelle . . . ;*

il/elle . . . A bridge is thus provided towards accepting grammatical gender as a feature of nouns. In the end, as Hawkins (1981: 205–1) writes: 'It is essential that the gender of the basic vocabulary should be rock-solidly known.' He gives many hints on how to promote this, such as the use of colour codes, spatial imagery and games.

It is also helpful to insist from the beginning on sharp auditory discrimination and distinct pronunciation of the different vowel sounds in articles and other determiners, particularly *un* and *une*.

As the course progresses, pupils may be able to make a few generalisations about the gender of nouns. Several concern word endings. For example, *-age, -ment, -oir* should suggest a masculine noun, *-aine, -ée, -ie, -tion* a feminine one. There are also a few semantic indicators: names of languages, trees and metals are mainly masculine, those of the sciences feminine.

Concord or agreement

The rule that adjectives and pronouns must agree in gender and number with the noun to which they refer, and that finite verb forms vary according to their subject constitutes a major way in which different elements in a sentence or paragraph are shown to hang together. The two paragraphs in the Camus text beginning respectively with *La sonnette de la porte* and *On l'a fait par la voie officielle* offer a good illustration of this. However, accepting the logic and importance of the concord rules to achieve cohesion does not by itself mean that learners find it easy to apply them, particularly in those forms of the adjective or pronoun where the grammatical distinction is not audible.

There are several *implications for teaching*. If the ability to communicate orally is truly a major aim of language courses, then pupils must learn to pay attention to the sound of the final syllable of adjectives and note how frequently it differs between the masculine and feminine form — a vowel sound *versus* a consonant sound (*vert/verte; heureux/heureuse*), a nasal vowel *versus* the consonant [n] (*certain/certaine*), [e] *versus* [r] (*premier/première*, [f] *versus* [v] (*actif/active*). Even more importantly, they must become accustomed to showing these differences in their own speech.

The cause of the differences lies in the change that an adjective undergoes in its syllabic structure, when the letter *e* is added to a final consonant. The syllabic basis to French phonology will be discussed in a future chapter. Understanding it is not difficult, and applying it will aid pupils in writing as well as speaking.

Plural agreement is a problem of the written language, which troubles even French children. The only advice one can give to pupils is to identify plural markers like *les, des, ces, sont* as warning signs that the following nouns and adjectives may be in the plural. Learning verses, 'comptines' and phrases that are amusing in themselves but also exemplify the agreement rules, and writing them out, as well as frequent short dictations, can help to instil good habits early.

The partitive article

The forms *du, de la, de l', des* are easy to remember in their meaning of *of the*, but they can cause confusion to English learners in their use as a partitive article. There are several reasons for this: the term itself is not used in English; in reality it applies only to the so-called non-count nouns *(beurre, courage)*, and not to the plural, since *des* is strictly the plural of *un, une*, and, thirdly, the explanation frequently found in coursebooks that the partitive article corresponds to the English *some* or *any* is only partly true. In fact English frequently uses no article at all. For example none would be used to translate the sentence in Camus: '*J'aimerais mieux que ce fût des hommes libres.*'

I believe that the danger of confusion can be avoided or at least lessened if *du, de la, de l'* are clearly linked to the concept of the unspecified quantity of a non-count noun, perhaps in contrast to a specifed quantity indicated in a measure *(kilo)*, container *(bouteille)* or a non-specific adverb *(beaucoup, peu)*. *Des* should be clearly linked to the concept of unspecified number of count nouns, perhaps in contrast to a precise number, to a few *(quelques)* or to all *(les)*.

Pronouns

Pronouns are important in French, as in English. First, every sentence must have a noun or pronoun as subject (unlike Italian or Latin) and, second, pronouns serve as major referents to people, things or events already mentioned, ensuring semantic connections within and across sentences. Personal pronouns are particularly frequent, 45 occurring in the Camus excerpt.

Although in both languages there are separate subject and object pronouns, French is more complex. Among the object pronouns it distinguishes between conjunctives, with a verb, and disjunctives, independent of verbs, except in the imperative. It also distinguishes in the third person of the conjunctives between direct and indirect object. *En* and *y* are etymologically adverbs of place, meaning 'from there' (Latin *inde*) and 'there' (Latin *ibi*), and they are still used as such. But they have also taken on the value of personal pronouns, meaning respectively 'of it, them' and 'to it, them'. With all the conjunctive pronouns there is a further problem in the position they occupy in relation to a verb and to each other. The role of the impersonal subject pronoun *on*, used in many cases where English would prefer a passive construction, and as a familiar substitute for *nous*, cannot be underestimated, while the distinction between a formal and a familiar pronoun of address needs to be learnt very early.

What are the *implications for teaching*? With the *tu/vous* distinction and *on* it seems mainly a question of choosing situations and role-plays where these pronouns would be used naturally.

The choice of object pronouns will appear less daunting if pupils keep in mind what would be the relationship between the verb and a noun object. This is summarised simply in Box 5.2. Examples are found in Bérard and Lavenne (1991: Chapter 10).

Box 5.2 The choice of object pronouns in French (based on Bérard and Lavenne, 1991: Chap.10)

Verb + noun (person or thing)	direct object pronoun
Verb + à + noun (person)	indirect object pronoun
Verb + noun preceded by *un/une*, a number or part. article	en
Verb + à + noun (thing or place)	y
Verb + other prepositions (person)	disjunctive pronoun

The Verb Phrase

There are several features of the French verbal system that can cause difficulties to the English learner. I will single out three.

The large number of verbal forms

A look at the *English* verbal system brings out starkly the size of the problem for English learners of French. In English, regular verbs, like *play*, which form the large majority, without necessarily being the most common of verbs, have only four separate forms, as shown in Box 5.3.

The present and the past are the only two tenses formed from the verb itself. For other purposes auxiliary verbs are used: the primary ones *do, have, be* and the modal ones *can, may, shall, must,* etc. Between them they express three concepts: *time, aspect,* 'the manner in which the verbal action is experienced or regarded, for example as completed or in progress' (Quirk & Greenbaum, 1973: 40), and *mood*, indicating the conditions under which the verbal action takes place, for example certainty, necessity, obligation, possibility. As Quirk and Greenbaum go on:' To a great extent these three categories impinge on each other: in particular the expression of time present and past cannot be considered separately from aspect, and the expression of the future is closely bound up with mood.' What is of interest here is the small number of inflected forms and the fact that a variety of meanings are expressed not by modifying the form of the

Box 5.3 The four basic verb forms in English

The base	play
The s-form or third person singular of the present	plays
The -ed form in past and past participle	played
The -ing form or present participle	playing

verb, but by using a number of independent, stable and easily recognisable items in different combinations.

By contrast a French verb can belong to four different conjugations classified by the ending of the infinitive: *-er* (the most productive), *-ir*, with an infix *-iss*, *-re* and *-oir*. There are significant differences between the first and the other three conjugations and some grammarians write of an *-e* and an *-s* conjugation, from the first person singular of the present, *parle, écris*. Two other features are even more important: first, the fact that each verb has 14 tenses (7 simple and 7 compound) in the active voice and a parallel 14 in the passive, and, second, the fact that each tense has 6 specific endings for the different persons. In the Camus extract 7 tenses and all the 6 persons are used. If one were to take any regular French verb conjugated with *avoir* in the *-er* conjugation and count the number of separate forms, a staggering total of 77 written and 51 spoken forms for the active voice alone would result, counting identically spelt or pronounced forms only once! (The detailed calculation can be checked in any grammar book.) The smaller number of spoken forms has some advantages, but it also presents problems, since the same spoken form can be rendered in writing in three different ways! [e] = *fermé, fermer, fermez*. The subjunctive cannot be entirely discounted, for in certain constructions and with certain verbs it is far from extinct (Nott, 1992), but even if it were disregarded, learning the other tense forms would still constitute a considerable load. If one adds the many common verbs whose endings are those of the *-s* conjugation, but whose stems undergo several changes, the learning load becomes heavy indeed.

There are several *implications for teaching*. The first, at beginners level, is that forms must become associated by the pupil, in their sound and spelling, with the appropriate subject. To put this more concretely, pupils must associate *j'ai* and other *je*-forms with actions performed or states related to themselves as individuals, *nous* with actions performed by two or more people, including themselves, and a third-person form with other people or things. All this implies presentation and practice activities that naturally involve certain person forms rather than others. Getting up in the morning calls for the *je* form, playing in a team game or going on a family holiday will call for the *nous* form.

The second and third implications are two sides of the same coin. I have mentioned the multiplicity of forms, aggravated by the number of irregular verbs, which, because of their importance, necessarily appear early in any course. This suggests that for a considerable time in the early stages verbal forms should be treated almost like vocabulary items, each one being learnt separately. On the other hand the verbal system displays many regularities — in the way tenses are formed from the stem, in the distribution of endings, in the fact that many irregular verbs form little groups with the same morphological pattern, for example *ouvrir, couvrir* etc. *venir, tenir* and their compounds. Once pupils have learnt a good number of verbs with the same pattern, they should be encouraged to develop and apply their feeling for the regularities in the system.

The fourth implication is the most important. Pupils are constantly having to learn and use new verbs as new topics are met. They cannot be expected to form the imperfect or future or other tenses from unfamiliar stems without making mistakes. Constant revision of tense forms involving old and newly encountered verbs is therefore needed.

The use of tenses and moods

The extensive French tense system is capable of expressing many of the meanings described by Quirk and Greenbaum, although the multiplicity of forms can also cause confusion: *arrivait* and *arriverait* do not sound very different. Learning the forms is essential, but it must go hand in hand with learning how they are used.

Here we touch upon a phenomenon found in many languages: however comprehensive the formal tense system may be, no single tense performs one function only. Thus, for example, the French *present tense* refers to actions or states occurring at all times (*L'eau est inodore*), in the present (*Qu'est-ce que tu fais? Je travaille*), at some time in the past (*Au bout d'un quart d'heure j'entends quelqu'un sur l'escalier*) and in the future (*Je reviens demain*). Similarly the *future* and *future perfect* are not only used of future events but also instead of an imperative (*vous me rapporterez cela cette après-midi*), to attenuate the strength of a statement, as in the Camus excerpt (*ce que j'appellerai les gros travaux*), to express suppositions about a past event (*il aura oublié*), or, in historic narrative, to look both backward to a given moment in the past and forward from it (*Pierre Dupont a commencé sa carrière politique en 1962. 4 ans plus tard il se présentera aux élections législatives et sera élu député*) (Bérard & Lavenne, 1991).

Some of these uses have their parallels in English, others require an adjustment of perspective. In *Ça fait deux heures que je t'attends* or *J'habite Paris depuis 1980* French stresses continuity through the use of the present tense, while the English *have been waiting* or *have lived* emphasise the origin in the past.

One of the most difficult points of French grammar is the distinction between, on the one hand, the *imperfect* and, on the other, the *perfect (passé composé)* or *past historic (passé défini)*. Bérard and Lavenne (1991) use the image of a film set for the imperfect, and of the events that suddenly happen on the set for the two action tenses. More precisely the contrast is between an action or state viewed as incomplete, with the starting or finishing point undefined, and an action viewed as complete, whether it be a single act, a series of acts or even a long period seen as a closed whole, as in *Louis XIV régna de 1660 à 1715*. Many English learners, accustomed to using the one past tense, have difficulties with this distinction and either choose the formally simpler imperfect or hesitate between the tenses. This is well illustrated by another extract from the French lesson quoted in Chapter 2.

Whatever definition or explanation one finds, it takes many years before one feels absolutely sure about an author's intentions in choosing one tense rather than another

Box 5.4 Excerpt II from the tapescript of a French lesson (Sanderson, 1982: 30)

Teacher:	*Après avoir mis les livres sur la porte. Oui.*
Pupil:	*Il s'est dés . . . déshabillé*
Teacher:	*Il s'est déshabillé.* You know, we had a whole series of these. *S'est déshabillé?*
Pupil:	*Il se lavait*
Teacher:	*Il s'est lavé*
Pupil:	*Il s'endormait*
Teacher:	*Il s'est couché et il . . . ?*
Pupil:	*endormait*
Teacher:	*Il . . .*
Henri:	*endorm . . .*
Teacher:	*s'est . . .*
Teacher & Pupils:	*endormi. Il s'est endormi, oui. Et puis il . . .*
Pupil:	*a dormi*

or absolutely confident in one's own use. Why for example has Camus chosen the imperfect *restait* in the paragraph beginning with *La sonnette de la porte retentit?*

The tenses mentioned so far are all in the indicative mood. In a full and illuminating article, Nott (1992) suggests the following distinction between indicative, conditional and subjunctive. With the indicative both speaker and listener understand that something is being put forward as if it were true or as a request for the truth. The conditional assumes that certain conditions will have to be met. The difference is illustrated in the following:

je connais quelqu'un qui **pourra** *vous aider* (will be able)
je connais quelqu'un qui **pourrait** *vous aider* (would be able, could)

The subjunctive implies that the speaker's intention is to *devalue* the information content of the subordinate clause. There may be a denial of the reality of what follows (*il est exclu que*), an expression of doubt (*je ne crois pas que*), or the facts may be made subordinate to the speaker's attitude (*bien que*). Nott then compares cases when the use of the subjunctive is automatic, because triggered by certain expressions (*il faut que*), and those where it depends on meaning and situation. Although the application of these principles is not beyond the capability of good intermediate and advanced students, the use of the subjunctive remains a taxing feature of the French verbal system.

What are the *implications for teaching?* The general one is the need to progress slowly, so as not to compound the difficulties presented by the formal complexity of the verb system. Starting with a tense use that has a parallel in English or is easily understood gives confidence.

If a tense has several uses, presentation and practice of one use, in a situation where its function is easily apprehended, before a second use is introduced, will avoid confusion and facilitate learning. Nor will this lead to contrived texts. For example, the imperfect is used for habitual actions, for descriptions, for reported speech and a certain type of *if-* clause. Each of these uses would naturally be associated with different contexts, though not exclusively. Similarly there are different uses for the action tenses. Concentrating on the functions of each tense before presenting them in contrast will help pupils to listen and read more sensitively and, later, make the correct choices themselves.

When a different tense is required in French from that expected by English learners, such as the future after *quand* in reference to future time, explanations of the reason and recurrent practice need to go hand in hand. There are times when it is sufficient to establish a mechanical link between one or more words and the choice of tense or mood (for example, with *il faut que* and the subjunctive). At other times, however, a 'rule of thumb' that precludes further amplification may be misleading. For example, despite the belief of countless pupils, *depuis* is not always used with the present or imperfect. It is the continuity of a verbal action from the past into the present that leads to the use of the present. In the two following sentences continuity is absent, and *depuis* is used with the perfect.

> *Je suis allé au cinéma plusieurs fois depuis mon arrivée à Paris* (the action took place at separate intervals in the past)
> *Je n'ai rien mangé depuis dix heures* (no action took place at all)

If pupils have understood the underlying concept, they will in time be able to see the connection between *depuis* and other time indicators such as *(ça) cela fait . . . que, il y a . . . que, depuis . . . que.*

The complementation of verbs

Verbs are often followed by a noun object, with or without intervening preposition, or by an infinitive clause, with or without preposition, or even by a noun object that is itself followed by an infinitive. The following are just a few of the different complementation patterns used in the Camus excerpt:

> *Il regarda sa mère*
> *Je pense à ce que tu fais*
> *Rieux fit asseoir le visiteur*
> *. . . obliger les hommes valides à participer au sauvetage civil*

English too uses different types of complementation, and sometimes the two languages use the same construction. But frequently, as in the previous examples, there are differences: one language uses a certain preposition, the other uses a different one or none at all. Pupils have to learn with each verb what complementation it requires. This is important, not only because complementation is essential in a very large number of sentence types, but also because, as was shown earlier, the relationship between a verb and a noun object determines the choice of the personal pronoun.

6 German Grammar: Problems for English Learners and Implications for Teaching

German is more strongly inflected than French, with three genders, eight plural forms in nouns, four cases, two declension patterns among adjectives in attributive position and all tense forms marked for person. Some of these features have their counterpart in French and do not need to be discussed in detail again. More space will be devoted to two features that cause particular difficulties to English learners: the case system and word order.

The Noun Phrase

Grammatical gender

The concept represents an initial hurdle for learners of German, as it does for learners of French. As in French, gender influences the form of articles, other determiners, pronouns and, additionally, that of adjectives before the noun. But getting the gender right is both more difficult and more important, because there are three genders instead of two, and because the influence of gender extends throughout the four cases.

There are some pointers to gender: days of the week, months and seasons are masculine, the endings *-ei, -in, -heit, -keit, -schaft, -ung* point to a feminine noun, diminutives ending in *-chen* and *-lein* and most terms for the young of persons and animals are neuter: *Mädchen, Fräulein, Kind, Lamm*. Yet these pointers are few and pupils simply have to learn the gender of nouns as they need them. As in French, it is possible to familiarise pupils with the concept by starting with living beings, such as *mein Bruder, meine Schwester, er heißt, sie heißt* and move from there to pets and then to inanimate objects.

The plural of nouns

English learners are familiar with a separate ending to mark the plural of a noun, but in German they are faced with a system of eight different forms in the plural

The way in which I have described these functions is drawn from the work of German grammarians and in particular from what has become known as *Valenzgrammatik* or *Dependenzgrammatik*, developed in the 1960s and 1970s and since then widely used in textbooks produced in Germany. The term 'valency' is borrowed from chemistry, where the valency of a chemical element determines the number of atoms of that element which are needed to form a compound. Adapted to grammar, the valency of a verb is the number and type of elements required to construct a sentence. Some elements are obligatory; they are called 'complements' (*Ergänzungen*), others are optional and are called 'adverbials' (*freie Angaben* or *Adverbialbestimmungen*). A verb may be followed by various complements, but the number of sentence patterns (*Satzbaupläne*) in the German language is limited. The Wahrig dictionary, among others, gives a list of these patterns, and refers to it in its entries for verbs. (For further details, see Hammer, 1991: 347.)

This work is of more than theoretical interest. It suggests that morphological mistakes may sometimes not be due to inadequate learning of the various case forms but to insufficient attention to a verb's valency, or, to put it more specifically, to the case it takes. This, in the opinion of Roberts (1986: 106) explains the following mistakes by his first-year university students: (the correct form is in brackets)

* ... *an die Testamentseröffnung teilnehmen* ... (*der*)
* ... *er glaubt sie nicht* ... (where *sie* refers to a person) (*ihr*)
* ... *fragten mir* ... (*mich*)
* ... *ich konnte das sie wohl kaum sagen* ... (*ihr*)
* ... *wasch dich die Hände* ... (*dir*)

The case system: implications for teaching from the multiplicity of forms and variety of functions

Take the long view

As was said at the beginning of this section, the case system is such a dominant and pervasive feature of the noun phrase, that it is worth dealing with it gradually and slowly. It does not matter if the forms for the different cases of different determiners or personal pronouns are introduced and practised separately. A complete declension or table may serve as a mnemonic device, but is no more than a formal entity without a semantic basis.

Begin with case after a preposition

It is a feature of all language learning, whether it be of L1 or L2, that a clear and stable link between form and meaning facilitates learning. If a grammatical structure resembles a fixed expression, if few choices have to be made or concepts understood, the learner's task is eased. A preposition, particularly one that must always be followed by a given case, provides just such a visible link. The distinction between a complement and an adverbial matters little here.

Box 6.2 The valency of German verbs: *state* and *direction* (based on Mebus *et al.*, 1987: 94)

Verben mit Lokalergänzung		Verben mit Direktivergänzung	
	Wo?		*Wohin?*
leben	*in Berlin*	*reisen*	*nach Berlin*
	in Österreich		*nach Österreich*
wohnen	*in der Schweiz*	*fliegen*	*in die Schweiz*
bleiben	*zu Hause*	*fahren*	*nach Hause*
	im Ausland		*ins Ausland*
	in den Bergen		*in die Berge*
	am Meer		*ans Meer*
sein	*bei Herrn Tossu*	*gehen*	*zu Herrn Tossu*
	beim Zahnarzt		*zum Zahnarzt*

Choose topics of intrinsic interest where certain prepositions occur naturally

With the dative different starting points seem equally valid. There is no need even to mention the terms 'case' or 'dative' with fixed expressions like *am Morgen, am Nachmittag*. 'Asking for and giving directions' requires only a binary choice in *wie komme ich zum Bahnhof, zur Post?* It can easily be followed by 'using means of transport', where the full form of the determiner is required, but mainly with one preposition *mit*, a few key verbs and a small number of nouns. Prepositions and verbs to express fixed spatial relationships are needed equally to describe one's room and house, shopping in a department store or even arrangements where to meet.

Stress the connection between verbs, cases and interrogative pronouns

Rhymes to remember which cases must follow certain prepositions have proved their usefulness to thousands of learners, but for prepositions that can take both the accusative and dative, any explanation about conceptual differences can be strengthened by bringing out the valency of verbs. Box 6.2 can be useful for reference, particularly when holiday plans are discussed.

With verbs requiring a dative or accusative object, emphasise learning by association. It is significant that among the mistakes quoted by Roberts (1986), all but the first occurred with verbs followed directly by the accusative or dative. The difficulty lies in the fact that the notional explanations of direct and indirect object are somewhat nebulous. To define the direct object in terms of an action going out from the doer to the receiver is helpful with verbs like *schlagen* or *finden* but less so with *haben* and *hören*. Similarly the etymological link between the word 'dative' and verbs of benefit is easily understood with *geben* and *schenken*, but hardly applies to *danken* or *glauben*. Rules of thumb comparisons with English 'if you would use *him/her* it's accusative, *to him/her* it's dative' cannot be dismissed outright, but are often misleading.

It is probably easiest to build up the concept of the direct object gradually, through the use of *haben* with siblings and pets, and later with enquiries in a shop, office, restaurant or hotel, to which can be added *ich möchte, nehme, trinke, kaufe, brauche* etc. In the same way some of the most common verbs taking the dative can be firmly linked to certain topics, for example *gratulieren* and *schenken* to birthday celebrations, *geben, leihen, reichen* to classroom discourse or meals, *passen* to clothes, and so on.

Verbs that take a prepositional object must be learnt individually.

Pay particular attention to practising the case forms of determiners other than the article (dieser, jeder, welcher) and of pronouns (personal, interrogative and relative).

Word Order

Getting the German word order right is notoriously difficult for English learners, because it runs counter in so many ways to the rules of English word order. In English the subject of a declarative statement normally comes before the verb, in German a statement may begin with a direct or indirect object. In English the verb normally follows the subject closely, in many German sentences subject and verb are at opposite ends of the sentence. In English there are no restrictions on the number of elements before the initial subject, in German one element only, however extended, normally occurs before the first verb. Conventions about punctuation within a sentence also differ in the two languages.

English learners therefore need to come to terms with some unfamiliar and strict *rules*, and in time with more flexible but equally unfamiliar *tendencies*.

In Box 6.3 two contrasting passages from modern German literature illustrate the main features of German word order.

The basic rules

The basic rules are those which cause most difficulties. They can be restated simply.

(1) *In a main declarative clause the initial position, called 'Vorfeld' or Position I by German grammarians, is often occupied by the subject.* (This is true for about two-thirds of all German declarative statements, according to Hammer, 1991: 461.) Alternatively, it may be occupied by any other element, causing the subject to move to Position III, after the verb. Position II is always occupied by the verb (or, more precisely, by the finite, conjugated part of the verb). In other words, the verb is like a pivot or weather vane, with the subject able to move either to the left or the right of it. The following are examples from the numbered lines in the two texts in Box 6.3.

Box 6.3 Extracts from (a) *Andorra* (Frisch, 1961: 25) and (b) *Und sagte kein einziges Wort* (Böll, 1973: 63)

(a) Wirt Ich gebe zu: Wir haben uns in dieser Ge- 1, 2
schichte alle getäuscht. Damals. Natürlich hab 3
ich geglaubt, was alle geglaubt haben damals. 4
Er selbst hat's geglaubt. Bis zuletzt. Ein Juden- 5
kind, das unser Lehrer gerettet habe vor den 6
Schwarzen da drüben, so hat's immer gehei- 7
ßen, und wir fanden's großartig, daß der Leh- 8
rer sich sorgte wie um einen eigenen Sohn. Ich 9
jedenfalls fand das großartig. Hab ich ihn 10, 11
vielleicht an den Pfahl gebracht? Niemand
von uns hat wissen können, daß Andri wirk- 12
lich sein eigner Sohn ist, der Sohn von unsrem 13
Lehrer. Als er mein Küchenjunge war, hab ich 14, 15
ihn schlecht behandelt? Ich bin nicht schuld, 16
daß es dann so gekommen ist. Das ist alles, 17, 18
was ich nach Jahr und Tag dazu sagen kann. 19
Ich bin nicht schuld. 20

(b) Ein paar Minuten hörte ich über den öden Bahnsteig hinweg 21
dieser Stimme zu, sah zugleich den rotgekleideten Mann dort 22
hinten am Lautsprecher stehen, mit einer Stimme sprechend, die 23
den Dialekt um eine kaum spürbare Quantität übertrieb, und 24
ich wußte plötzlich das Wort, das ich jahrelang gesucht hatte, 25, 26
das aber zu einfach war, um mir einzufallen: Der Bischof war 27, 28, 29
dumm. Mein Blick wanderte über den Bahnhof zurück, wo das 30
Mädchen seine weiße Schürze immer noch mit unruhigen Be-
wegungen den Schoß herauf- und hinunterrollte und die Frau 31
auf der Bank nun dem Kind die Flasche gab. Mein Blick wan- 32
derte über die bräunlichen Mäandermuster an der Backstein- 33
wand, kam über die schmutzige Fensterbank in mein Zimmer, 34
und ich schloß das Fenster, legte mich aufs Bett und rauchte. 35, 36, 37

(a) Subject in Position I:
ich bin nicht schuld (20)
Wir fanden's großartig (8)
Mein Blick wanderte über den Bahnhof zurück (30).

(b) Subject in Position III:
Natürlich **hab ich** geglaubt (3)
Ein paar Minuten **hörte ich** . . . dieser Stimme zu (21)
[Als er mein Küchenjunge war], **hab ich** ihn schlecht behandelt? (15)

(2) *Whatever the position of the subject, if there is a non-finite part of the verb in the main clause (past participle, infinitive, separable prefix), that goes to the end of the clause.* The finite and the non-finite parts of the verb thus form the two pillars or brackets in this basic framework of the sentence, alternatively called in German *Verbklammer, Satzklammer, Verbrahmen*, with the clause sandwiched between them.

Wir **haben** uns in dieser Geschichte alle **getäuscht** (3)
Hab ich ihn vielleicht an den Pfahl **gebracht**? (11)
sah zugleich den rotgekleideten Mann dort hinten am Lautsprecher **stehen** (22).

(3) *Subordinate clauses can precede or follow the main clause. In all subordinate clauses the finite verb goes to the end.* In a subordinate clause introduced by a conjunction, Position 0 is taken up by the conjunction and Position I by the subject.

Als er mein Küchenjunge **war** (14)
daß Andri wirklich sein eigner Sohn **ist** (13).

In a relative clause, if the relative pronoun is the subject, it occupies Position I, otherwise the subject is in Position II.

[eine Stimme], **die** den Dialekt um eine kaum merkbare Quantität **übertrieb** (24)
[das ist alles], **was ich** nach Jahr und Tag dazu sagen **kann** (19).

(4) *'Und' 'aber' 'oder' 'denn' 'sondern' do not affect the word order;* they take up Position 0. If two main clauses are linked by one of these conjunctions, either may be inverted, without affecting the other. In two clauses joined by *und*, if the subject is the same in both, it may be omitted in the second clause.

Ein paar Minuten **hörte ich** . . . dieser Stimme zu, **sah** zugleich den . . . Mann dort stehen . . . , **und ich wußte** plötzlich das Wort . . . (21–25)

If both are subordinate clauses, the subject of the second, if named, is in Position I and the verb is at the end of the clause.

wo **das Mädchen** seine weiße Schürze . . . **herauf- und hinunterrollte und die Frau** . . . dem Kind die Flasche **gab** (31–2).

(5) A fifth rule may be added which does not affect word order, but relates to the structure of a written German sentence: every clause *within* a sentence should begin and end with a comma. (For exceptions, see Hammer, 1991: 517–19.)

Ich bin nicht schuld, daß es dann so gekommen ist (17)
ich wußte plötzlich das Wort, das ich jahrelang gesucht hatte, das aber zu einfach war, um . . . ' (25–6).

As Hammer states (1991: 516): 'the comma in German is used to mark off grammatical units, *not* to signal a pause when speaking'. In neither case would the corresponding English sentence have contained a comma. An important corollary of this rule is that adverbs and adverbial phrases within a sentence are not separated by a comma, as frequently happens in English. If the following sentence were to be translated into German, no comma would be required: 'May I add a point that was not, however, brought out in the article' (*Independent* 15 March 1993).

The central part of the clause

A detailed discussion of the word order in the central part of the clause (*Mittelfeld*) would take up too much space. A few comments on the basic pattern, taken from Hammer (1991: 469), and with references to the two literary extracts in Box 6.3, will suffice.

The basic order of the elements in the German sentence

Position I: Various

Position II: Verb (Pillar 1) — Pronouns (N.A.D.) — Dative Noun — Most
                Adverbials — Accusative Noun — *nicht* — Adverbials of Manner —
                Complement — Verb (Pillar 2)

Position I

The essential point about the element ocupying Position I, whatever its grammatical form, is that it functions as the 'topic' of the clause, 'that element which we put first in order to say something further about it' (Hammer, 1991: 462). This is most often the subject, and examples from the extracts were quoted earlier: numbers (20), (8) and (30).

The first element often refers to something previously mentioned. The subject itself may provide that link through a pronoun: *Das ist alles, was ich . . . dazu sagen kann* (19). But frequently the connecting link in Position I is not the subject. Expressions of time, in the form of adverbs, phrases or clauses, are common, giving information about what happened before, during or after the situation already known to the listener or reader: *Ein paar Minuten* hörte ich dieser Stimme zu (21); *Als er mein Küchenjunge war* (14). Other adverbials, not all represented in the extracts, indicate place, result, opposition, attitude: *Natürlich habe ich geglaubt* (3).

One consequence of the topic role of the first element is that new information is placed towards the end of the sentence. In line with this principle, when the subject itself carries new information, it moves towards the end of the sentence. This occurs, for example, with verbs of happening (*geschehen, sich ereignen, stattfinden*): *Im Juli findet in München eine große Kunstausstellung statt.*

One other point has sometimes to be explained even to advanced students: only one element, however extended, normally precedes the verb in main clause statements.

Thus one would not find parallels in German to English sentences that start like this: 'Firstly, and most importantly, I would argue . . . 'or' If, as is often claimed, this country . . . '.

Pronouns

The principle of end-focus explains why pronouns, which refer to known people or things, occur early in the clause, usually directly after the finite verb or the conjunction and before noun objects. This means that in an inverted main clause or in a subordinate clause the pronouns push the subject further to the end: *Zum Glück hat es mir der Professor noch einmal erklärt.* However, if the subject is itself a pronoun, it stays in Position III: *Zum Glück hat er es mir noch einmal erklärt.*

Noun Objects

The normal order is dative before accusative, as exemplified in (32): *„wo . . . die Frau . . . dem Kind die Flasche gab.* The order may sometimes be inverted if stress is put on the recipient.

Adverbials and complements

The position of adverbials is flexible. Modal particles such as *aber, also, doch,* attitudinal adverbs like *wahrscheinlich, vielleicht* and short unstressed adverbs like *hier, dort, damals* tend to come early. However in (4) *damals* is deliberately stressed by the speaker and even stands outside the second bracket. *Natürlich hab ich geglaubt, was alle geglaubt haben damals.* The usual order of adverbials is Time — Manner — Place.

7 The Learning of Grammar in L1 and L2 as the Learning of a Cognitive Skill

Much of the huge literature on the learning of foreign languages centres on the learning of grammar, almost equating the two. Yet there is no theory or set of experimentally proved facts about the learning of languages and the role of grammar in it on which there is general agreement. Ellis (1990), at the end of a book wholly dedicated to answering the question 'How does second language learning take place in the classroom?' quotes, rather pessimistically, the conclusions of a fellow researcher (Chaudron, 1988: 204): 'Despite the obvious increase in the amount of classroom-oriented research in recent years, few of the suggestions offered here can be made with great confidence, for the existing research is difficult to synthesize.'

The main problem is a general one: learning is a mental activity, whose nature can only be inferred, not observed, and whose results may not be immediately apparent. As Ellis (1990: 201) states: 'The most serious problem is how to investigate the *relationship* between instructional events and learning outcomes.' Any comprehensive theory would have to encompass many variables of learner and teacher characteristics and external conditions. But there is also a specific problem associated with the learning of foreign languages, the fact that L2 learners have already acquired a first language.

An account of the L2 learning process would therefore have to address questions like the following:

Can the process by which L2 is learnt be compared at all with the process of L1 acquisition? Or do the greater cognitive maturity of L2 learners and the fewer and less motivating opportunities for contact with the foreign language inherent in school learning make the conditions for learning so different that the two processes cannot be compared?

The question can also be widened: are the acquisition of L1 and the learning of L2 both manifestations of a unique human faculty for the acquisition of language? Or can they both be explained by reference to general theories of learning cognitive skills?

My own view, to be elaborated in the next two chapters, is to consider the learning of a foreign language, particularly its grammar, as the learning of a cognitive skill. First, I am intuitively inclined to favour a theory which places the learning of a foreign language within a general theory of human learning, rather than as a special case. Second, the cognitive skill model is supported by research. Third, at present it seems to offer the most fruitful basis for teaching, whereas it is not clear how other models can be applied in practice. On the other hand I admit that the cognitive skill theory does not fully take into account the presence of the first language in the learner's mind and other features peculiar to language learning.

This chapter will thus be devoted to a detailed analysis of the cognitive skill view of language learning, covering the acquisition of grammar in L1, the learning of intellectual skills in general, a comparison between the two processes and the application of the resulting model to the learning of grammar in L2.

The next chapter will deal with other theories of language learning, based on characteristics of language and language acquisition. It will also present some examples of classroom performance and finally offer a summary and conclusions.

The Cognitive Skill Model

The development of grammatical competence in first language acquisition

The development of the first language can be seen as the gradual elaboration from simple to complex utterances, as children seek to map their meanings onto linguistic forms (Clark & Clark, 1977). From one- and two-word utterances children add more and more detail, begin to add word endings to show the plural or past tense and produce the first coordinate sentences. The *order* in which grammatical forms are acquired is the same for most children, and in all languages, even if the *rate* varies . Children use a kind of *interlanguage*, with its own progression, resistant to any attempts at speeding up or correction.

Two factors play a role in deciding which structures are learnt first. One is cognitive complexity. Children do not use words and word endings for which they have no meaning. For example, studies in both French and English show that children under six often use the definite article where adults would use the indefinite, because they assume that what is known to them is also known to their listeners.

The other is formal complexity. The more complex a linguistic device is or the more exceptions there are to a rule, the longer children will take to learn them. For example, the concept of plurality, of more-than-one, appears with all children at virtually the same age and stage of development. Yet there is a startling difference between English-speaking and Arabic-speaking children in the age by which they have learnt the required forms. In English *s* is a regular and transparent marker of the plural, and is used correctly by age six. In Arabic, where the forms are more diverse, children do not seem confident in their use until age 14 (Clark & Clark, 1977: 338).

After investigating over 40 languages, Slobin (1973) suggested that children apply a small number of *operating principles* to language, which influence the order in which structures are learnt. They look for systematic modification in the form of words and for a transparent relation between grammatical markers and underlying semantic distinctions, as with English plurals. They overregularize in order to avoid exceptions. For example individual irregular past forms appear first, then the use of the regular suffix -*ed* is applied to all tense forms, producing both *jumped* and *runned*, and only in the end do they follow adult usage. Another principle is not to interrupt other linguistic units. Events are first described in their order of occurrence, with a separate sentence for each event or else a series of clauses joined by *and* or *and then* or *et puis*. When they begin to use adverbial clauses, these are first attached to the end of the main clause, and only later are they placed initially. Both in English and in German negation is first expressed by *no* and *nein* at the beginning of a sentence, while *not* and *nicht* in the middle of the sentence do not appear till later.

Altogether the development of grammatical competence takes longer than is often realised. 'Eight or ten years is probably an underestimate of the time children require to master the structures of their first language' (Clark & Clark, 1977: 363).

The interesting question is: by what process do children acquire the relevant rules? A five step sequence is suggested by Berman (1986), with the term *step* indicating segments of development which may vary in length from a few days to several months.

(1) *Rote-knowledge*: initial acquisition of individual items as unanalysed amalgams. A pre-grammatical, context-bound stage: a child may use a plural form without knowing that it has a singular counterpart.
(2) *Early modifications*: a few familiar items are alternated contrastively. The child realises that two or more surface forms may be instances of 'the same thing'.
(3) *Interim schemata*: interim generalisations, productive and creative, expressed through overregularization and overextension.
(4) *Rule-knowledge*: rules based not on words, but on classes of words. Rules may be formal or have a semantic basis. Some gaps remain.
(5) *End-state usage*: rule-application is constrained by adult norms and conventions, with increasing variations of style and register.

As Bialystok (1990) sums up, movement from initial to proficient use of the linguistic system occurs through the analysis and organisation of existing knowledge.

Other researchers (Bowerman 1982, Karmiloff-Smith 1986) also interpret the process as one in which children move from an implicit representation, closely tied to the performance of individual operations, through a spontaneous process of analysis and restructuring of their performance to a more explicit representation, of wider applicability.

Analysis should not be equated with consciousness. Talking to 482 French children aged between four and six, Karmiloff-Smith noted that even the younger children would spontaneously reformulate utterances to fit adult usage. If asked to explain their changes, they might give 'extra-linguistic' reasons. However, increasingly after age six, and dramatically after age seven, they showed themselves aware of the linguistic system. The timing of this change coincides with the age at which French children learn to read. This makes them aware for the first time of the symbolic nature of letters in relation to sounds, and thereby sharpens their existing powers of analysis.

In addition to this first process of analysis of linguistic knowledge, Bialystok (1990: 125) also posits a second component: control of linguistic processing, which she defines as 'the ability to control attention to relevant and appropriate information and to integrate those forms in real time'. The key factor is selective attention, the ability to attend to the required information without being distracted by irrelevant or misleading cues. Skilled selective attention creates a performance that appears automatic and effortless.

Bialystok does not discuss in any detail how this control develops during children's language acquisition, but the concept of skilled attention devoted to performance is one that will be discussed again.

The learning of intellectual skills

By the age most pupils begin the study of a foreign language, the difference between their assured use of the native language and their slow, stumbling progress in the new one is so stark that few teachers see any parallels between the two processes. Yet the account by psychologists of how cognitive skills are learnt contains several similarities to the description of language acquisition given earlier. The following summary is based chiefly on the life-long work of Gagné (1985) on the psychology of learning and its implications for teaching, and also on concepts derived from information processing, summarised in McLaughlin (1987).

Gagné sees the learning of intellectual skills as a hierarchical process, represented in the diagram below, where each form of learning requires as a prerequisite the learning of the form below.

Higher order rules

↑

Rules

↑

Concepts

↑

Discriminations

↑

Basic forms of learning

The key element in this process is the formation of *concepts*. Gagné quotes a simple rule such as young children might be led to discover 'Round things roll'. It involves two concepts only, both concrete in the sense that they are verifiable by observation. Let us assume that the children will have learnt from experience that balls roll, but have not yet formed the full concept *round*. They need to have encountered, perhaps at different times, a number of objects that possess this feature, in the shape of spheres (balls), discs (hoops, coins, saucers), cylinders (toy drums and pots, sticks). They would be familiar with them and know the verbal label attached to them (basic learning). If one wanted the children to learn the concept *round*, one would draw attention to the fact that they all shared this feature, even though they might differ in other respects, such as size, colour, material and use. Other objects would be compared, perhaps similar in a number of ways, but not in regard to roundness, so that the distinction is established between relevant and non-relevant features, instances and non-instances of the concept (discrimination). This discrimination is then generalised by introducing *new* objects, not previously used, thereby reinforcing the concept. Forming a concept thus involves both *abstraction* — distinguishing one or more critical features, and *generalisation* — classifying a number of objects or events as equivalent for the making of a particular response. In this case the children would have recognised a number of the objects as belonging to the class of round things.

School subjects often involve abstract concepts, defined through words, such as *mass, fulcrum, democracy, noun, passive, direct object*. Since abstract concepts cannot be perceived by direct observation, the first step in their presentation should be through concrete references to examples, pictures and diagrams. As with concrete concepts, negative examples should be brought in to strengthen discrimination. Ideally the initial situation used to exhibit the concept should be sufficiently representative, but it may be necessary sometimes to proceed by stages and present an *incomplete* concept, making it clear that it will be filled out later. Incomplete does not mean inaccurate, and it is important that any definitions given should be clear and leave the way open for amplification and refinement. The role of *language* is important here. Teachers constantly use abstract terms proper to their discipline, but they have to check regularly that the meaning of these terms is understood. Once that is so, the mind is freed from reliance on specific examples, and the learner can proceed to the understanding of rules.

Rules

Rules are described by Gagné (1985: 112) as 'probably the major organising factor ... in intellectual functioning', because they guide the individual's behaviour in a huge variety of situations. They are thus placed at the top of his learning hierarchy.

A rule expresses a relationship between concepts. It can take the form of a statement: *Round things roll; a + b = b + a; the mark of the plural in French nouns and adjectives when written is normally -s.* They may also be formulated in *if/then* or operational terms: *If a + b = c, then b + a = c; to form the plural of French nouns and adjectives you normally add -s.*

Some rules are simple, if the concepts related are few and easy to grasp, and any relational concept, such as + or =, is unambiguous. An example might be the rule about the formation of plurals. Others are harder, either because they depend on the successful application of simpler rules or because the concepts are less easy to understand.

Evidence of 'knowing a rule' does not come from being able to state a proposition, but from appropriate performance. However Gagné is emphatic about the value of verbal statements.

> While 'knowing the verbal statement' does not necessarily mean 'understanding the rule', it is important to recognise that verbal statements usually are crucial in the process of *learning* a new rule. Once a child has learned to use language, the process of learning is vastly facilitated by the use of verbal statements as *cues* to the learning of new defined concepts and rules. Adult learning, in many spheres, is largely carried on by the use of verbal statements read in textbooks or other written materials. (Gagné, 1985: 120)

He acknowledges that children learn the rules of their native language without being able to state them, but maintains that verbal statements are helpful in the learning of foreign languages, as in the learning of other intellectual skills.

Learning rules is a cognitive process because it involves understanding concepts and the relation between them. But there is also an *action* quality about rules: calculations have to be made, problems solved, language forms chosen. That is why rules have been given the collective name of *procedural knowledge*, in contrast to *declarative knowledge*, such as is required for knowledge of content and facts. The test of whether a rule has been learnt is not the ability of learners to talk about it, but to apply it correctly and swiftly. Learning rules therefore is also learning a *skill*. As McLaughlin (1987: 133) writes, in describing the cognitive approach to the learning of a second language generally: 'To learn a second language is to learn a *skill*', because various aspects of the task must be practised and integrated into fluent performance. This requires the automatization of component sub-skills.

This recalls Bialystok's (1990) 'control of linguistic processing'. However, whereas she describes this globally as 'skilled selective attention', Shiffrin and Schneider (1977, quoted in McLaughlin, 1987), distinguish between two phases: controlled and automatic processing. Any new task requires close attention to each aspect or to each step in a series of procedures. They call this *controlled* processing. Through repeated practice, the performance becomes smoother and the different steps become integrated with each other, until the performance becomes *automatic*, and attention is freed for higher order tasks. (The learning of motor skills, such as driving a car, playing an instrument or engaging in sport provides obvious parallels, though at a lower level of complexity than with intellectual skills.)

The aquisition of grammar in L1 and the learning of cognitive skills compared

Box 7.1 shows a comparison between the development of grammatical competence in L1 as described by Berman and the learning of cognitive skills as described by Gagné.

It would need detailed discussion to determine whether Berman's schemata can be equated with Gagné's concepts, but the overall similarity between the two models is striking. Both contain two parts: analysis and processing. In both, concrete, unanalysed operations are performed first, then contrasts and similarities are noticed, next a generalisation is made or a concept formed, in which items or events with the same attributes are grouped together; finally a rule is worked out which defines the conditions under which the common items or events occur. The second part, processing, first requires selective or controlled attention, and then becomes increasingly skilled and automatic. In many cases a rule may need elaboration and restructuring before it fits all the facts (end-state-usage) or, to put it differently, several rules may interact to form a complex, higher-order rule.

This similarity suggests that first language acquisition is not unique in character, but falls within the general category of learning of intellectual skills, (although this is not universally accepted). It seems legitimate therefore to assume that the same process

Box 7.1 The development of grammatical competence in L1 and the learning of cognitive skills compared (based on Berman (1986) and Gagné (1985))

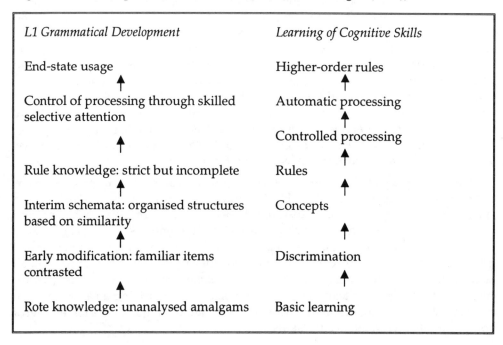

L1 Grammatical Development	Learning of Cognitive Skills
End-state usage ↑	Higher-order rules ↑
Control of processing through skilled selective attention ↑	Automatic processing ↑
	Controlled processing ↑
Rule knowledge: strict but incomplete ↑	Rules ↑
Interim schemata: organised structures based on similarity ↑	Concepts ↑
Early modification: familiar items contrasted ↑	Discrimination ↑
Rote knowledge: unanalysed amalgams	Basic learning

is at work in the learning of a foreign language and its grammar, involving in turn context-bound contact, analysis and processing of the new knowledge.

Application of the Cognitive Skill Model to the Learning of L2 Grammar

Before the different stages of the model are examined in detail, it is important to define the specific functions of grammar rules, compared with rules in other subjects. This means specifying the characteristics of words viewed from a grammatical instead of a lexical perspective.

(1) *Variability of form.*
(2) *Variability of position.*
(3) *Membership of a word class.* The variability of form and position is neither infinite nor random: it is constrained by membership of a word class.
(4) *The variations in a word's form and position are determined by its relation to other elements within or outside the sentence.* This is the most important characteristic of all.

Grammar rules therefore express the relation between elements and indicate what form or position of words should be chosen within the range of variations permitted in their word class.

The first stages in the analysis

According to the Berman/Gagné model, the first encounter with a new element does not yet involve analysis. The learner's emphasis is on meaning, on understanding, recognition or production as required in specific contexts. *Je m'appelle . . . ich heiße* may appear as formulaic expressions, as single unanalysed wholes (basic learning). Once other expressions are introduced, *j'habite à,.. j'ai onze ans, ich wohne in . . . ich bin elf Jahre alt*, what seemed a single whole is revealed as being made up of separate parts, each of which can be slightly modified or used in new combinations (discrimination). This is confirmed and reinforced when the question formulas are learnt. Regularities are noted or pointed out: phrases with *je* or *ich* refer to a learner as speaker, those with *tu* or *du* to another as addressee. In French the different phonetic and graphic forms of *je, j'* may have to be clarified. Form and meaning are now more explicitly linked, both in regard to the subject pronoun and the corresponding verbal form (generalisation), and the relationship is expressed, however informally, as a rule.

A judgement has to be made by teachers how soon to draw attention to these variations or, in other words, how soon to categorise the relevant forms and formulate the relevant rules. Do they wish to reject explicit analysis at this stage, and simply provide their pupils from the start with useful phrases for social interaction? If they wait, more examples of a particular form–meaning correspondence will have been met and any recapitulatory statement will thus have a broader basis.

On the other hand, if pupils do not know how to take the phrases apart and reuse individual elements in new combinations, or at least come back to them in a cyclical progression and integrate them with new acquisitions, there is a strong risk that an unanalysed amalgam may have been drilled in so firmly that its limited applicability to a particular context is not realised and the formula is produced where it is not appropriate. Weinert (1987, 1990) quotes several examples from an investigation into classroom learning where that risk was not avoided, and whole formulas were confused. For instance 'Wie heißt du?' evoked the response 'Ich bin zwölf Jahre alt', or an adverb was thought to be an integral part of the verb: 'Wo spielst du Gitarre?' 'Ich spiele nicht gern Gitarre'.

The importance of discrimination and conscious analysis as steps towards developing the right concept and as prerequisites for learning a rule may be illustrated through another example, again from German.

A favourite topic during the first year is learning the names of civic buildings, followed by expressions for asking and giving directions. Pupils may thus have learnt in one lesson *der Bahnhof, die Hauptpost* etc., perhaps through actual photographs. Soon after, they may hear on tape or read in their textbooks requests for directions like *Wie komme ich am besten zum Bahnhof, Stadtpark, Rathaus, Freibad, bitte?* and *Wie komme ich am besten zur Hauptpost, Sporthalle, Jugendherberge, bitte?* They will recognise the nouns and will concentrate on the meaning, which can be made clear through photos of one person talking to another and pointing in a certain direction. Many of them will just accept the new formula, without recognising that the same determiner has been used, but in a modified form. They may even be able to frame questions themselves about those particular buildings by imitation.

However they can only produce questions with other nouns they know, and *any new ones*, if they pay attention to form and analyse it. They need to:

(1)   discriminate carefully between the requests, perhaps writing out two lists,
(2)   link the *zum* occurrences to masculine and neuter nouns, and *zur* to feminine nouns; and
(3)   generalise the connection into an operational rule.

The concept of *zum/zur* and the rules relating to its use would gradually have to be clarified and elaborated. The first step would be to make clear that these are contractions of *zu* and *dem/der*, so that the link with the article becomes visible (and later in the course allows *zu* + *den* in the plural). The next step would be to highlight the connection between *zum/zur* and verbs of motion such as *kommen* and any other that is known, and bring out the fact that *zum/zur* are used to express direction. To drive the point home, one would wish to contrast expressions of direction with those of identification or location, where the nominative is used, as in *das ist/wo ist?/hier ist das Postamt.* (To use Gagné's terminology, instances and non-instances of the concept need to be shown.)

Once the concept of *zum/zur* and the relevant rule has been grasped, it can be practised in a variety of interesting ways. But the following anecdote shows how learners' natural tendency to generalise from what they know sometimes leads them to erroneous conclusions. In a class that I observed, where the giving of directions was being taught, I overheard one girl whispering to another: 'I get it. English "to the" is translated into German by "*zum/zur*". In the following chapter of her textbook she would find out that her rule only applied to names of buildings and that she had to use *nach* with names of places. At a later stage, when verbs of giving, telling, writing etc. were introduced, which require neither *zum/zur* nor *nach*, but whose English counterpart was followed by 'to the', further restructuring of her own internal representation of the rule would be urgently necessary.

It should be emphazised that the time to move from an unanalysed whole to a changeable form can vary enormously. Phrases like *J'ai oublié mon stylo* or *Est-ce que je peux aller aux toilettes?* can be taught at an early stage and used as wholes for a long time until the teacher thinks that other instances of the perfect or the question form should be introduced. Analysis begins when it is important to attend to significant relationships, that is similarities and distinctions.

Concepts required for the learning of grammar

Understanding a concept, as was stated earlier, means recognising individual elements as members of a class. For the learning of grammar two types of concepts are required: *grammatical* and *semantic*.

The *grammatical* concepts comprise first those of different word classes, such as verbs, nouns, pronouns and subdivisions within them, for example infinitive, past participle, direct and indirect object pronoun. *Zum/zur* combine members of two classes. The list is long. With each new grammatical concept, say, the infinitive, the process will have to be repeated, from context bound use, through discrimination to the discovery of similarities with other instances of the concept, until finally the concept for the whole class is formed, and all its members and their common distinguishing features are known.

At some stage teachers will have to grasp the nettle of using grammatical terminology. In Britain there is a possibility that knowledge of the most common terms will have been acquired within the English syllabus within the National Curriculum. If that occurs, the conceptual basis will have been laid, and only minor changes or additions will be necessary. If no such knowledge can be relied on, foreign language teachers will have to provide it themselves, at the appropriate time and after a sufficient number of concrete examples have been met. In all disciplines, as Gagné points out, abstract terms are used as general descriptors of a large number of specific examples, and the pupils' experience in their own language facilitates understanding.

One has to accept, nevertheless, that unfamiliar grammatical concepts will need time to develop. As pupils' knowledge of the system increases, the deductive approach, presenting the complete picture of a class or category, to be exemplified subsequently, can save time; similarly, a table can serve as a visual summary.

Even if the use of grammatical terms is delayed or reduced to a minimum, learners need to be able to demonstrate in practice that they can differentiate between one class and another. Whether it is as the result of explanation, correction or repeated exposure and production, they must feel, for example, that *plus* and *très* cannot be made feminine or plural and that *mal* and *seulement* must be treated as adverbs and not as adjectives.

A second kind of grammatical concepts that need to be acquired are the terms used to describe some of the 'dimensions' or 'features' of words, such as number, gender, person, case, subject and object (Hudson, 1992), or the relationships between forms, such as agreement or inversion. Some of these concepts, like subject and object or agreement between noun and adjective, are difficult for English learners, because they do not express semantic relationships, or because they are expressed differently in English.

The *semantic* concepts required for learning grammar include relatively easy ones , like agent or actor, speaker, third party, past and future time, ownership, purpose. But others, some of which have been mentioned in the previous chapter, are more complex, for example, continuity and discontinuity, completed and incompleted actions, certainty and doubt, realisable and unrealisable hypotheses. Some rules only bring together grammatical concepts, such as *'durch* takes the accusative' or 'In French the adjective agrees in gender and number with the noun it qualifies', others involve both grammatical and semantic concepts, as 'If an action is performed by a number of people, including yourself, use *nous* or *wir* and the first person plural form of the verb'.

Rules

One of the reasons why generalisations about grammar are unhelpful is that all rules are treated as similar in nature. Yet this is not so. Their function, as stated earlier in this chapter, is to determine the form or position of words within a range of variations. This already implies that some rules are concerned with form, others with position. They can also differ according to whether:

- the rule covers two adjoining elements in a phrase, as with plural markers (*à sept heures*), or expresses a relationship between different elements in a sentence (*en été il se levait à sept heures*);
- the rule is specific (*devoir* is followed by the infinitive), or applies throughout the language (agreement);
- the rule can be applied mechanically, because the concepts are grammatical (*ich weiß nicht, ob sie morgen kommt*), or involves choice, because the concepts are semantic (*passe-moi le pain/du pain, s'il te plaît*);
- the rule applies to both the spoken and written medium, or to a specific medium (*la pomme est verte*: write *e*, pronounce /t /;
- the rule is invariable (the first and third person of the German past tense have the same form) or needs elaboration and restructuring (choice of tense with *depuis*).

A further way of classifying rules in relation to learning is to divide them into four broad groups.

I. Rules affecting individual forms and their immediate neighbours

(1) The gender of nouns. The range of variations only amounts to two in French and three in German, although several elements are affected (articles, pronouns, adjectives).
(2) Forms of irregular verbs, especially in the most common tenses.
(3) The complementation of verbs. The range of variations may be small (*pouvoir* + one verb phrase, *zuhören* + one noun phrase, *ordonner* + a direct or indirect object) or large (*habiter*).
(4) The case of the noun phrase after German prepositions, where it is fixed (*mit, durch*, etc.).

The range of forms covered by these rules is large. The point to stress is that here the boundary between grammar and vocabulary has almost disappeared. Learning therefore is partly a matter of learning and remembering a great number of individual lexical items (irregular tense forms, nouns and articles) and partly learning small syntactic patterns, where the second slot can be filled by a large number of lexical items, as with complements of verbs or after prepositions (*dans cet établissement il faut/ il ne faut pas . . . ; ich komme mit dem Zug, mit dem Bus . . .*). Because they are not subject to larger constraints, the rules do not need further modification or restructuring. Learning therefore is not so much an analytical process, where the difficulty is to understand the concept, as one of memorising individual features, and carrying out variations that affect only a particular form and its immediate neighbours.

On the other hand, the communicative force of some rules, such as those for gender, is limited, and accuracy may tend to be sacrificed under the stress of production, when the wish to express meaning is uppermost.

II. Morphological rules

They form the grammatical infrastructure of the whole language at phrase level. They deal with:

(1) elements dependent on the noun (these are shown diagrammatically in Box 7.2).
(2) the conjugation of regular verbs: relation between stem and endings for different tenses and persons.

In the noun phrase, the range of variations within each of the cells or sub-groups is not large, but each phrase commonly consists of members from two or three cells and each member will probably be affected by the gender, number and, particularly in German, the function of the noun within the sentence (*les liaisons dangereuses; sie kam mit ihrem kleinen Bruder*). The learning difficulty therefore is partly conceptual, that is knowing which factors relate to the choice of form, and partly one of control in applying this knowledge swiftly. Identifying the factors, keeping the different forms

Box 7.2 Elements dependent on the noun

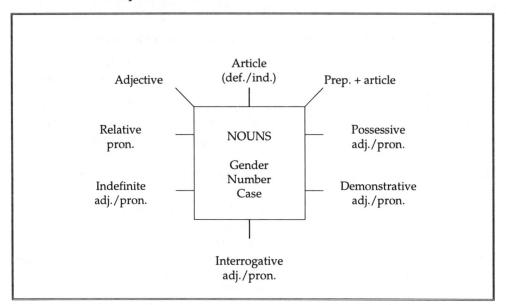

distinct and combining them as appropriate correctly and quickly ('multiple discrimi-nation' in Gagné's terms), requires much informed practice. The greater the number of factors and forms, the greater the processing load (see the reference earlier to *ihr (neues) Portemonnaie*).

Multiple discrimination is called for even more with verbs. The potential multiplic-ity of forms is daunting, and even the limited number of tenses in frequent use demands the rapid choice from 20–30 different forms, and also requires much practice.

The learner's reward for gaining confident control of morphological rules is the freedom to concentrate on the shaping of larger discourse units.

III. Word-order rules

These rules apply to:

(1) The position of specific elements. Rules affecting separable verbs in German can be applied mechanically, those determining the order of pronouns in both languages require some preliminary operations, those concerning the order of adverbials in German involve fairly subtle semantic criteria.

(2) The position of the verb in German in main, inverted and subordinate clauses. The rules are relatively few, but they affect German sentence structure so pervasively that they take a long time to acquire.

(3) Word order in declarative, negative, interrogative and imperative sentences. Sometimes the rules simply involve the appropriate insertion of a word, such as *est-ce que, ne . . . pas, nicht,* sometimes the social context or the medium may play a role, for example in deciding between *comment t'appelles-tu? comment tu t'appelles?, tu t'appelles comment?*

Alertness to particular grammatical elements that trigger a rule, the model of poems and sayings learnt by heart and repeated exposure can all help in the learning of word order rules, but the influence of L1 sentence patterns is often strong.

IV. Semantic rules

These rules determine, among others:

(1) the choice of article: definite, indefinite, partitive;
(2) the choice of tense, mood (indicative/subjunctive), voice (active/passive).

Some difficulties facing English learners under (2) have already been discussed in the previous chapter. Rules in this category do not come into force mechanically by the presence of a certain grammatical element, but because of certain configurations in a situation, such as the relation between one action and another in regard to time or the aspect under which it is viewed, or the degree of explicitness about the reference to an object. Practice therefore cannot be mechanical, but must aim at increasing depth and sureness of understanding through the presentation of different situations, where instances and non-instances of the various semantic concepts are realised.

The distinction made between small syntactic patterns such as *il est défendu de parler* and more complex rules which produce *il parle depuis une heure* suggests different degrees of difficulty and different kinds of learning. A mechanical rule that only affects one or two forms is likely to prove easier than a rule that is arrived at through a chain of decisions or one which demands sensitivity to wider semantic constraints. On the other hand some morphological rules, which require choice, have to be learnt early in any course of study.

I hope that teachers will not be put off by the term 'rules'. It is used here in the sense stated at the beginning of the section as expressing systematic relations between elements in a sentence. Nor does the use of the term imply an emphasis on formal exercises, divorced from meaning. It allows for the teaching of a large number of relatively simple patterns, which can be practised in life-like dialogues and role-plays, but it also underlines the fact that learners need to know about those systematic relationships, so that they can extend the range of their communicative resources. and go beyond the 'function speak' quoted by Johnstone (1989: 30)

P1: *Tu aimes le football?*
P2: *Non, je déteste le football*
P1: *Tu aimes le tennis?*
P2: *Oui . . . Tu aimes le rugby?*
etc. etc.

Effective communication and interaction depend both on a stock of vocabulary and on the ability to generate utterances through internalised grammatical knowledge.

Processing and restructuring rules

The Berman/Gagné model may have suggested through its typographical layout that analysis, leading to the internalisation of a rule, has to be completed before processing, leading to its automatisation, can begin. This is seldom the case.

Processing begins as soon as learners turn their attention to one particular language form. This may occur already during the first phase of understanding meaning; it is reinforced when learners try to produce the form themselves. They may have to concentrate at first on getting the pronunciation or the spelling right, then on choosing one form rather than another, selecting features that are relevant and discarding those that are not. All this requires deliberate mental operations, called, as stated earlier, *skilled selective attention* by Bialystok (1990) and *controlled processing* by Shiffrin and Schneider (1977). (The question whether learners do this consciously or unconsciously will be discussed later.) Gradually, through practice, the processing becomes *automatic*, although the time this takes may vary greatly between individuals and for different rules. (Different kinds of practice will be discussed in the chapter on teaching approaches.)

With a few rules the sequence of controlled, then automatic processing need only occur a few times, as for example in the choice of *les* as the definite plural article. With others some minor adjustments are needed. For instance the rules governing the formation of the present tense of *-er* verbs apply unchanged to thousands of verbs and in pronunciation to all. It is only in spelling that a few verbs require slight modifications.On many occasions however a rule will need to be elaborated from its first version and restructured to take account of new factors. An example of such restructuring was given earlier in relation to *zum/zur*. In French the examples would include the different functions of the imperfect or the tense to be used with *depuis* or *quand*.

Until restructuring is achieved and forms are mapped exactly on the functions they serve in the target language, the existing system is likely to show variability. As in the acquisition of the first language and indeed in the historical evolution of a language, two forms may be used in free variation. What seemed so firmly established a term or year ago now seems disturbed. For example, every teacher of French is familiar with 'subjunctivitis', the disease that seems to afflict learners after their first introduction to this mood, when they use it indiscriminately for a time.

Gaining Skilled Control through Practice

In describing the learning of L2 grammar as a cognitive skill, the emphasis so far has been on the cognitive, knowledge element. The present section is devoted to the attainment of skill, or language processing, as it is called in the model.

Skill is mainly achieved through practice, which is normally organised by the teacher. Yet practice is above all an opportunity for learning and therefore properly deserves to be discussed in the present chapter. The characteristics of learning grammar skills will be considered within general accounts of skill learning, such as are given in the psychological literature. Details of particular exercises will be left to the chapter concerned with teaching.

A clear and full account of skill learning is given in Cronbach (1954: 356). He introduces the topic thus:

> Skill is easy to describe, but hard to define. One person may be more skilled than another, if he reaches the goal faster, with fewer errors, and with less need to pause to find his way. We can describe skilled performance in such words as automatic, rapid, accurate, and smooth. It is wrong, however, to think of a skill as some single perfected action. Any skilled performance, even writing the letter *a*, is a series of hundreds of nerve-muscle coordinations. A skilled movement is a very complex process involving differentiation of cues and continual correction of errors.

Cronbach illustrates the difference between unskilled and skilled performance by comparing the behaviour of a motorist in unfamiliar territory with that when he is on a well known road. In the first, he is engaged in problem-solving; he makes a trial decision and pushes hesitantly down the chosen route, watching closely for signs which will help him check his decision. When he is on a well known route, he still subconsciously continues to interpret the cues provided by the conditions of the road, but he is so confident that he changes gears, gives extra power on a hill and takes curves without interrupting his conversation with his companion.

For language users the cues are the words that come into their minds, as they plan what they wish to say or write. Just as a road sign of a steep gradient acts as a cue to the driver to slow down, so the presence of a noun should signal the need for the right article, that of a verb for the right form, that of *daß* for the verb to go the end of the sentence.

In learning a skill, according to Cronbach, one should start with a general conception of the required response, which is then refined into more rapid and coordinated action through practice. Practice on its own is not so effective as practice assisted by demonstration and explanation.

Practice, properly organised, plays the major role in learning a skill. It does so in two ways: it gives learners experience with the cues that they must use to guide responses, and it shows them how adequate their response is, and where correction is particularly needed.

Conditions for effective practice

Practice does not guarantee expertness. As was said earlier, it is only an opportunity for learning. Whether that opportunity is used effectively depends on: (1) motivation and readiness, (2) suitable material, (3) proper amount and spacing of practice and (4) feedback.

Motivation and readiness

Little mention has been made so far in the book of pupils' attitudes to the subject, the teacher and to learning generally, but they are clearly of the utmost importance. To a certain extent they are influenced by the degree to which the other conditions for effective practice are met.

Suitable practice material

Suitability must obviously be related to the learners, their knowledge, ability, maturity and interests, but the material itself, according to Cronbach, should possess certain characteristics.

(1) *Practice material should present cues like those to be used later.* In relation to grammar this means that it should reflect both linguistic and contextual realities. Questions, requests and commands provide the natural contexts for addressee forms, whether polite or familiar; longer stretches of discourse are needed for realistic practice of pronouns and tenses.

(2) *Students should practise in the greatest feasible variety of situations.* Aiming for automatic response has sometimes been interpreted as calling for repetitive drills. This is not so. Varied situations require the students to isolate the essential elements and give practice in recognising what responses are needed. In language this means that even in practising, say, nouns with their genders or the forms of some irregular verbs, the material should vary.

(3) *Using a response in the context of a significant problem is a superior form of practice.* This is mainly a question of motivation, as students will be keener to learn, when their response is part of a larger undertaking. However *it may be impossible to practise some essentials sufficiently in significant projects.* Short but targeted practice may be necessary.

The relevance of both quotations to language learning is generally appreciated. On the one hand a visit abroad, a school play or class display evoke greater readiness by individuals to practise so as to enhance their contributions to the whole, on the other hand the discovery of a weakness requires special practice. The fact that immediate constituents, the noun and verb phrase and the clause, play an important role in both comprehension and production of language, justifies attention to these grammatical units.

Proper amount and spacing of practice

Larger amounts of practice are required when the responses (1) depend on delicate cues (in French this might apply to a choice between the imperfect and the perfect, or the indicative and the subjunctive), (2) involve a series of operations (in German this occurs when a possessive adjective has to agree with its noun) or (3) are easily forgotten (as with the gender of nouns). Considerable practice is desirable at the outset. This is not only to establish the basic response, but to do so correctly. At a later stage distributed practice, with shorter periods and lengthening intervals, is preferable to blocks of massed practice, since it reveals elements that have been forgotten.

Feedback and monitoring

Knowledge of results is important as a guide to further action. Those learning motor skills may receive intrinsic feedback from the situation itself. Letting the car drift to one side obviously requires the steering wheel to be turned in the other direction. It is possible to work this out for oneself, as it might be to fathom out why one's service action in tennis always sends the ball into the net. However extrinsic feedback, that is monitoring by an instructor, can identify what needs to be changed. It is particularly important to prevent bad habits from being fixed, because they are difficult to eradicate later.

The learning of a foreign language in the classroom offers fewer opportunities for intrinsic feedback than the learning of motor skills. The monitoring role of teachers thus becomes all the more important, because it is they who can evaluate the appropriacy of the performance in given contexts. Though the desirable level of attainment may vary with circumstances, the evidence from skill learning about the difficulty of eradicating bad habits reinforces the value of insisting on accuracy at the beginning.

Final Comments on the Cognitive Skill View of L2 Grammar Learning

This account has been rather lengthy, for two reasons. First, I wanted to show the different stages in the model clearly, yet supply enough examples. The sequence of unanalysed wholes, discrimination, concept and rule formation, followed by practice seems to me to reflect my own experience as a struggling learner of Russian and that of many adolescent learners whom I have taught, observed and examined. Second I wanted to show that the model can account for many different problems that are encountered by foreign language learners. Sometimes they have to go through a series of mental operations to produce the correct form, sometimes they have to understand an unfamiliar concept.

However this general cognitive theory does not specifically take into account the existence of the learner's first language, and the influence which this can exercise. Thus while in mathematics a coherent system of rules can be built from first principles, L2 learners start in full possession of an alternative and thoroughly familiar language system to which they inevitably relate any new language phenomenon they meet. Nor does the cognitive model allow for the possibility that there may be after all some special features about language learning which distinguish it from other kinds of learning.

It is therefore time to consider other theories of second language learning.

8 Other Theories of Foreign Language Learning: Extrapolating from Performance: Summary and Conclusions

Other Theories of Foreign Language Learning

According to cognitive theory, if the meaning of concepts and the working of a rule have been accurately, vividly and fully demonstrated and understood, and the rules have been practised appropriately and adequately, learning should ensue. However, as every teacher knows, this does not always happen, input does not become intake. According to some, this is because cognitive theory does not take account of the special nature of language and language learning. Alternative theories have therefore been put forward, some of which will be outlined below. (For a full account see McLaughlin (1987) or Cook (1991).)

The interlanguage theory

This is probably the most comprehensive of the theories that have their basis in the human faculty of language. The idea goes back to the discovery in the late 1960s and early 1970s that children develop the grammar of their L1 in a common order, which is independent of the input they receive and cannot be significantly speeded up. Corder (1967) in a seminal article entitled 'The Significance of Learners' Errors' speculated that L2 learners, like L1 learners, have a built-in syllabus determining their grammatical development, causing them to accept and integrate some external inputs but reject others. By studying the systematic errors that learners make, we are able to reconstruct their underlying knowledge to date, their *transitional competence*. This transitional competence or *interlanguage*, as Selinker (1972) called it in another seminal article with that name, is an interim grammar, distinct from both the learner's first language and the target language, and evolving all the time.

According to Selinker, five central processes involved in second language learning can influence a learner's interlanguage:

(1) language transfer: items, rules and sub-systems transferred from L1;
(2) transfer of training: features specifically due to the teaching received;
(3) strategies of second language learning: features resulting from an identifiable approach to the material to be learned;
(4) strategies of second language communication: features linked to the way a learner communicates with native speakers;
(5) overgeneralisation of semantic features and grammar rules of the target language.

Each of these processes, according to Selinker, can lead, either singly or in combination with others, to *fossilisation*, the retention in the learner's interlanguage of erroneous items, over time and despite corrections. Thus some persistent errors in pronunciation and grammar may result equally from language transfer and from strategies of second language communication: learners decide that their proficiency enables them to communicate to a degree they consider appropriate, and consequently no longer seek to improve.

The articles by Corder (1967) and Selinker (1972) led to a veritable explosion of research activity and the creation of a new research field: Second Language Acquisition (SLA). Learners' language was investigated in a number of ways: by listing, classifying and explaining errors (a task which often proved quite difficult), by measuring levels of accuracy or types of error at various stages, with learners from the same or different linguistic background, by testing learners' ability to distinguish grammatical from ungrammatical sentences, and the relation betwen this ability and explicit grammatical knowledge. Many of the studies have been of naturalistic learning, for example Spanish- or Chinese-speaking children in the USA or adult Spanish and Italian immigrants in Germany. (For a full discussion of the studies see Ellis (1990).) The main issues for research have been indicated by Hawkins and Towell, (1992: 97–121) as follows.

- How systematic are the developing interlanguage grammars?
- What are the sources of variability?
- What is the extent of language transfer and where does it occur?
- Does conscious knowledge influence learning?
- What is the relation between age, aptitude and attitude and success?   ·
- How is success to be defined?

To some teachers such questions may appear theoretical, yet to many they are very pertinent to their experience. Would one not wish to know, for example, why a university student of French, after 11 years of study, including a year spent in France, still shows non-systematic variability in her use of *c'est difficile de/à* and *pas de/ pas de la, des*? (Towell, 1987: 113–27).

Again, some teachers may be disappointed that despite this intense research activity, no comprehensive set of answers has yet been given to such questions. One can only point out that in every scientific discipline there is an initial period of hypothesis-building and testing, before practical issues can be confidently addressed. That is why many researchers (though not all!) have been cautious in extrapolating from their findings any recommendations for teaching. To the complexity of the issues one must add the difficulty of applying unreservedly to one's own classes findings reached in different or insufficiently specified circumstances.

In spite of all these reservations, I believe that some of the theories and some of the studies, particularly those conducted in familiar contexts, offer thought-provoking findings.

The natural-order hypothesis

One of the most controversial questions regarding the nature of interlanguage is the so-called 'natural-order hypothesis'. Corder (1967) suggests that some L2 *strategies* might be the same as those used in L1 acquisition, but he does not state that the actual course or *sequence* of learning is the same. A stronger claim for the existence of a natural order is made by Krashen (1985: 1):

> We acquire the rules of language in a predictable order, some rules tending to come early and others late. The order does not appear to be determined simply by formal simplicity and there is evidence that it is independent of the order in which rules are taught in language classes.

Krashen drew his evidence from studies which showed that learners from different language backgrounds reached similar levels of accuracy in some aspects of English grammar (Dulay & Burt, 1974), but later studies produced contradictory results, showing the influence of different linguistic backgrounds.

Studies of naturalistic L2 learning provide some support for the natural-order hypothesis, but the evidence from classroom learning has so far been meagre.

That is why a longitudinal study of grammatical development in a British classroom (Weinert, 1990) is of particular interest to British readers. Weinert studied the development of negation and interrogation in 42 pupils aged 11–16, drawn from each of the first four years of learning German as their first foreign language in an Edinburgh secondary school. The textbook used was *Deutsch Heute* (Sidwell & Capoore, 1983), which embodies a task-based approach, but with some grammatical explanation and practice.

I show first in Box 8.1 the order in which negation with finite verbs is acquired by L1 and naturalistic L2 learners (L2 examples from Felix (1982, quoted by Weinert, 1990):

Kein is rare, learners first use *nicht ein* and later *nicht kein*.

Weinert found in Year 2 and even in Year 3 many examples of similar non-target-like forms, for instance examples of the second stage, absence of verb, *ich keine groß*; *Zola*

Box 8.1 Order in which negation is acquired by naturalistic learners of German (Felix, 1980: 23–30)

1. External negation	*nein spielen Katze*
2. Sentence internal negat. (no verb)	*Milch nicht da*
3. Pre-verbal negation	*du nicht spielen Keller*
4. Post-verbal negation	*ich weiß nicht das*

Budd nicht ein Schwimmer and of the third stage, pre-verbal negation *Zola Budd nicht spielt Fußball; ich nicht gehen zu Schule am Sonntag.*

As for information questions beginning with *wie, wann, wo, was,* on which the study focused rather than on *yes/no* questions, the order used both in L1 and in naturalistic L2 learning is first the uninverted and then the inverted form. Here too in pair work conducted in Year 2 and based on pictures, half the information questions produced by the pupils followed this naturalistic order, that is, they were uninverted *wann F.S. schläft?*

The intriguing point is that these incorrect forms appear in Year 2, whereas in Year 1 the proportion of correct forms is much higher. With information questions, for example, correct performance drops from 98% in Year 1 to 59% in Year 2, improving again in subsequent years, as the graph in Box 8.2 indicates.

Weinert's explanation is that in Year 1 a few formulas were taught, both in regard to questions *wie heißt X?; wie alt ist X?* and to negatives *ich habe kein* (siblings or pets) and *ich spiele nicht (gern) X.* These were drilled intensively in a small number of contexts and without the internal structure of the expression being broken down, that is, they were used, in Berman's terms, as unanalysed chunks. When in Year 2 input was

Box 8.2 The order in which a group of secondary school pupils in Scotland learnt inversion in German information questions (Weinert, 1990)

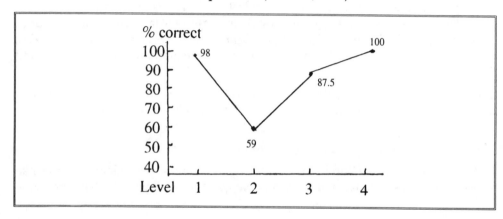

extended and drilling reduced, classroom learners processed the material in a manner independent from the input they were receiving in class and nearer to the natural order.

Weinert does not draw any teaching implications from her study, except to suggest that *nicht* should perhaps be introduced sooner. (*Kein*, introduced 12 weeks before *nicht*, was overgeneralised in negative sentences for a long time.)

What conclusions is one to draw from Weinert's study? Considered narrowly, it supports my view, advanced earlier, that prolonged reliance on an unanalysed whole without an understanding of its structure prevents learners from making personal recombinations of its elements and thereby retards their progress.

More importantly in this context, Weinert's study tells us something unexpected about learning strategies. The errors made in Year 2 are not simply due to carelessness or to transfer from English but seem to follow a deeper order similar to the order attested in L1 and naturalistic L2 acquisition and independent from the teaching received. It thus seems to lend some support to the idea of an in-built syllabus.

At this stage it is probably impossible to go further: we need to test whether the motivating effect of social phrases can be achieved without overlearning and with a more analytical approach. Whatever has been discovered about the grammatical development in L1 and naturalistic L2 learning of French and German needs to be more widely known outside the home countries. Further longitudinal studies about classroom language learning and about the relation between input, intake and output are needed. Even then, the implications for teaching are not obvious. Would one for example wish to introduce negation in German in the L1 order?

In the meantime, teaching will probably have to follow the old criteria of progression from the simple to the complex and attention to student needs, but teachers may show more understanding of their pupils' errors, if they know more about the course of development.

Linguistic universals and Universal Grammar

Weinert's findings prompt two further questions.

First, why should English-speaking adolescents use pre-verbal negation and uninverted questions at an early stage of their learning, like German children? One possible explanation is that they fall back on the order in which they acquired negation and questions in *English*. This starts with *no* or *where* at the beginning of the utterance (*no sit there; where milk go?*) and then progresses to internal negation (*I not hurt him*), the use of auxiliaries and, in questions, inversion. (For details, see Clark & Clark, 1977: 347–54.)

Second, going even further back, why should English and German children follow this order, which does not correspond to what they hear? The answer probably lies in Slobin's (1973) operating principles referred to at the beginning of Chapter 7. The child is concerned with semantic salience and simplicity of surface form. One of Slobin's operating principles is 'avoid interruption or rearrangement of linguistic units'. By placing a negative or interrogative word at or near the beginning, children emphasise the aspect that matters most to them, without having to rearrange the rest of the utterance.

Slobin was following an approach pioneered by Greenberg (1966), in which many languages are examined in order to discover what they have in common, how they vary and what principles and constraints govern this variation. The common features are called *linguistic universals*. Since languages can be classified according to different types, features found throughout a given type would be called *typological universals*. Pre-verbal negation, that is the pattern subject + neg + verb phrase, qualifies as a typological universal because it is the most frequent and geographically the most widespread. Thus, because of its universality, pre-verbal negation may occur as a stage in the acquisition order not only of the first but also of a second language. If this hypothesis is correct, the same may apply to other strong typological universals, *irrespective of the adult form either within the native or the target language*.

A different approach to explain the child's capacity to construct grammatical rules is that taken by Chomsky. The argument is highly abstract. It posits an innate language faculty, distinct from general cognitive capacity. 'When children are exposed to speech, certain general principles for discovering or structuring language automatically begin to operate' (Crystal, 1987: 234). These principles constitute a *Universal Grammar*, they are properties that apply to all languages, although parameters are left open, to be fixed according to individual languages. Universal Grammar may be present from the beginning, but its operation is influenced by non-linguistic factors, such as memory and cognitive ability, which together constitute *channel capacity*.

The rules that children discover with the aid of Universal Grammar form the *core* grammar of their language. However every language also contains *peripheral* elements, rules borrowed from other languages or derived from the history of the language. Related to this distinction is one between *unmarked* and *marked* rules. Unmarked rules are said to accord with the general tendencies of the language, or even the generality of languages, to be simpler or have wider application. For example, *big, long* and *fast* are unmarked in relation to *small, short* and *slow*, because the former can occur in both statements and questions. One does not say 'How slow does she run?' or 'How short is a piece of string?'

Teachers may ask whether these general theories are relevant to the practice of teaching. The answer is almost certainly 'no' at present, but they *may* shed some tangential light on problems related to learning and non-learning which teachers frequently meet. If concepts like *core, periphery, unmarked, marked* can be clarified and fully applied to French and German, and if it can be empirically shown that learners find core elements in a foreign language more accessible than peripheral ones and unmarked features easier than marked ones, teachers would be helped to predict probable difficulties or at least understand the learning process better.

For example, the possibility that linguistic universals may cause learners to choose more basic ways to express themselves has already been mentioned in connection with negation and questions in German.

The notion of core, with its connotation of basic, may explain why *I am driving a car now* was considered as more acceptable than *I am flying to New York tomorrow* and *He broke his leg* than *He broke his word* by foreign learners of English (Davies *et al.*, 1984: 9–10). In French, the pattern *Combien d'oranges voulez-vous?* may be considered unmarked by comparison with *Combien voulez-vous d'oranges?* French learners of English did not transfer the marked form (McLaughlin, 1987: 89).

Research into linguistic universals and Universal Grammar is very active and therefore deserves to be mentioned. It may contribute more to our understanding of language learning in the future.

The conscious/subconscious issue and Krashen's monitor model

The next theory to be discussed is more specific than those considered previously and its relevance to teaching more evident. It deals with the relative roles of conscious and subconscious learning in the study of foreign languages. Though the matter was raised by early writers such as Sweet (1899) and Palmer (1917), it came into prominence again in the 1980s through Krashen's monitor model. This theory has several strands, but the fundamental idea is the distinction between *acquisition* and *learning*. For Krashen (1985: 1), acquisition is 'a subconscious process identical in all important ways to the process children utilize in acquiring their first language'. It occurs through meaningful interaction in a natural communicative situation. Learning, on the other hand, is a conscious process that results in 'knowing about language'. Utterances are produced only as a result of acquisition, learning comes into play only as a monitor, when learners have time to edit what they have produced, when they concentrate on form and when they know the relevant rules. Whereas cognitive theory maintains that performance can become automatic through appropriate and adequate practice, Krashen denies any link between acquisition and learning. What is consciously learnt through explanation and practice of grammar cannot turn into acquisition.

Two important issues need to be addressed: (1) Can the distinction between acquisition and learning be proved? Is it true that consciously learnt rules do not become integrated into our comprehension and spontaneous production of the foreign language? (2) Have the implications for teaching been shown to be valid? Can proficiency result entirely from acquisition activities?

In respect of the first issue, all accounts of the development of grammar in children stress the role played in it by analysis. Consciousness may not play a part in this analysis with young children, but with adolescents and adults it normally does. The girl I quoted earlier, who formulated her own rule about the meaning and use of *zum/zur* was bringing her analysis to consciousness by verbalizing it. According to

Gagné (1985), by this very act her learning would have been strengthened. 'Verbal statements usually are crucial in the process of learning a rule' (see earlier). It is the need felt by learners to see connections and understand relationships in the data before them that has led teachers over the years to provide explanations or elicit from the learners themselves the rules which render their analysis conscious.

One can willingly accept that sometimes the concept emerges so clearly from the data that it is grasped without the need for an explicit formulation. Alternatively it may happen that an explanation is given before learners have had enough concrete experience of the relationship involved, so that the explanation makes no impact. In that case further examples have to be given, and the process of discrimination, of noting instances and non-instances of the concept has to continue, often for a long time, until learners are ready to truly understand the rule. This applies particularly to rules expressing semantic distinctions. However it is also part of our normal experience as learners that for many, more mechanical rules, what was consciously learnt at one stage gradually becomes part of our subconscious operating procedures, so that we judge or perform by what feels right, even though the rule may be only partly or even wrongly remembered. Unless a certain rule or vocabulary item is associated in our memory with a particularly striking occurrence, few of us would be able to disentangle which elements in our language competence spring from conscious learning or subconscious acquisition. In other words, unless one has never in the course of one's study received any formal explanation or engaged in deliberate learning, the source of one's knowledge cannot be identified precisely. The rigid demarcation between the results of acquisition and the results of formal learning suggested by Krashen thus seems difficult to test.

This issue was partly addressed in an experiment by Green and Hecht (1992), in which they set out to investigate the relationship between explicit and implicit knowledge in pupils' judgement of grammaticality. Three hundred German learners of English were shown 12 sentences in a connected text, each of which contained an error. The error was underlined and infringed one of the rules which are normally taught within the German school syllabus (see Chapter 4 for an account of German practice). For each sentence the testees were asked to put in a correction and also to write in an explanation or rule which might help the author of the text to avoid the mistake in future. Six groups of 50 of different levels of academic ability and at different stages in their study of English were tested.

If one takes the group as a whole, the main results were:

(1) Only 46% were able to produce a correct rule. Those that produced a correct rule nearly always (97%) produced the right correction.
(2) 78% produced the right correction. In other words, learners were still able to correct even when they had an incorrect explicit rule or no explicit rule at all.

On the theoretical issue the authors speculate as follows (p. 178):

What does seem to be the case here is that classroom learners with *learned* rules

Box 8.3 Proportion of pupils in different types of German schools able to correct mistakes and state a rule (Green & Hecht, 1992: 169–84)

	Gymnasium		*Realschule*		*Hauptschule*	
	Correction	Rule	Correction	Rule	Correction	Rule
Correct:	92%	55%	72%	34%	33%	7%

under their belt and confronted by a grammar test — a classic Krashen *Monitor* situation — operated to a large extent by *feel*. That is to say, they corrected largely by implicit rules, which very possibly had been facilitated by explicit rules. The explicit rules resurfaced when they were specifically called for and were then wrongly remembered in some cases. This is a possible explanation of the consistently greater success rate that the German pupils had with corrections when they gave a wrong rule than when they could offer no rule at all.

Two other results of the experiment are also of interest. First, as one might expect, success both in rule formulation and in error correction was closely linked to general academic ability. This emerges most clearly in comparing the performance of pupils from the three types of secondary school in the German system, the *Gymnasium* (academic), the *Realschule* (practical) and the *Hauptschule* (non-academic), after 5–6 years of English (Green & Hecht, 1992: 174).

Second, testees performed better, both in the statement of rules and in corrections, with some rules than with others. Easy rules were those that (1) referred to easily recognised categories; (2) could be applied mechanically; (3) were not dependent on large contexts. Green and Hecht (1992: 180) deduce from this that 'straightforward, mechanically governed linguistic categories can be usefully taught to learners as rules and readily practised in the context of short linguistic exercises'. Hard rules were those that demanded an appreciation of a speaker's perspective on an action, such as is required in English in the choice between a simple and a continuous tense or the simple past and the present perfect. The authors argue that drawing the attention of learners to how such semantic distinctions are realised in longer contexts and organising meaning-focused activities would be a more efficient use of time than prescriptive rules and formal exercises.

These reflections, which recall the distinctions between different kinds of rules made earlier in the chapter, touch upon the second issue raised by Krashen, that is the usefulness to learners of receiving explanations and corrections. When his theories were first put forward, they evoked a strong reaction on the Continent, because they contrasted sharply with the approach that had been followed there for a long time and continues to be followed today. One noted Danish teacher and researcher wrote (Faerch, 1985):

One occasionally comes across fairly sweeping generalisations about the utility of grammar explanation in the classroom or about the effect of corrections. Whether such generalisations are valid in certain social contexts is a question that I do not want to discuss here. But when we discuss foreign language teaching in relation to countries that have a long tradition in teaching foreign languages, and often with very successful results, such generalisations are considered extremely arrogant by practicing teachers and may well sever the communication between second language researchers and teachers.

A comment that similarly questions the extreme position taken up by Krashen and reasserts the usefulness of giving some attention to form comes from Canada, a country with wide experience of immersion programmes and school subjects taught in the foreign language. English-speaking children following such programmes display remarkable comprehension ability and obtain high scores in subjects like mathematics and science which they have studied in French. However, even after 6 or 7 years in an immersion programme, their productive use of L2 differs considerably in grammatical and lexical ways from that of native-speakers (Harley & Swain,1984). The results of an extensive research programme into both immersion programmes and core study of 1 hour per day led one observer to conclude that, while a return to a *principally* form-based teaching was not desirable, experiental teaching by itself was not sufficient and some analytic teaching was necessary (Lightbown, 1990: 90–1).

> French immersion, extended French, intensive courses, and exchange programs are successful mainly because they provide more time than traditional courses, and do so in contexts where learners' attention can be engaged and held for extended periods . . . Whether students have many hours of contact with the language (as in immersion) or few hours (as in core French), it is important that some attention be given to teaching the language itself, to providing some formal, analytic teaching that can help students see where their use of the target language differs from that of native speakers.

Drawing their evidence from a wide range of studies, Lightbown and Spada (1993: 105–6) give a balanced assessment that reasserts the contribution of form-focused instruction and correction 'within the context of a communicative program':

> Classroom data from a number of studies offer support for the view that form-focused instruction and corrective feedback provided within the context of a communicative program are more effective in promoting second language learning than programs which are limited to an exclusive emphasis on accuracy on the one hand or an exclusive emphasis on fluency on the other. Thus, we would argue that second language teachers can (and should) provide guided, form-fo-cused instruction and correction in specific circumstances. For example, teachers should not hesitate to correct persistent errors which learners seem not to notice without focused attention. Teachers should be especially aware of errors that the majority of learners in a class are making when they share the same language background. Nor should they hesitate to point out how a particular structure in a learner's first language differs from the target language . . . It may be useful to encourage learners to take part in the process by creating activities which draw the

learners' attention to forms they use in communicative practice, by developing contexts in which they can provide each other with feedback and by encouraging them to ask questions about language forms.

Krashen's views were publicized at a time when the importance of communicative competence as the goal of language learning and teaching was being emphasised. This probably explains much of the attention they have received. However I believe that his extreme position of denying altogether the value of conscious attention to form as a help to learning has been refuted by the evidence of the kind I have quoted. As so often in the history of language teaching, there has been a tendency to 'throw the baby out with the bathwater'. In the reaction against barren formalism or uncontextualised drills, the role of analytic teaching has been downgraded.

This does not deny the validity of the claim that subconscious learning also occurs. We cannot know for certain what use the learner will make of the language we teach. When language is associated with a truly felt experience, it may be retained for a long time. In the words of Stevick (1976: 44):

> The surrealistic story which on paper looks asinine may, in the hands of a teacher who understands its use and evidently believes in what he or she is doing, become an instrument for producing astonishing degrees of retention, both lexical and structural . . .

Elsewhere he (1976: 109) states: 'Other things being equal, the *"deeper" the source* of a sentence within the student's personality, *the more lasting value* it has for learning the language.'

The following conclusions seem to emerge:

- conscious learning, explanation of grammar and correction play a positive role as elucidation of experience and support for further learning and practice, particularly with mechanical rules;
- with semantic rules, the role of explanations is more one of raising awareness; exposure and use in different contexts is likely to be more productive;
- personal involvement by the learner can produce subconscious learning.

Extrapolating from Performance

So far I have tried to grasp how the learning process is conceived in different theoretical models. The arguments have been general and rather abstract, even though an effort has been made to illustrate them through reference to specific language difficulties, classroom responses and empirical studies. In the following I present data from actual performances, unfortunately mainly for the elementary stage, and try to relate them to the account of grammatical development given earlier.

The elementary stage: the APU survey

The data come from the surveys conducted over three successive years between

1983 and 1985 by the Assessment of Performance Unit (APU) of the then Department of Education and Science. They tested 24,000 pupils in over 1000 schools towards the end of their second year of learning a first foreign language, whether French (surveyed each year) or German or Spanish (surveyed in 1983 only). Each of the four skills was tested through five separate tasks, appropriate for 13-year-old pupils, and scored on a six-point scale from 0 to 5. The main criterion was communicative effectiveness. Results, detailed analyses and implications for teaching were published in three survey reports (DES, 1985–7) and four booklets for teachers (NFER–Nelson, 1986–7).

I will concentrate on speaking and writing because the analysis of the other two skills focused on the effectiveness of different task types rather than on pupil performance. As one might expect in such a large survey, the range of proficiency was very wide. (A similar range was found in the German study reported earlier in this chapter.) I shall seek to describe and illustrate the characteristics of performances at three levels: level 1, where only a minimum of communication was effected; level 3, intermediate; and level 5, the highest.

Level 1

The results of three speaking tests were analysed in detail: a structured conversation, role-plays and extended speaking about a situation or series of events cued by pictures. In the first task pupils at this level answered between one and four of the 14 items, in the second and third they produced only one or two words. These were greetings and nouns, mainly cognates or items of food and drink. Pupils relied heavily on the scaffolding provided by the assessor's questions.

Box 8.4 Performance at level 1 in a speaking test (role-play) after two years of study (APU, 1985: 145)

A. Bonjour monsieur
P. Bonjour . . . . je remis la fromage
A. Oui. Combien de fromage? . . . . Un kilo?
P. Oui.
A. Un kilo de fromage
P. Tu remis la . . . . vin?
A. Oui . . . . rouge ou blanc?
P. Blanc . . . . Tu remis la pommes
A. Combien de pommes?
P. Oui . . . .

Box 8.5 Performance at level 1 in two writing tests after two years of study (APU, 1987c: 5, 21)

Ils grande ville, une café, les enfants, les icés, la sadie, les bien.

Guten tag Frank
Ich sonstag ich buzy ich Haus. Varter ich Krank. Eine schwester ist werking. We go to der Kirche on sonntags. Und we go tanzen.

Box 8.4 gives the transcript of a role-play scoring 1. It is about buying food for a picnic.

In writing (see Box 8.5), two strategies were common: to string together a series of nouns in L2 or to use English, with an occasional word in L2. The first is illustrated in a description of a seaside town based on a picture, the second in a report on a day at home.

In the receptive skills, level 1 pupils relied mainly on recognising lexical items. Where they could not do so, they omitted the answer.

Level 3

In the speaking tests, level 3 learners showed more independence from the assessor and were readier to initiate questions *kannste ich habe?* They occasionally resorted to

Box 8.6 Performance at level 3 in a speaking test (role-play) after two years of study (APU, 1985: 171)

P. Guten Morgen.

A. Guten Morgen

P. Ich would like eine piece of Kartoffelsalat.

A. Ach so . . . Kartoffelsalat. Möchten sie sonst was?

P. Und eine Flasche Rotwein

A. Ja . . . Wurst vielleicht auch?

P. Und eine Pfund Apfels.

A. Gut, ist das alles?

P. Ja . . . I don't know . . . How much kostet's?

A. Das kostet insgesamt 9.75 DM.

P. Danke schön.

A. Bitte sehr. Wiedersehen.

P. Wiedersehen

English. The role-play reproduced in Box 8.6, again about buying food, but in German, is fairly typical of performances scoring 3.

Another common strategy was to use the phrases which they had learnt. This was often adequate, but at times pupils confused two phrases *je voudrais un café près d'ici*, or were unable to make the necessary adaptations, simply adding another lexical item *quelle heure est-il . . . arriver à l'école?*

In writing, level 3 learners constructed simple sentences and some attempted to express more complex ideas. In reporting, there was sometimes confusion between the two tenses normally learnt by this stage, the perfect and the immediate future. Within one script there might be correct L2 structures and transfers from English *Mein Vater ist lesen*. The use of English was less common than at level 1, though complete transfers ('calques') were not uncommon, such as *ich habe ein wasche*. The report on a day in town in Box 8.7 is typical for writing at this level. The account is clear, though not very full. Some useful knowledge has been learnt, semantic as well as grammatical, such as how to negate, the feminine and masculine form of the possessive, the plural of the indefinite article. On the other hand verb forms are confused, *je vais acheter* and *j'ai acheté* being used alternatively. The repetition of *dans en ville* indicates a systematic error. The idiomatic phrase *je suis fauché*, though not applicable to the girl writer, strikes a pleasant note.

Recognition of individual words in reading and listening was better at level 3, but

Box 8.7 Performance at level 3 in a writing test after two years of study (APU, 1987c: 17)

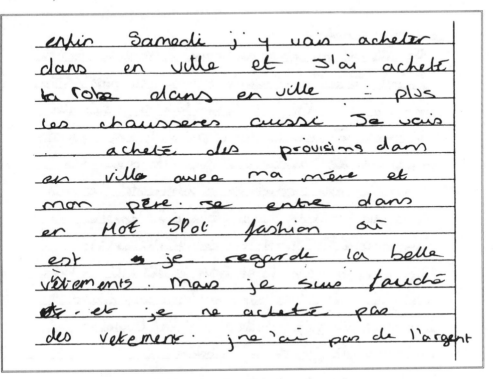

it was only at level 5 that deduction and inference were used to relate individual words to larger contexts.

Level 5

In speaking, pupils at this level could manage well formed utterances, use paraphrase and correct themselves, though mistakes were still frequent. In writing, they hardly ever used English; they attempted coordination and subordination, modals and separable verbs. In the report of a day in town in Box 8.8, the account is full and well structured, with details introduced through subordinate clauses beginning with conjunctions and pronouns. The perfect tense is expertly handled. However it is also typical that there should still be inconsistencies *je suis entré/j' y est entrée*.

Discussion

(1) From a psycholinguistic point of view the most interesting result is the similarity between the first steps in classroom L2 learning and the process of L1 acquisition, at least when the teaching emphasises communicative interaction. As was

Box 8.8 Performance at level 5 in a writing test after two years of study (APU, 1987c: 19)

> Le dernier samedi,
> Je suis allé au place du Marché à neuf heures moins le quart. Je suis entré dans le bureau du poste. «Trois timbres» ai-je dit. Après ~~entrato~~ je suis Sorti et je suis allé au Tabac, j'ai je demandé trois pains et cinq baguettes. Je suis sorti. Et j'ai attendu au arrêt d'autobus. L'autobus est arrivée et je suis monté. Je suis descendu près de supermaché qui s'appelle «Hypermarché». J'y est entrée et j'ai achite deux verres et trois livres. Enfin je suis allé au Tabac où j'ai achète trois journaux. Jusqu'aux douze heures je suis parti la ville et j'ai pris l'autobus au Tours où ~~j'ai habi~~ j'habite.

mentioned at the beginning of Chapter 7, young children initially rely on one- or two-word utterances to express a number of meanings. In the same way L2 learners at level 1 seem to rely mainly on nouns strung together. In L1, elaboration begins when children start to add endings to show plurality or tense and to produce the first coordinated sentences. Similarly L2 learners at level 3 begin to form simple sentences and those at level 5 have advanced further along the route of linguistic elaboration and complexity by adding more detail and using more complex sentence structures.

(2) Language users, whether in L1 or on L2, try to communicate with whatever means they possess. The difference is that L2 learners have available to them as a natural and reliable vehicle of communication their own language. It is thus understandable that they should fall back on English when their limited knowledge of the foreign language does not allow them to express their meanings as they wish. Hence the temporary mixture of English and L2 at level 1, and the occasional resort to English at the intermediate level, often with some communicative success.

(3) As more is retained of what has been taught, more of the foreign language becomes available for communication, and the need for English diminishes. But what is known of the foreign language so far are individual words (together with often undifferentiated articles), and fixed phrases. In terms of grammatical development then, level 3 pupils are beginning to move past the stage of using unanalysed wholes.

(4) The next stage is when modification of individual elements begins. Rules of agreement have to be applied in French, case endings added in German, verb forms learnt. Level 5 students have reached the stage when the concept has been understood and an awareness of rules is present, but the actual performance is still inconsistent. This applies in particular to the gender of articles, agreement, verb forms and, in German, to case endings and word order. Some influence of English may still be noticeable *nach Fußball; j'ai pris l'autobus au Tours*.

(5) The development of grammatical knowledge seems to go hand in hand with the increase in vocabulary.

Open questions

In the discussion I have suggested that the difference in L2 proficiency between pupils at level 1 and those at level 5 bears similarities to the different stages in grammatical development as described by Berman and Gagné. I think that this interpretation is supported by the data. Nevertheless some questions remain unanswered.

First, did those pupils who performed at level 5 go through the earlier phases of relying on nouns and fixed phrases? Only longitudinal studies from the start could provide the answer.

Second, would a similar exercise in another country provide similar learner profiles? For example, would there be as many references to fixed phrases, or are they specifically associated with teaching approaches developed in Britain in the mid–1980s through the Graded Objectives in Modern Languages movement and functional syllabuses, and sanctioned in 1988 in the new form of the examination at 16 for the General Certificate of Secondary Education (GCSE)?

Finally, one needs to remember that the APU surveys only deal with the first two years of language study in school.

The intermediate and advanced stages

One can assume that grammatical and general language proficiency improve after the elementary stage. The pupils observed by Weinert may have been held back by inappropriate drilling at the beginning, but by the their fourth year they were using question and negation forms correctly. Official statistics show that in the 1991 GCSE summer examination, the same percentage of candidates, 44%, gained an acceptable level of proficiency in French and German as in mathematics (Grades A–C). On the other hand the same variation in performance was noted by G.C.S.E. examiners after five years of study as in the APU survey after two. One report for 1992 stated:

> The best candidates showed excellent control of verb structures and a pleasing range of vocabulary and idiom. At the other end of the scale, anglicisms were frequent, and virtually incomprehensible French was punctuated by almost equally incomprehensible English. (Southern Examining Group, 1992)

However there are almost no research studies or analytical surveys about the later stages. In one of the few relevant studies, Hecht and Green (1993) comment that their literature search had yielded accounts of L2 development in general and of research with beginners, but no empirical studies of groups of learners over a prolonged period. In their own project, entitled 'Wie wachsen Wissen and Können?', they investigated the development of L2 knowledge and L2 use over six years by pupils in various Gymnasien, the German academic secondary school. A number of identical tests on discrete items and global tasks were administered three times, after three, five and eight or nine years of learning English. The results are complex: in the performance tasks progress speeds up between the intermediate and advanced stage, pointing to a long 'incubation period', as the authors call it. Progress is most marked in the expansion of vocabulary, on the other hand the proportion of lexical and discourse errors also increases by comparison with grammatical errors.

Inferences from findings obtained in another educational context are always questionable. Nevertheless the results from Germany, where grammar is still explicitly taught and practised, confirm British findings from a period where the teaching of grammar was emphasised. In 1968 an error analysis was made of an essay about a train journey written by British first-year university students of German (Grauberg, 1971). Morphological errors about the gender and declensions of nouns or verb forms were very few; the number of syntactical errors, mainly in the government of verbs and prepositions, was only half that of lexical errors. Among these the largest group was due to a faulty equivalence of English and German words, for example *ich sollte meinen Freunden in Nottingham begegnen; ich wollte den Zug halten*; another substantial group involved a transfer of a complete English expression, for example *Ich dachte, daß Sie mir sagten, Sie wohnten in London*. It looks as if during their course of study the learners had concentrated on achieving formal accuracy at the expense of semantic skills. As a result, when they were uncertain about the correct way of expessing ideas in L2, they fell back on patterns in their L1.

Twenty years later, the performance of learners at GCSE and the revised A-level examination seems to reflect a rather different set of priorities. I quote here from the report from one of the boards setting A-level examinations. The syllabus is based on the study of topics, and the examination, taken by over 8000 candidates in French, German, Spanish and Italian, is conducted entirely in the foreign language. The performance of many candidates in the summer of 1992 was highly praised by the examiners. In the oral, which includes a 20 minute discussion of a selected topic, 'many candidates were fluent and were able to speak accurately with a good range of vocabulary and constructions'. In relation to the written papers, 'Many candidates wrote very good French, and did not seem at all inhibited by the task of writing about their topics in the foreign language; for the best, writing in French seems a natural extension of their study.'

On the other hand the examiners also noted that in the oral 'an alarming number of candidates experienced serious problems of accuracy, with elementary errors occurring in verb forms and tenses, adjectival agreements, case endings, pronouns, prepositions and word order'. After praising the written performance in French, the examiners continued: 'but there is a continuing tendency to spoil the effect of their often very good French by errors in elementary areas of language' (University of Oxford Delegacy of Local Examinations, 1993). This situation has so alarmed modern language departments in universities that there have been references to a crisis, and formal grammar courses now figure in many timetables.

It appears that changed teaching priorities have led to changed learning outcomes. Pupils have concentrated on the semantic skills and in their topic study they have successfully absorbed the vocabulary and grammar needed to express their opinions. On the other hand many have failed to consolidate through analysis and practice grammatical features of the language that do not contribute directly to communication.

If this conclusion is correct, what light does it throw on the nature of the grammar learning process? Does it mean that the influence of an internally driven syllabus, resistant to teaching, is seriously questioned? Does it suggest that we are left with a cognitive skill theory, in which performance depends on which aspects of the language have been stressed most? Only a long-term study could answer that question.

Summary and Conclusions

In this last section I want first to review what each of the three parts of the discussion on the grammar learning process — the cognitive skill theory, other theories and learner performance — has contributed to our understanding, and subsequently to suggest a way in which the three perspectives can be brought together.

Chapter 7 started with a demonstration that children's grammatical development in their first language can be accommodated within a general theory of learning intellectual skills. The special function of grammar rules was defined as expressing the relations between sentence elements, and determining their form and position accordingly. The application of the cognitive skill model to the learning of grammar rules was pursued through all its stages, from the use of context bound items, through the gradual identification of concepts by noting instances and non-instances of their use to the formation of rules. Different types of grammar rules were distinguished, together with the kind of learning each requires. Finally, the conditions by which practice can be made effective and lead to smooth performance were described.

In the first part of the present chapter some theories were discussed in which the learning of language is held to have some unique features. Within the general concept of an evolving interlanguage, different from both the source and target language of L2 learners, the possibility that their grammatical development follows a natural order, in line with an inbuilt syllabus, was considered. Some evidence for this was found in the emergence of naturalistic negative and interrogative forms in the German of Scots learners, once the effect of early intensive drilling had worn off. The hypothesis that all language learning is influenced by linguistic universals or Universal Grammar was outlined briefly. Greater attention was paid to the claim that the grammar of L2 can only be acquired subconsciously and not learnt consciously. Findings from a number of studies seem to refute this claim, although subconscious acquisition through memorable associations is well attested.

In the second part of the chapter the performance of 13-year-olds after learning a foreign language for two years, as tested in a nation-wide survey, was characterized. Weaker pupils rely heavily on English, those at an intermediate level of proficiency seem about to emerge from the initial stage of context bound use, while abler pupils show awareness of rules, though with inconsistent performance. These findings seem to confirm the developmental path proposed in the Berman/Gagné model.

At an advanced stage a difference was noted between performance in the late 1960s and that in the early 1990s. In the former a sure grasp of basic morphological and syntactic rules was accompanied by much lexical uncertainty, in the latter semantic appropriateness, resulting from a topic based syllabus, has been gained at the expense of grammatical accuracy. The level of grammatical proficiency thus seems influenced by teaching priorities rather than by any inherent language constraints.

Can the different perspectives and findings in the three parts of the discussion be brought together? I believe that a useful framework is provided by the account in Clark and Clark (1977: 223–58) of how speakers plan and execute speech in L1. The framework can also, in my view, apply to writing.

Clark and Clark (1977) distinguish five steps in the decision-making process. They are in order:

(1) *Discourse plans*: the structure for a particular kind of discourse is decided. (Giving instructions, describing a house, reporting an event etc. all show characteristic structures.)

(2) *Sentence plans*: the global structure of the sentence to convey the intended message is selected. What is being talked about? What is said about it? Is it to be through a statement or a question? What does the interlocutor know already and what is new information?

(3) *Constituent plans*: words and phrases (noun phrase, verb phrase, clause) and their order are chosen.

(4) *Articulatory programme*: phonetic segments, stresses and intonation pattern of the words in a constituent are called up into memory.

(5) *Articulation*: the articulatory programme is executed.

Commenting on this process, which skilled speakers perform very rapidly, Clark and Clark (1977: 257) write: 'Within discourse, each sentence is . . . planned broadly, roughly one at a time . . . The words within a sentence however, are not all planned at once . . . Speakers appear to work from a skeleton plan of a sentence and select the words roughly constituent by constituent'. The constituent may vary in size from two words, as in *the man*, up to seven or eight words, for example a short clause (p. 260). The importance of constituents in the organisation of speech is shown by the fact that pauses, hesitations and new starts in L1 tend to occur at the boundaries between constituents.

If one re-interprets the content of Chapters 7 and 8 within this framework, Chapter 7 in its detailed, almost schematic account of how grammar is learnt, keeps to the constituent level. Some of the rules deal with elements within one constituent (agreement in the noun or verb phrase), others with relations across constituents (complementation of verbs, choice of tense and mood).

Chapter 8 is concerned both with actual performance and the presumed learning process, and in different ways throws light on the manner in which learners handle the relationship between constituents and the message of the sentence. In Weinert's study it was shown that some pupils had to re-learn almost from scratch in Year 2 how to express negation and information questions. Perhaps the reason was that the drilling in Year 1 offered them complete, sentence-length messages, and thus ran counter to the natural process of building a sentence constituent by constituent. Learners therefore had to go through this process in Year 2, before they could set out on the route towards adult use. The possibility that this route might start in a developmentally simpler way is not excluded.

The APU survey again shows learners keen to construct messages. At level 1 words are either strung together without linking grammatical structures, or they are connected by English. At level 3 learners have sufficient lexical and grammatical knowledge to build simple sentences from constituents, but, as with Weinert's pupils, fixed messages are sometimes used, with varied appropriateness: *Quelle heure est-il . . . arriver à lécole* or *Je suis fauché*. The better pupils of level 5 are able to fill out constituents with adverbials and vary the clause structure.

The 1968 essays show advanced learners with good control at constituent level but deficient in semantic knowledge, unaware that certain messages require different constituents altogether. On the other hand, students in the early 1990s, according to examiners' reports, have been encouraged to concentrate on the transmission of messages and not been pressed to assimilate the many form-related rules at constituent level.

To sum up, the discussion has progressed from an examination of how grammar rules are learnt to a sampling of how they are used. It has confirmed the interdependence of vocabulary and grammar: for the learner there is an undoubted tension between the desire to communicate and hence reliance on vocabulary, and the disciplined effort needed for the learning of grammar. In the end semantic and grammatical knowledge have to work together. It is a conclusion that echoes earlier statements about children mapping meaning onto forms (Clark & Clark, 1977) and about the dependence of grammatical knowledge on an adequate knowledge of vocabulary (APU). The connection between grammatical and lexical knowledge, and between control of language forms and the use of language to communicate will be reaffirmed in the discussion of teaching approaches.

9 Teaching Different Kinds of Grammar Rules in French and German

The Case for Explicit Teaching of Grammar

The question whether grammar should be taught at all is not rhetorical. The previous chapter has shown that some serious scholars doubt or even deny the usefulness of explicit grammar teaching, arguing that the grammar of a foreign language can only be learnt subconsciously, perhaps according to an internally determined order. There are teacher's books, intended to accompany coursebooks for schools, which devote page after page to information gap exercises, games or the uses of information technology, but never specify what grammatical knowledge is required by the learner to complete these exercises successfully, or indicate how such knowledge may be learnt or taught. The case for teaching grammar therefore needs to be made anew.

It needs only a little reflection to agree that in a school course of four or five years learners, in order to engage in even relatively simple communication, will need to do all or most of the following:

- distinguish between what they as speakers do and what the addressee or a third party does;
- ask questions;
- make negative as well as positive statements;
- refer to people or things previously mentioned;
- indicate possession;
- make comparisons;
- talk about the past and the future as well as the present;
- show who performed an action and who or what was the object of the action.

They need grammatical knowledge for these basic notions. Even if one organises a course round the purposes which the learners want to achieve through language, such as identifying, reporting, expressing likes, dislikes and other feelings, making plans and arrangements, enquiring about health, costs and transport, grammatical knowledge is needed.

Obviously they will need the vocabulary appropriate to the subject matter and will find it helpful to memorize illustrative phrases, but neither vocabulary nor phrases will be enough. Learners will have to make choices between words, according to word class, decide which verb form, which pronoun to use, how to signal the distinctions between singular and plural, statement and question, and so on. In other words, they need to learn the rules of grammar that will guide them in choosing the form and position of words. The necessity of choice implies the necessity of understanding and applying the necessary rules.

And the more one wishes to nuance one's meaning, by indicating doubt, hypotheses or polite disagreement, the more grammatical forms one needs. Conversely, the greater one's knowledge of the resources offered by the linguistic system, the more flexibly, precisely and tellingly one can communicate one's meanings and understand the meanings expressed by native speakers and writers. As one of the pioneers of the communicative approach, Littlewood (1981: 6) writes: 'We communicate by exploiting the creative potential of linguistic structures.'

On the same page Littlewood describes the four broad domains of skill that make up a person's communicative competence. The first is linguistic competence.

> The learner must attain as high a degree as possible of linguistic competence. That is, he must develop skill in manipulating the linguistic system, to the point where he can use it spontaneously and flexibly in order to express his intended message.

To linguistic competence must be added, according to Littlewood, an awareness of the communicative function of the forms that have been learnt, communication strategies to deal with concrete situations, and an awareness of the social meanings of language forms.

Bialystok (1990) argues that communication strategies, the third skill mentioned by Littlewood, cannot be taught separately, but are a by-product of teaching the language. Using the two terms *analysis* and *control*, which were defined earlier in the account of the learning model, she concludes that by giving learners the knowledge about rules of grammar, rules of use, vocabulary, and the like, which they need for analysis, and by enabling them through practice to develop control of processing, teachers are providing all that is necessary to deploy communication strategies. Her final words are (p. 147):

'The more language the learner knows, the more possibilities exist for the system to be flexible and to adjust itself to meet the demands of the learner. What one must teach students of language is not strategy, but language.'

One has to admit, however, that not all rules of grammar perform a communicative function. Mistakes can be made in French and German with the gender of nouns, in German with adjectival endings or in written French with the plural ending of nouns without communication being materially affected. Why then should learners be encouraged to aim at correctness even in those aspects of the linguistic system?

One answer can be given on educational grounds: it has to do with learners' self-esteem, and their desire to achieve their own highest potential. But there is also another answer, based on what Littlewood calls the fourth domain of communicative competence, *social acceptability*. This means following the conventions in regard to the language of the community where the target language is spoken. As Littlewood (1981: 44) writes, this is partly a question of using the appropriate level of formality, but also, particularly for beginners, of achieving a satisfactory level of grammatical accuracy. French people in particular are sensitive to mistakes of gender.

Another of the pioneers of the communicative approach in Britain, Page (1990: 104–5), takes this argument even further (and further than I would), seeing in the social function of language the main reason to achieve correct grammar.

> Correct grammar, like pronunciation, serves a social function . . . Our use of language, including the accuracy of our grammar, invites interlocutors to regard us in a certain light and therefore to treat us in certain ways. Grammar does indeed have a communicative value but not necessarily in the transmission of the objective message. It transmits an image of the speaker. Most speakers wish to be accepted by their hearers, so the use of correct grammar is mostly integrative in intent rather than instrumental . . . [We can tell our learners]: You should try to get your adjectives right and acquire as wide a vocabulary as possible because then you will communicate to your native speaker friend a much truer picture of yourself. S/he will be able to respond in a more natural manner and your relationship will be the richer and the more interesting.

On several grounds therefore, including all the evidence from research quoted earlier, the case for teaching grammar as a means towards developing communicative competence is strong.

The place of grammar in the syllabus

If grammar is to be taught, what is to be its place in the syllabus? There are two extreme positions. On the one hand there is the *grammatical syllabus*, common in Britain until the mid-1980s and still found in many countries. Its organising principle is systematic coverage, presenting all or several forms of a grammatical category together and progressing from the formally simple to the formally complex. Exercises are mainly aimed at securing grammatical knowledge, leading from controlled to automatic processing and finally to free use in realistic contexts. The strengths claimed for it are that the systematic and transparent presentation of forms gives learners a secure basis to create their own sentences. The weaknesses of which it is accused are that presentation based on grammatical categories, which are abstract constructs, does not allow appropriate practice of separate forms and disregards the variety of functions for one form and of exponents for one function. It is more suitable for academic than for average or weaker pupils, to whom it offers insufficient motivation.

At the other extreme is the *notional-functional* syllabus, semantically based, as its name indicates, on notions, e.g. *time*, and functions, e.g. *making plans* within a defined context. This allows several exponents of a function to be presented together and across categories e.g. *möchtest du? hast du Lust?* and a cyclical progression with more differentiated realisations and changed contexts. Exercises are mainly aimed at promoting fluent performance of a task. The measure of the learner's success is the extent to which the task has been achieved. The strengths claimed for this kind of syllabus are: grammar and lexis are linked naturally as in L1 for the performance of a defined task; presentation and practice are realistic and have a clearly visible and motivating purpose, and some degree of communicative success is available to most learners. The weaknesses of which it is accused are that forms are presented in isolation from the rest of the grammatical category, so that they can become tied to particular contexts. It encourages the learning of set phrases and fails to provide learners with the knowledge to recombine elements and create new messages. Inaccurate language, though roughly communicative, becomes fossilised.

Increasingly the two extreme positions are being softened and there is convergence. Many course writers show through their table of contents that they seek to link topics, notions and functions and grammatical structures. The evidence presented by Lightbown and Spada (1993) and their conclusions quoted earlier in favour of 'form-focused instruction and corrective feedback within the context of a communicative program' would probably find support with many teachers, who vary their approach according to the ability, proficiency and age of their learners and the particular language element they are teaching. In the end what matters is that new acquisitions of vocabulary and grammar should be integrated with old ones and used in stimulating ways. The teaching of grammar, as described in this chapter, is not viewed as an aim in itself, but as making an essential contribution to the teaching of the language as a whole.

General principles

In the last chapter the special characteristics of grammar rules were set out (p. 65). Accordingly, grammar teaching aims to teach how words can vary in form and position. In addition, since grammar does not operate in a vacuum but combines with vocabulary in communication, grammar teaching also aims at enabling learners to understand and produce meaningful messages.

In what follows there is no intention to insist on one approach to the exclusion of others. Any objective and experienced observer must have noted that success can be attained by different routes. In the end it is the willingness and capacity of learners to absorb and integrate new knowledge that is crucial. However I believe that, if teaching means causing to learn, it should proceed in accordance with what is known about learning. It is useful therefore to be reminded briefly of the six stages in rule learning, described in Chapter 7.

(1) A language structure is met, understood and used as an unanalysed whole. It is tied to a particular context and to a small number of lexical items; if it has component parts, they are not distinguished.

(2) Similarities with other structures or other contexts begin to be noticed.

(3) Through continued use and comparison (discrimination), the learner becomes aware of distinctive, critical features in the structure and regularities in its use. A concept is being formed.

(4) A provisional rule is derived about the conditions determining the use of the structure.

(5) The rule is put into practice, first with deliberation and mistakes, then, as the mind takes in appropriate cues more quickly, with greater speed and accuracy. To be effective, practice should take into account the learners' readiness and motivation, reflect common linguistic and contextual use, be plentiful, varied and well spaced, and provide feedback on progress.

(6) A rule may need restructuring. Sometimes this occurs as an early extension of the provisional rule, and before the practice stage. Sometimes considerable time elapses before further conditions qualifying the use of the rule are discovered, and practice of its more complex form needs to be as thorough as it was of the simpler form earlier.

One possible model

One approach that almost provides a mirror image of the learning process is to be found in the chapter on the teaching of grammar in *Methodik: Englisch- und Französischunterricht* (1978), produced by a team led by Pohl, Schlecht and Uthess. Their approach falls into two parts: learning (*Erarbeitung grammatischer Kenntnisse*), and consolidation and use (*Festigung und Anwendung*). The two terms recall those used by Bialystok: analysis and control.

The learning stage is again sub-divided into two: an introductory practical stage (*der sprachpraktische Vorlauf*) and the generalisation stage (*die Verallgemeinerungsphase*).

In the introductory stage learners use the new grammatical structure as an unanalysed whole in the form and context in which they first met it, and without variation. It may even be introduced earlier, as a lexical item and without any use being required, as the first step in the familiarisation process. During the introductory stage learners may carry out information transfer exercises, answer questions on a recorded or written text, respond to visual stimuli, reconstitute a dialogue, etc. For instance an account of what children do after school in which the French perfect tense with *avoir* is introduced, might contain the statement *Pierre a rangé l'appartement*. In one activity, pupils are cued by flashcards to use *il a rangé* with words they already know, such as *il a rangé sa chambre, il a rangé la salle de séjour, il a rangé la salle de bains* and so on.

In my view, the importance of the text on which the introductory work is based cannot be overstated. It should deal with a topic of interest to the learners, building on lexical and grammatical knowledge acquired earlier, yet having the attraction of novelty. If a grammatical structure is to be taught, it should be introduced in a context which lends itself to varied and interesting practice and where form and function are brought out clearly and without distortion to normal use. The following are a few examples. One way (not the only one!) of introducing possessive adjectives is through photographs of family members and environment; two pictures of the same room, the one belonging to a teenager, the other to the same young person as an 8-year old offer a visible context for the use of the past tense of description; the account of a removal or plans to change the furniture in one's bedroom around prompt the natural use of spatial prepositions, and, in German, of the appropriate case.

The generalisation stage begins when the teacher decides to draw attention to the new grammatical structure. A few of the now thoroughly familiar sentences would be written up on an OHP or the blackboard as examples of the structure, and the class would be invited to discover its critical features. According to the structure, this task of analysis may involve the learners in:

- comparing different examples
- breaking down larger forms into their component parts
- identifying the component parts in each example
- discriminating between relevant and non-relevant features
- identifying the function of the structure
- comparing the form or function in the target language with those in the source language.

If a new term is required, it might be written over the relevant form. This stage corresponds to Steps 2 and 3 in the learning model (similarities and critical features noted) and also to the suggestion by Lightbown and Spada (1993), quoted in the previous chapter, that pupils should have their attention drawn to the forms they were using in communicative practice.

The next step in Pohl et al.'s (1978) model, is for the teacher, by means of concrete and carefully focused questions, to steer the pupils to work out a rule. For instance, with the French partitive article, they might be asked to work out (1) what the component parts are (de + definite article); (2) what determines the different forms (the number and gender of the following noun, whether the noun begins with a vowel or a consonant); and (3) what its function is compared with that of the other articles (indicate an indefinite amount).

Finally, one of the abler pupils might be asked to summarise the new rule. Under the guidance of the teacher, the pupils would write it down as simply and clearly as possible, adding at least one example from those on the OHP or blackboard. This part of the teaching procedure matches the next step in the learning model, that is Step 4 (provisional rule worked out).

Pohl *et al.* (1978) clearly prefer this inductive, bottom–up approach, but mention the possibility of working deductively, without the introductory stage, when a rule is only needed for reception, or with individual elements that do not lend themselves to a general rule.

Before proceeding to the teaching of specific rules, I want to state briefly why Pohl *et al.*'s approach to analysis appeals to me. First, it seems to fit the known process of natural learning, the teacher simply making up for the shorter exposure and contact time available in the classroom by supplying enough linguistic data to work on. Second, to judge by the observations of Peck (1988), it represents in its essentials the approach of experienced teachers in various countries. Third, it is educationally valuable, training learners to make their own observations and draw their own conclusions from the data available to them. In this way the study of foreign languages, which has often been too dependent on the authority of the teacher, can become as exciting as the use of discovery methods in other subjects.

On the other hand, there are times when the form and function of a structure are almost self-evident and an elaborate build-up to rule formulation is therefore not necessary. This applies in particular to the rules of type 1, such as the forms of irregular verbs or the gender of nouns, which can be treated as vocabulary. A considerable number of words or expressions useful for simple communicative exchanges like *je voudrais* or *ich möchte*, or classroom language such as *je peux aller aux toilettes, Madame?* do not need to be placed into a grammatical framework until much later.

It is also obvious that pupils will vary in the speed with which they can carry out the analysis and in the number of concrete examples they need both before and after.

Finally, as cognitive skill theory as well as teachers' experience make abundantly clear, understanding the rule is not enough. Practice is essential. One needs therefore to pass to the second part in Pohl et al's approach: consolidation and use, and deal with specific rules.

This practical part is going to be long. There are two reasons for this. First, I want to examine rules in each of the four categories mentioned in Chapter 7 and drawn from both French and German. Second, unless the approach is described in some detail, it will not prove convincing or helpful.

To aid readers who may wish to check on one particular rule, I list here and in order the rules treated. They relate to both French and German, unless a language is specifically mentioned:

(1) *Rules affecting individual forms and their immediate neighbours:*
    gender of nouns pp. 106–108.
    complementation of verbs pp. 108–111.
(2) *Morphological rules:*
    Verb phrase: (a) Eliciting the forms for the different persons of the verb pp. 114–117.
                  (b) Promoting discrimination between verb forms pp. 117–118.

(c) Practising tenses pp. 118–121.
(d) Written practice of verbs pp. 121–124.
Noun phrase: (a) The possessive adjective pp. 124–125.
(b) The comparative of the adjective p. 125.
(c) The relative pronoun pp. 125–126.
(d) The personal object pronoun pp. 126–131.
(3) *Word order in German* pp. 131–137
(4) *Semantic rules:*
Choosing between the imperfect and an action tense in French pp. 137–139.

Finally, it is worth restating that, although the focus here is on the nuts and bolts of teaching, the aim is always to improve learners' ability to use the language for their own ends.

Teaching Grammar Rules Affecting Individual Forms and their Immediate Neighbours

As stated in Chapter 7, there are a very large number of forms to which individual rules apply and where the boundary between grammar and vocabulary has almost disappeared. Teaching procedures, or, from the pupil's point of view, learning activities, have as their aim:

- to introduce these forms through a text, spoken or written, which is interesting and easily understood, where the language is appropriate and the content offers scope for extension;
- to fix the forms until they can be used freely;
- to revise regularly.

The goal of practice activities is therefore not to consolidate the understanding of a concept and make the application of the rule automatic, but to ensure remembering.

I will deal first with teaching the gender of nouns and next with the complementation of verbs.

The gender of nouns

Despite a few signals about gender given by endings (see Chapters 5 and 6), each noun poses a new learning and teaching task. Since the pupils cannot have recourse to a general rule to guide them in their choice of determiner, the teacher's aim must be to fix the initial link between noun and determiner firmly, with as much and as varied repetition as possible. The nouns in the introductory text that are to be learnt for production can be matched individually with visual representations, through drawings, photographs or symbols, on flashcards, the OHP or the coursebook, with the chosen determiner elicited each time with the noun. Clear pronunciation of *un/une, le/la* provides a frequently undervalued auditory support, which can be strengthened further by short dictations. The use of different colours or different positions on an OHP for nouns of different gender can mediate a useful visual association.

It probably does not matter much through which determiner or topic the concept of grammatical gender is introduced. Some coursebooks start with a possessive adjective and move on to the definite article. Family photographs have as their caption *Voici* or *C'est mon père, ma mère* and lead on to *le père de Luc*. Alternatively, there may be a class photo, showing among the captions: *Das ist Klaus, mein Freund; Das ist Astrid, meine Freundin; Das ist meine Schule; Das ist die Klasse 7a; Ich bin die Klassenlehrerin.* Others start with objects and the indefinite article, defining them subsequently in some way.

Whatever route is chosen, two points are important:

(1) The concept of gender applying to non-animate as well as to animate entities needs to be introduced soon.

(2) The indefinite article and the definite article should each be introduced and practised in ways that clearly reflect their different use, the former with a noun as yet unspecified, the latter with a noun made specific by earlier reference, or by additional information (*le père de Luc*) or uniqueness (*Ich bin die Klassenlehrerin. Das ist das Rathaus*). It will probably not be necessary to make that distinction explicit to beginners; English learners in particular will be familiar with it from their own language, but confusion can ensue if the teacher or an exercise in the coursebook demand now one and now the other article without apparent reason.

Most teachers will want to proceed very soon from rehearsing nouns in isolation to practising them in the context set by the topic or the function highlighted in the chapter. At first the practice may still relate to the introductory text, but soon the same nouns will be used in a different configuration (rooms in a different house from the one met first, clothes worn by other people or for other occasions), through role-play and information gap exercises between partners, at first guided by prompts, then unplanned.

How can this association between noun and gender be preserved, as new topics are introduced and new vocabulary threatens to displace the old? There is probably a case both for the systematic revision of individual nouns with their gender and for the contextualised revision that occurs naturally as topics are recycled.

Various exercises have been used over the years for revision practice of the gender of nouns and irregular forms of verbs. In 1935 a noted inspector, Marc Ceppi, suggested that the first five minutes of every lesson, from the second year onwards, should be spent on *copying* the present, perfect and future of two irregular French verbs. In the 1980s one coursebook (*Deutsch Heute*: Sidwell & Capoore, 1983) concluded every unit in its Books 2 and 3 with a revision quiz to be carried out in pair work on 10–15 nouns and verbs. In the 1990s, crossword puzzles, games and mobiles have become familiar. One of the ideas suggested in 1993 at a conference by another inspector, Mr E.A.L. Bird, was to let pupils find from texts displayed around the walls 10 nouns on a certain subject or 10 past participles, to be written down with their gender or infinitive respectively.

Other exercises seek to provide some context. Some textbooks rework at regular intervals the story of earlier chapters through a gapped text, with the pupil being expected to write in a noun and article or an irregular verb form. In a different exercise the teacher simply puts on an OHP or the blackboard a few nouns or verbs, and invites pupils to make sentences with each orally. This exercise is quick, can be fitted in whenever convenient and adapted to the needs and abilities of the learners. It also allows learners to provide their own contexts and generate their own combinations, integrating new with older vocabulary and learning from each other. Teachers can spot and act on weaknesses and misunderstandings quickly.

Gapped exercises are necessarily meant to be read, though they may be performed orally. They also tend to be *testing* exercises, in which a form is introduced only once. An oral exercise like the one mentioned earlier is a *teaching* exercise, because one form at the time is practised. The distinction between teaching and testing exercises is not absolutely rigid, but it is important and will be mentioned several times in this chapter.

The extension of topics that proceeds throughout a course and the introduction of new grammar forms onto familiar vocabulary will by themselves provide practice. The vocabulary of clothing, for example, will be revised through the introduction of adjectives of colour and accounts of shopping expeditions, that of parts of the body when illnesses are discussed, accommodation terms can recur in the description of one's room, removals or holiday experiencs. As different parts of the morphological system are introduced and practised — possessive adjectives, personal pronouns, etc. — control of gender is again revealed as fundamental.

The complementation of verbs

Knowing the complementation of verbs is important. It allows learners to move out from the verb to the rest of the sentence, to communicate complete messages.

References to complementation have already been made in the discussion of the German case system in Chapter 6. But it was limited to German, and no details of exercises were given, whereas below I will deal with both French and German and focus on practice activities.

As mentioned in the earlier chapter, verbs can be divided into three major categories in respect of complementation. One comprises verbs that are followed by an obligatory complement of place or direction, without which the sentence would not be complete, for example *habiter, se jeter*, or by an optional adverbial, providing additional information, for example *jouer*. If the adverbial is a Noun Phrase, various prepositions can provide the link (*j'habite derrière la gare, près du parc; les enfants jouaient avec leurs jouets, dans leur chambre*).

On the whole, this category poses few problems in regard to complementation. Prepositions are chosen according to intended meaning, for many specific combinations, such as *est né(e) en/à; fährt/fliegt um . . . Uhr von . . . ab*, it is not difficult to find compendia of information, such as a genealogical tree, a biographical dictionary or a timetable to provide practice material.

Complementation is more problematic when learners have to remember whether a verb is followed by a direct or by an indirect object or both. There are no generally valid rules to guide one's choice: why is *treffen* followed by the accusative, and *begegnen* by the dative? The act of asking a person is expressed in German by *fragen + acc.* and in French by *demander + à*. How can one ensure that learners remember the right complementation?

For certain verbs no special effort is needed. They are the core ones, followed by a direct object, which are used in so many contexts that the required complementation is constantly being practised. For example, the basic meaning of *avoir* or *haben*, possession, appears in a wide range of everyday topics — family, pets, personal possessions, items in shops, rooms in a hotel, playing cards, school subjects, illnesses. Another example is *prendre* which occurs not only in its basic meaning of seizing, but also with food and drink and means of transport.

Then there are verbs with the same complementation which, though perhaps first encountered separately, can later be practised as a group because they also fall within the same broad semantic field.

One such group comprises verbs broadly expressing the idea of *giving*, such as *offering, passing, buying, bringing, showing, lending*. The most natural introduction and practice is provided by classroom discourse, starting with the pronoun rather than with the noun. Pupils constantly share items in class. Why therefore not teach at an early stage expressions like *Tu peux me prêter ta gomme, un crayon? Kannst du mir deinen Bleistift leihen*? Other verbs useful for pupil interaction could be introducd as the need arises. One could expect the teacher to use such verbs too: *Annick, tu pourrais montrer ton dessin à Yvette? Passez votre feuille à votre voisin(e)*. Thus a stock of phrases is already in learners' memory when they need to use a Noun Phrase complement or relate what has happened to a third party. *Reichen/passer* would be practised again during table talk, *montrer/zeigen* would occur when shopping for clothes, *donner/schenken* when it is time for seasonal gifts.

If more comprehensive practice is thought necessary, a written completion exercise

Box 9.1 Exercise to practise complementation after verbs of *showing, bringing*, etc. in French

Les touristes	*envoyer*	*des cartes postales*	
Le garçon de café	*apporter*	*une bière*	
Le professeur	*rendre*	*les copies corrigées*	*à un, à une*
Les parents	*donner*	*l'argent de poche*	*au, à la, aux*
Un jeune homme	*offrir*	*sa place*	
La banque	*prêter*	*de l'argent*	
La vendeuse	*montrer*	*des vêtements*	

like the one in Box 9.1 revises the complementation of these verbs in a more scholastic manner, with room left for personal invention.

The exercise can be made easier by specifying, in jumbled form, some possible recipients, or harder by deleting the direct object and letting pupils use their imagination even more.

Another set of verbs that could be revised as a group centres on *saying*, such as *telling, explaining, replying, writing*. Practice can be arranged through contexts where instructions or messages are reported, or through exercises like the previous one.

There are also the verbs referring to inanimate objects (food, clothes, pictures, parts of the body, etc.) which cause pleasing or unpleasing sensations, such as *plaire, aller* in the sense of 'fit', *faire mal, schmecken, gefallen, passen, weh tun*. The number of items within each field is large enough to provide natural practice, particularly with pronouns.

At a more advanced stage it is possible to group together for revision verbs of permission, advice, command, prohibition, where some kind of influence is exerted on another person. The common pattern is *verb + indirect object of the person + de/zu + infinitive*

Mes parents ont dit que je dois rester à la maison — m'ont ordonné
Meine Eltern haben gesagt, ich darf mitkommen — haben mir erlaubt

Practice is most difficult for the third category of verbs, those followed obligatorily by a preposition. They are relatively few in French, where only two prepositions, *à* and *de* are used (*penser à, se souvenir de*), but considerably more numerous in German, where any one of 12 prepositions can link verb and complement *bitten + um, denken + an, warten + auf* etc. They are so disparate and numerous that few can be practised together naturally.

Yet revision is necessary. In the chapter on the learning of vocabulary, stress was laid on the speed with which individual words are forgotten unless they are constantly re-used, and the same is true about the gender of nouns and the complementation of verbs. Revision becomes even more pressing as the full range of interrogative and personal pronouns is learnt, animate and non-animate, direct, indirect and oblique object, and as learners wish to use relative clauses. What was known in simple sentences is often forgotten with more complex patterns.

One form of revision is to go back to teaching exercises that focus on one verb at the time. One can, for example, ask pupils to recall a memorable event, so that they use *se souvenir*, or produce definitions, using *servir*, or look forward *sich auf etwas freuen*. Or one can use chain drills. *Moi, je pense souvent à Yvonne, et toi?, Moi, je pense souvent aux vacances, et toi?* In the intermediate stage one can refine the drill and ask pupils to put the question in full: *À qui* or *à quoi est-ce que tu penses?*

Training pupils to listen carefully to the questions used by the teacher or speakers in a recording can itself remind them of the appropriate complementation. Hearing *Wofür interessierst du dich?* or *Worum geht es in dieser Sendung?* can act as useful prompts for their own utterances. It is a preliminary step towards learning to use the question forms themselves. This not only revises and extends control over complementation,

Box 9.2 Exercise to practise the choice of prepositions in German

Jörg ist ein Junge,	. . .	den man sich verlassen kann
	. . .	den man immer warten muß
	. . .	dem ich Angst habe
	. . .	dem man viel Gutes sagt

but, more importantly, enables learners to communicate more effectively, by asking a wider range of questions in role-play and, later, in real conversation.

Exercises that practise several verbs have their place. Box 9.2 shows an exercise at the intermediate level where the right preposition has to be inserted. Like other gapped exercises, it has to be seen, but it is most economical and instructive to pupil and teacher if done orally. It might form part of the preparation for a pen portrait.

So that such exercises teach as well as test, it is worth going over them more than once, the third and fourth time covering up the relative pronoun, so as to practise also the case taken by the verb.

A few concluding comments are called for. I have devoted several pages to complementation, both because, as stated earlier, it helps learners to communicate complete messages and because of its importance in the grammatical system. If, as some theorists believe (see Willis, 1990), it is possible to organise a course round a lexical syllabus, learning the complementation or valency of verbs would be an important element in it.

Various approaches and exercises have been suggested. For most of them I have indicated contexts in which practice would not be an aim in itself, but lead to a better performance of some communicative task. However some learners would benefit from seeing a common pattern clearly apparent in a structural exercise. And some might remember the complementation of a few important verbs best through memorizing a poem like *Grammatik mit Herz*, reproduced in Box 9.3.

Teaching Morphological Rules

With each morphological rule teachers have to ask themselves:

(1) What form(s) within the range of variations do I want to teach in connection with this particular text or this particular communicative task?

(2) What determines these variations, that is, which elements in or outside the sentence are in relation with each other?

- If the determining factors in that relation are to be brought out explicitly, as in the Pohl *et al.* (1978) model, what are the points which I will wish to stress and ask pupils to formulate a rule about?

Box 9.3 Poem: *Grammatik mit Herz* (Mebus *et al.*, 1987: 84)

Ich lerne Deutsch.
Ich lerne dich kennen.
Ich sehe dich an.
Wir lesen einen Text.
Ich verstehe nichts.
Ich sehe nur dich.
Ich frage dich.

Du antwortest mir.
Du hilfst mir.
Ich höre dir zu.

Du zeigst mir das Heft.
Du gibst mir en Beispiel.
Du erklärst mir.
Ja, was erklärst du mir eigentlich?

- What are the steps in any explanation? Will I need any new terms? What previous knowledge do the pupils need?
- If I hope that the rule will be understood without any explanation, how can I ensure that the examples in the introductory text (a) occur naturally, that is, would be used by a native speaker in that context and have not been introduced artificially, (b) are nevertheless sufficiently numerous to illustrate the range of variations and (c) can be referred to, if necessary, as the essential cues to which, in Cronbach's (1954) terms, pupils have to attend to?

(3) In what contexts, through what exercises, can I get the forms and the rules practised, bearing in mind that practice should:
  - ensure control of each form (teach) and also quicken discrimination between various forms (test),
  - strengthen the understanding of the relation,
  - conform to normal language use and, as far as possible,
  - lead to a smooth performance of a meaningful task?

Morphological rules are too numerous for each to be discussed. I give below a few examples of how these three sets of questions might be dealt with in regard to some rules commonly covered in a school course. Rules applying to the Verb Phrase and to the Noun Phrase are treated separately.

Verb Phrase

Range of forms to be taught

Forms have to be taught for

- each of the six persons,
- in each tense,
- for each regular conjugation,
- and for each of the most common irregular forms.

Fortunately the earlier custom of presenting all the six persons of a tense together in the same chapter has been abandoned, at least for the present tense, in favour of a more gradual introduction. In later years there is still a tendency to present the whole pattern of a tense at once and to allow relatively little time before a new one is introduced. This can cause confusion, unless discrimination between the many forms is constantly practised.

Both the spoken and the written forms have to be taught. The divergence between them in French adds considerably to the teaching and learning task. More will be written about that later.

Rules to be taught

These are:

- the semantic relationship between each verb form and its subject (1st person = speaker/writer about him/herself),
- the rules for the formation of each tense,
- within each tense, the relationship between a common part and specific parts for each grammatical person,
- the distinction between polite and familiar modes of address,
- the use of the different tenses.

As I interpret learning theory, three elements contribute to rule learning: (1) initial transparent presentation and unanalysed use, (2) gradual understanding of the relevant concepts and of the relation between them, aided by explanation and (3) extensive practice. For English pupils in particular, accustomed to the virtual uniformity in sound and spelling of verb forms in all six persons of a tense (except for the third singular -s in the base), all means must be employed to bring home to them that in French and German almost every verb form has a specific ending, with a characteristic sound and spelling.

The role of explanation therefore, at a suitable time after exposure and initial use, is to draw attention to the semantic function of the particular subject + verb form, to its relation to the form that is found in a dictionary, the infinitive, to the contrast with any form already learned, to the way each tense is formed and the distinction between stem and endings. As each new tense is learnt, the process needs to be repeated, with time allowed for the new information to be assimilated and integrated with the old.

I believe, with Gagné, 1985, (see Chapter 7), that consciousness has a role to play in learning. I believe, for example, in the usefulness of knowing that in French the stem of the imperfect is the same as that of the *nous* form of the present, or for German that only verbs stressed on the first syllable of the infinitive form the past participle with *ge*. On the other hand I also believe that the role of conscious knowledge has its limits, as was clearly demonstrated in the experiment conducted by Hecht and Green (1993) on the relation between implicit and explicit knowledge (see Chapter 8). Practice is essential to make the pupil produce the right tense and the right verb form automatically.

Aspects of Practice

Eliciting the forms for the different persons of the verb

The first person This is the most important verb form for the majority of learners. After all, most of us use language principally to talk and write about ourselves and our concerns. In speech the first person is often used in response to a question, hence questions are widely used in the classroom as an eliciting device, whether put by the teacher or by a fellow pupil. The three most common types of question are:

(1) yes/no questions: *Tu aimes le français?*
(2) either/or questions: *Bist du mit dem Schiff oder mit dem Flugzeug gekommen?*
(3) the so-called 'wh-questions', e.g. in English 'when, where, how', bearing on an attendant circumstance: *Comment viens-tu à l'école?*

However the answers to these types of question would normally be short, without a verb. In relation to these three questions above they might be:

(1a) *Oui, beaucoup. Non, pas tellement.*
(2b) *Mit dem Flugzeug.*
(3c) *A pied. En autobus.*

Teachers will certainly want to use these types of question, for two reasons. They are common in everyday one-to-one situations, and pupils need to become accustomed to them. They also offer a model for pupils to use themselves in pair-work or role-play. So, should short answers be demanded from the start?

There may be a conflict here between the claims of authenticity in language use and pedagogic considerations. Allowing pupil to use the verb in a longer answer offers them a prop with which to build their utterance and some thinking time. It also gives some practice in the verb form. There may be a case therefore for some leniency in the early stages. On the other hand, as pupils gain confidence, they should be encouraged to switch from long to short answers, so that their speech does not remain stilted. One can also hope that, as their linguistic resources increase, they themselves will want to amplify or qualify their replies, thus using the first person quite naturally.

Box 9.4 Revision exercise on the day's activities, practising the perfect (based on Piepho, 1980: 143)

Was hast du/ habt ihr heute gemacht?
Heute habe ich gespielt — gerechnet — gelacht — gestritten — geschrie[e]n — geschrieben   *haben wir*
schön   *toll*   *viel*   *gut*   *gar nicht*   *im Hof*   *in der Pause*   *vor der Schule*
Kreuze an, was stimmt. — Lies vor. — Frage nach, wenn andere vorgelesen haben.   *Wann denn? Mit wem denn? Wo denn? Warum denn? Wobei denn? Wieso denn das?*

There are other ways open to teachers to elicit a statement in the first person.

(4) Make a general request to members of a group to say, for instance, at what time they get up, how they come to school, etc.

(5) Deliberately make a false statement, which provokes a correction *Tu t'appelles Dracula, n'est-ce pas?*

(6) Occasionally pretend to be hard of hearing

(7) As a stringent elicitation device, put an open question, using *faire* or *tun/machen* or otherwise leaving out the verb: *Qu'est-ce que tu fais le samedi? Comment est-ce que tu fêtes ton anniversaire? Wie hast du die Ferien verbracht?*

After a while, revision will become necessary. Revision exercises can take different forms. The object is to set before the pupils a context which allows several possibilities. The more it stimulates them to talk about themselves, the more motivating it will be, and the better it will revise verb forms. The exercise in Box 9.4, recommended by Piepho (1980), revises several verbs in the perfect, but can obviously be adapted to other tenses. The framework is fixed by the verbs selected, but the rubric at the bottom suggests how it can lead to unrehearsed and lively interaction in class, groups or pairs.

Completion exercises are more open-ended. A phrase is put up on an OHP or the blackboard, and pupils are asked to complete it by giving some personal information. The following are just a few examples:

Le samedi,
Pendant les vacances,

Quand je m'ennuie,
Pour gagner un peu d'argent,

The format of such an exercise is flexible. It can deal with personal matters or with a topic from the course, for example what one does on arrival at a camp site or at a youth hostel, when arranging a holiday or planning a party. Instead of the present, as here, other tenses can be revised. As many contributions as possible can be sought from each pupil or groups of four can be formed, with each pupil offering two sentences and no verb being used more than once. The exercise can be done orally as quick revision or in writing, as preliminary to a careful draft.

The verb forms of address

In the current approach to teaching modern languages, where so much stress is laid on communicative interaction, the verbal forms to address an interlocutor are constantly used. In the early chapters of school textbooks the most common situations involve young people talking to each other. The appropriate verb form is therefore the second person singular, in which pupils ask each other about their name, age, address, interests, etc. Its use is closely linked to the introduction of interrogative particles for where, when, what, how, how much, etc.

The polite address form will be practised through the formal contacts with the parents of friends, passers by, shop assistants, as well as the teacher. Flexible switching between polite and familiar according to interlocutor needs deliberate and continuous practice. In German, situations must be created where the familiar plural verb form with *ihr* is used.

The forms of the third person singular and plural

Even though interaction and dialogue have achieved pre-eminence in modern textbooks, speaking and writing *about* people and things is still necessary. The third person is essential for description and also very important for narrative. The opportunities for practice abound.

One important aim of teaching verbs must be to establish the link between nouns and the third-person form. In my view, if pupils are asked to write down the paradigm of a verb, nouns *must* figure in it as well as subject pronouns.

The form of the first person plural

Activities performed together with a friend or as members of a family or group are sufficiently important to be treated in a school course. Topics could include common family routines, including ways of celebrating traditional festivities, holidays and the planning of joint entertainments.

Teachers of French need to consider seriously how much weight should be given to the teaching of *on* as the subject of joint action in everyday language. '*ON est très souvent utilisé par les Français, de préférence à nous*' (Bérard & Lavenne, 1991: 11).

Promoting discrimination between verb forms

Previously I have given some examples of contexts in which the verb forms associated with different persons would be used naturally and could therefore be practised naturally. The examples may have seemed rather obvious, but I believe that the first and most important step in practising the different forms is to concentrate on one form at the time, so that the link between a given subject, pronoun or noun, and a verb form, with its specific sound and spelling, is established firmly enough to resist confusion with other forms.

In the 1960s and 1970s the contrast between verbal forms used to be brought out through drills, and a number of textbooks used on the Continent and in the USA still contain drills based on the text of a chapter. For example, one of the earliest chapters in *Échanges* (Grunwald *et al.*, 1981) widely used in Germany for the teaching of French, is set on a campsite and describes two families getting to know one another. The drills in Box 9.5 are used to practise the first and second person plural of *-er* verbs and *être*, as well as two ways of asking a question and the names of some French-speaking towns.

The argument against drills is that they impose a relationship between two propositions which is based only on structural similarity, and not on the reality of the situation. The repetition of the same type of response to a given stimulus can suggest to the learner that this response is the only one acceptable. On the other hand, it is possible for the teacher to engineer situations where, through a temporary suspension of belief, the contrast between forms is made manifest and hammered home through drills that are predictable yet also offer an opportunity for humour and pupils' own invention. Two examples of chain drills are shown in Box 9.6.

Short drills can be improvised by the pupils themselves and introduced at any place in the course, adding the spice of guesswork.

Box 9.5 Examples of structural drills (Grunwald *et al.*, 1981: 18)

M. Cartier:	*Est-ce que vous habitez à Tours (aimer le camping, jouer aux boules, travailler aussi à Tours, préparer quelque chose à manger, etc.)*
Mme Durand:	*Oui, nous habitons à Tours, etc.*

Tu est de Tours?
Oui, et vous, vous êtes aussi de Tours?
Non. Nous sommes de Poitiers (Paris/Reims, Genève/Lausanne etc.)

Box 9.6 Examples of chain drills

Je me suis lavé le cou ce matin (brossé les cheveux, coupé les ongles, etc.)
Quoi, tu t'es lavé le cou ce matin? (Jamais de la vie!)
Ce n'est pas vrai! (C'est un mensonge!) Je suis sûr que Pierre ne s'est pas lavé le cou ce matin.

Wir haben Karten fürs Rockkonzert (fürs Fußballspiel, fürs Theater) bekommen
Was, ihr habt Karten fürs Rockkonzert bekommen?
Hört mal — Petra und Gerda haben Karten fürs Rockkonzert bekommen!

Box 9.7 Examples of short drills improvised by pupils

Rat mal, was ich gekauft habe. Es fängt mit einem A an.
Du hast . . . gekauft
Rat mal, wohin wir im Sommer fahren. Es fängt mit einem M an.
Ihr fahrt nach . . .

Half way between drills and entirely contextualised activities are exercises where the same material is viewed from different points of view, so that there is repetition but also a change in the verb form. In *Échanges* (Grunwald *et al.*, 1981a) chapter dealing with the future tense includes a full page of horoscopes. Some of the information from it is summarised in the form of a circle in an exercise reproduced in Box 9.8. With only slight variations in the text three forms of the future are practised at least times each.

Practising tenses

On some aspects of practice there will be general agreement. Practice must be set in contexts appropriate to the interests and likely needs of learners and bring out clearly the function of the tense. Since indications of time are signalled as much by adverbials as by tense, practice must be much concerned with linking verbs, in questions as well as statements, with adverbs and phrases expressing a point in time, duration, relation in time of one action to another, etc. As mentioned earlier, practice must be distributed over several persons.

There may be less agreement on how to proceed when a variety of forms have to be learnt for a given tense. In German compound tenses, for example, pupils have not only to remember the sentence final position of the past participle, but learn its form in regular weak and the most common strong verbs, separable and inseparable verbs

Box 9.8 Practising different forms of the future through horoscopes (Grunwald *et al.*, 1981: 42)

a) *D'après l'horoscope de cette semaine, les Béliers découvriront un nouveau passe-temps.*
b) *Sylvie est Bélier: elle découvrira un nouveau passe-temps. Et Pascal?*
c) *A vous. Je suis né(e) le . . . . Je suis . . . . D'après l'horoscope, je . . .*

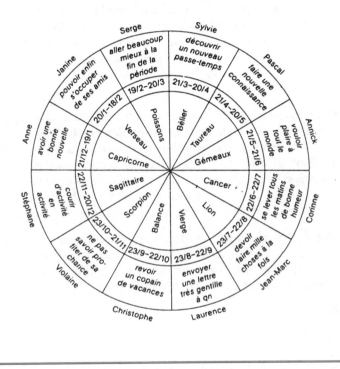

of either class, and know which verbs are conjugated with *haben* and which with *sein*. Coursebook writers in fact differ considerably in the order in which they present these different classes. Nor is the problem solved by stating that the topic or intended task determines the language. Accounts of journeys across the Channel in two textbooks read equally well, yet one uses predominantly the perfect of weak verbs, the other mixes weak and strong verbs. The difference in the language chosen is not important in itself, but it has implications for practice. With the first account the teacher can count on the regularity in the form of the past participle to aid production, with the second the teacher has to rely entirely on repetition to bring about memorisation.

My own approach is to make use of whatever regularities are offered by the system, while recognising that repetition remains indispensable.

Practice might start with information transfer or familiarisation exercises. As pupils listen to several short texts, they are asked to focus on some detail, such as a date, time, place, but in the process they hear verbs of which they know or can guess the meaning used in a new tense. Production might follow with gradually diminishing support from within the exercise, moving from completion exercises where one verb form in the correct tense has to be chosen from several, to the framing of questions to elicit given answers, and to dialogues or statements guided by pictorial prompts. In the Pohl *et al.* (1978) approach, once pupils have gained confidence by using the new form as an unanalysed whole, they are led to formulate and write down what they need to know at this stage about its use and forms. The old topic may then be taken up again and extended, or a new one may be introduced, confirming the patterns. Practice can now move more quickly to independent production, the individual or joint creation of texts of different kinds.

In revising tenses, use and form cannot be easily separated. This is particularly true about those tenses which differ in their use from English. In others, one can take the grasp of function for granted and concentrate on forms. Regular short periods devoted solely to the revision of verbs and tenses have been mentioned already. Revision of forms can be incorporated in the revision of tasks. Excerpts from earlier chapters may be reproduced exactly, so that the context is brought back to mind, but the verb may be either put in the infinitive or even omitted, if the choice is obvious.

Any list, whether it be of things to be done in preparation for a journey, diary entries for a week, or errands to be run, lends itself to revision of the perfect, or the future. In *Échanges* 2 (Grunwald *et al.*, 1981) a German boy is preparing to go to France and has made a list of things to do. The exercise is in three parts:

(a) *Il faut . . .*
(b) *A midi Jörg dit: Je n'ai pas encore . . .*
(c) *Mais le soir il a tout fait. Il a . . .*

Exercises in which pupils are simply required to replace one tense with another have been justly criticised because they ignore the context, but a case can be made for oppositions which bring out the function of a tense as well as its forms.

D'habitude je ne suis jamais malade en hiver. Mais cet hiver il a fait si froid, que . . . malade trois fois.
Ma soeur va acheter une Renault 19. Moi, à sa place, . . . une voiture britannique. Les pièces détachées sont moins chères.
Wann macht ihr eure Schulaufgaben? Wir haben sie schon . . .
Warum arbeitest du nicht? Ich hab doch den ganzen Vormittag . . .

Finally, one would hope that revision would allow pupils to express their own ideas, however simply, and with appropriate help. Here are a few suggestions, probably familiar to experienced teachers.

Perfect: Two things which you have not yet done that day
One good thing that happened to you during the last month
A day when everything went wrong
A mini-biography (so far) of a friend, or a famous person

Future: A portrait of yourself at 20 or 30
Three things which will still be the same in 20 years and three things which
will be different

Imperfect: Life in a certain period in the past
How your bedroom looked when you were a child compared with how it
looks today

Box 9.9 reproduces a poem in which a young adolescent looks back at his childhood.

Written practice of verbs

Much of verb practice will be oral — as part of various tasks, in answer to questions,
completion exercises, descriptions of pictures, drills and, above all, dialogues, whether
guided by prompts or created jointly by two learners.

Yet written practice of verbs is also needed, particularly for not so able pupils. There
are several reasons:

- According to the APU Survey of Foreign Language Perfomance in Schools after
  two years (APU, 1987a), weak pupils could only write words and short phrases,
  whereas average and above average pupils succeeded in writing sentences,
  however simple. Learning to use verbs, as the key component of sentences, is
  therefore important.
- As pupils proceed up the school and often begin to correspond with partners
  abroad, they will want to use verbs in all six persons, in at least the most common
  tenses. To do so correctly in writing will be a daunting task for some pupils,
  however the majority of pupils should be encouraged and helped to achieve
  accuracy as an aspect of social acceptability.
- The actual operation of writing out a verb form acts as a prop for the memory
  and thus for spoken production.
- Finally, practice in writing is needed to disambiguate the numerous cases where
  the same sound can be represented graphically in different ways. This applies
  particularly to French, as will be shown later.

Written practice can thus have different purposes. It may be geared specifically to
supporting spoken performance, when dialogues are copied from the coursebook or
created by pupils. It may serve as a preparation for a particular task, such as a letter,
when the writing of certain verb forms that often cause spelling problems is practised,
for example *je m'appelle, j'espère, je vais arriver.*

Box 9.9 Poem: *Quand j'étais petit* (quoted by E.A.L. Bird at a conference in Leicester, 1993, and reproduced with his permission)

> Quand j'étais petit
>
> Quand j'étais petit
>   je buvais du thé
> Maintenant, je préfère le café.
>
> Quand j'étais petit
>   j'allais à la plage
> Maintenant, j'embrasse Nicole
>   dans le garage.
>
> Quand j'étais petit
>   j'aimais l'éducation physique
> Maintenant je préfère la musique.
>
> Quand j'étais petit, je regardais Play School
> Maintenant, j'aime jouer aux boules
>
> Quand j'étais petit je mangeais le pain
> Maintenant je bois du vin
>
> Quand j'étais petit je jouais au ballon
> Maintenant je regarde la télé
>   dans le salon.
>
> Quand j'étais petit
>   je ne savais rien
> Maintenant je me sens bien - - - - -

But as new verbs and new tenses are introduced, the need may also be felt for targeted exercises, both for initial fixing, when awareness follows unanalysed use, and for revision, restoring order into the growing number of forms. The aims of practice may therefore differ, and pupils should be made aware of what the aims of a particular exercise are, so that, in Cronbach's (1954) terms, they can look out for relevant cues. The purpose of such targeted exercises may be as follows:

(1) *To consolidate the relation between subject and ending.* For example, the relation in French between a plural noun and the ending *-ent* in the present, or between a plural noun and *-ont* in the future, would be practised half a dozen times. Pupils would receive feedback on what they had written either from the teacher or a computer program after each sentence, so that the terms of the relation are firmly established. A sequence on another, previously learnt ending could follow, and then a third *testing* sequence could ascertain how well the learner could now discriminate.

In order to be set in context, the exercise could be composed of three short paragraphs, describing, for example, activities by the writer, a third party and the two of them in contrast. However, separate sentences may be easier to construct. The verb could be presented in the infinitive or with the stem only.

(2) *To disambiguate between two or three forms with the same sound.* Examples of this are too numerous and well known to be mentioned. The purpose of practice, as with the earlier set, is to develop the learner's awareness of the relation between the subject and the verbal form, and similar exercises can be used.

Special care is required for verbal forms with [e], where there is the possibility of confusion between *-ez*, *-er* and four forms of the past participle. Fewest errors occur with the *-ez* form, since pupils associate it with *vous* from the beginning. For the other two, exercises would stress, on the one hand, the link between the past participle and forms of *avoir* or *être*, and, on the other, draw attention to a preceding preposition or to one of the modal verbs, including *aller*. Short but frequent exercises, concentrating on one combination at the time, may in the end establish connections. Short dictations of one or two lines, drawn from a currently or recently studied text, or of phrases needed for a future written task, often prove helpful.

All these exercises should help pupils to write as accurately as they can. However most teachers will probably not want to make a fetish of written accuracy. They will know that French and German children too make spelling mistakes. To aid me in the preparation of this book, a French friend of mine, teaching in a comprehensive school in the West of France asked a whole class of 38 pupils, aged 12–13, to write down sentences which they might typically use in class to other pupils or the teacher, and sent them to me uncorrected. Examples of 'phonetic spelling' are shown in Box 9.10. (A full list of expressions suggested by these pupils, as well as by German and Swiss pupils, is given in the Appendix.)

Box 9.10 Some spelling mistakes in a list of classroom expressions written by 38 French pupils aged 12–13

j'ai oublier	7 pupils
je n'est pas (fini, compris, fait mon exercice)	5 pupils
Vous pouvez fermez (2), fermé, répétée, allez?	5 pupils
je peu (2), tu peu, je peut sortir?	4 pupils
je ne comprend pas	4 pupils
je n'ai pas fais	3 pupils
A few other mistakes:	
on ma volé un crayon — il ma mis un coup de pied — il a prid — tu me prête ta gomme? — quelqu'un aurai une gomme?	

The Noun Phrase

Pupils must groan sometimes as yet another determiner or pronoun is introduced. Yet they form part of the basic infrastructure of the language and must therefore be learnt. The fact that they are not tied to any specific topic or noun means that one of them may be needed at any moment. On the other hand it also means that opportunities for practice constantly recur.

I will limit myself to discussing four grammatical forms, where coursebook presentation may not always reflect normal language use.

The possessive adjective

(Other terms are common in modern linguistics: possessives, possessive determiners, possessive pronouns. 'Possessive determiners' probably reflects the special nature of these adjectives best, but the traditional term is the one familiar to most teachers, and has therefore been retained.)

In spoken English and German the possessive adjective can be stressed for emphasis *Das ist mèin Buch*. In French, emphasis is expressed differently *C'est mon livre à moi (ça)*. Contrasts sometimes found in coursebook exercises, as in *Ce n'est pas ton livre, c'est mon livre*, can lead to a false intonation. Practice of one person at the time is therefore preferable. Examples might be: *J'ai tout pour l'école aujourd'hui: mon cahier de français, ma règle, mes sandwichs, etc.* or *Je trouve X adorable, détestable: j'aime/je déteste ses yeux, son nez etc.* For revision in either language one needs a topic with a number of people, objects or places related in some way to the speaker or to each other. One topic might be a photo of our class, in front of our school, showing me and my best friend, Mary and her friend Joan, our teacher, etc. Another might be holiday snaps of our hotel, the window of our room, the owner or a fellow guest with his wife and their children, etc., a third could be a genealogical tree. Dialogues, as between an interested friend and the informer, can easily be devised on any of these topics. Realistic exchanges can similarly be improvised and kept going by the pupils themselves:

J'ai perdu ma gomme, etc. or *Où est ma gomme?*
Ta gomme? Tu as regardé dans ta poche, ton sac (elle est peut-être . . .)?
Non, elle n'est pas dans ma poche . . .
Tu as regardé . . . ?

The comparative of the adjective

This is almost always introduced and practised in coursebooks with the two entities in the comparison explicitly named. *London ist größer als Huddersfield.* Yet there is little practice of the cases, which are quite common, where the second entity has been previously mentioned or is understood, and therefore need not be repeated.

Ici c'est plus tranquille (que là-bas). Il y a moins de bruit, on a une meilleure vue, on est plus à l'ombre.

As this example shows, comparisons with nouns often occur together with those with adjectives and therefore deserve to be learnt at the same time.

The inflected forms of the comparative adjective in German require considerable practice.

Dieser Pullover ist schön, aber zu groß. Haben Sie auch kleinere?
Hätten Sie eine kleinere Größe? Ich brauche einen kleineren. Ein kleinerer wäre genau das, was ich suche.

There are many contexts suitable for practising the comparative: choosing a site for pitching a tent, choosing items of clothing, discussing how to spend a free afternoon, the merits of two teams, bands, routes, etc. Dialogues, with arguments for both sides, and without necessarily overusing the comparative, can easily be devised.

The relative pronoun

Using a relative pronoun to link two clauses is a fairly sophisticated device. Anyone listening to young children's speech or reading children's books like *Le petit prince* or *Emil und die Detektive* will not find many occurrences of the relative pronoun. And when children begin to produce relative clauses, they attach them first to the object of the main clause, as in *I want the ones you've got.* In this they follow one of Slobin's (1973) operating principles to avoid interruption or rearrangement of linguistic units. *Zeig mir (Wo ist) das Fahrrad, das du bekommen hast,* in which the relative clause comes at the end of the sentence, seems a more useful pattern with which to begin than *Der Mann, der dort steht, kennt den Weg nicht* (Dreyer & Schmitt, 1985).

Since the function of the relative clause is to expand the noun to which it refers, indicating special characteristics or purpose, practice need not be confined to any one topic. Definitions can be a good starting point, from fairly easy ones like *Briefträger,*

Taschenlampe, Wartezimmer to more challenging ones like *Friseuse, Fahrrad, Zeitschrift*. Anyone needing or asking for someone or something to provide a particular service is likely to use *ich brauche, ich suche*, followed by a noun, or *jemanden/etwas* and a relative clause.

The personal object pronoun

This is a part of the grammatical system where the paradigm on the page conveys an illusory picture of uniformity. Learning the object pronoun of the first and second person is not only easier in practice than learning the pronoun of the third person, but is set in contexts that are different in kind. When the first and second person pronouns are used together, they operate in a closed, self-contained relationship. In contrast, the third person pronoun serves as a shorthand referent to people, things and events previously mentioned, thus connecting past and present.

An extract from the poem *Grammatik mit Herz*, reproduced in Box 9.3, illustrates the use of the first and second person pronouns.

> *Ich sehe nur dich.*
> *Ich frage dich.*
> *Du antwortest mir.*
> *Du hilfst mir.*

In these four lines, as in the whole poem, in any dialogue or letter, any reference to the originator and the addressee of the message will be understood, because they know each other, and no other indication of identity except the pronouns is required.

Knowing the first- and second-person forms thus enables learners to initiate and respond to a large number of messages. Learners of French only have to remember one form for each person, although they also need to learn a different set of forms for pronouns after a preposition and in the singular imperative affirmative. In German, with its separate forms for the dative and accusative, the learning task is harder, as the valency of the verb or the case taken by the particular preposition have to be recalled.

There are several contexts where the first- and second-person object pronouns would occur naturally and can therefore be practised realistically. There are those which come under the broad term of personal relationships, particularly on the practical side, for example: *je vais t'écrire, téléphoner, je viendrai te chercher, ich danke dir, wir erwarten dich*. Then there are the verbs denoting pleasure and pain, for example *gefallen, schmecken, weh tun*, and verbs of giving and sending with a noun. Finally, learning reflexive verbs consolidates the forms.

Learning the forms of the third person, particularly in the singular, is harder. I give here three examples with the direct and three with the indirect object pronoun.

- *Vous prenez cette chemise, Mademoiselle? (Cette chemise te plaît, Annick?)*
  Oui, je la prends.

- *Tu as vu Marie et Yvonne ce matin? (Marie et Yvonne sont à l'école ce matin?)*
  Oui, je les ai vues dans la cour.
- *Wie findest du dieses Buch? (Was hältst du von diesem Buch?)*
  Ich finde es sehr gut.
- *Est-ce qu'elle ressemble à sa mère? (Elle est comme sa mère, tu ne trouves pas?)*
  Oui, elle lui ressemble beaucoup.
- *Tu as téléphoné à tes parents? (Tu as écrit à tes parents?)*
  Je vais leur téléphoner ce soir.
- *Hast du schon mit Frau Müller gesprochen? (Weiß es Frau Müller schon?)*
  Ja, ich habe heute mit ihr gesprochen.

In order to answer with the right object pronoun, pupils must know two things:

(1) the valency or complementation of the verb they are using (in German they also need to know what case is taken by different prepositions);

(2) the gender and number of the noun to which the pronoun refers in the previous sentence.

Their attention must therefore span two sentences — they must keep in mind the noun in the previous sentence as well as the verb and its complementation in the sentence they are formulating. The examples have been in the form of questions, such as would occur in conversation, but exactly the same conditions apply in two consecutive statements in any written text. *Birgit hat John voriges Jahr kennengelernt. Seitdem schreibt sie ihm oft.*

Remembering the valency of the verb is the harder task because of the large number of verbs. It is made easier if the verb occurs in the question, because this gives the pupils some cues. If the verb is followed directly by a noun in French or by a noun in the accusative in German, the choice will be from the set of direct object pronouns. If the verb is followed by *à, au* etc. in French or by the noun in the dative in German, the set of indirect object pronouns must come to the fore.

Choosing within a given set of pronouns is easier because the noun to which the pronoun refers will have been explicitly mentioned, accompanied generally by a determiner which signals its gender and number.

This analysis of the learning task suggests the directions that practice can take. But before one can start practising, indeed before pupils are explicitly taught the object pronoun, they will need to possess some preliminary experience and knowledge. One should be able to assume that they will be familiar with classroom phrases incorporating pronouns, and that students of German will have learnt about the accusative and dative in the main determiners and recognise the respective endings. If some introductory exercises have been carried out, as suggested in our learning model, the new forms will already have been used, though without analysis. Any explanation would seek to bring out the two relationships described earlier.

Initial teaching

One further assumption must be made: that the direct and the indirect object pronouns are taught and practised in different chapters, with an interval between them.

For the direct object pronoun one sequence could be:

- start by revising the valency of some familiar verbs in sentences containing a noun. One would point to the direct proximity of the noun object to the verb, and for German, where present, to markers of the accusative;
- using the same verbs, quote from the text or construct pairs of sentences with a noun in the first and a pronoun in the second, bringing out the different forms and their position before the verb;
- carry on with a large number of nouns, but still with a very small number of verbs, so that the pupils' attention is wholly focused on the relation between noun and pronoun.

The valency of the verb is not in question; the first objective is to learn the forms of the pronoun. Since the aim of the practice is to teach rather than test, one would use at least three or four nouns of the same gender: *Est-ce que vous prenez cette chemise, robe, blouse, cravate?* before moving on to practising with another gender or number. A mixed, testing sequence could conclude the exercise.

The schematic description given here makes the exercise look dry, but in the right context it can be developed into natural dialogues. Some of the verbs that can be used appear in the examples. Card games such as 'Happy Families' provide excellent practice for *haben/avoir*. *Finden/trouver* collocate with a large number of adjectives of approval or disapproval. They can also be used in the negative as a possible reply to a question about objects to take to school or to pack for a journey: *Hast du deine Turnschuhe? Ja, ich habe sie hier. Nein, ich finde sie nicht.*

The number of verbs taking the indirect object pronoun is smaller, but the same sequence can be followed in realistic contexts with, for example, *écrire, téléphoner, parler.*

Accepting answers with a verb that was used in the question may offer support initially, but, as I have suggested earlier, such repetition can sound artificial. Once pupils are confident about the various pronominal forms and the valency of important verbs, they should be encouraged to use these verbs rather than rely on the scaffolding of the question. The next stage in the practice therefore, at least with abler pupils, is to vary the words of the question, so that pupils have to rely on their own resources to provide the appropriate answer. (That is why the examples include possible alternative questions in brackets.)

Revision practice and the next stage

Every new chapter will provide opportunities for revision, with new nouns and new verbs and practice extending to the position of pronouns in compound tenses, negative and interrogative sentences and with modal verbs. At the same time, it may be worth repeating a small stock of questions over three or four weeks to make the connection between cue and response automatic:

Vous avez vu Monsieur X/Madame Y ce matin? (with names of teachers)
Vous avez parlé à Monsieur X/ Madame Y ce matin?
Qu'est-ce que vous dîtes à vos parents avant de vous coucher?
Est-ce que vous allez regarder la télévision, faire vos devoirs ce soir?

The next stage is practice with ditransitive verbs, mainly concerned with giving, showing, sending, which are followed by two objects, normally indirect for the person and direct for the thing. The drawing in Box 9.11 can serve as basis for one possible approach. It shows the presents which the girl in the middle — let's call her Nicole — has given to relatives and friends.

The first two steps could be to check that the words for the presents were known and to have eight sentences written out for reference: *Nicole a donné des disques à Silvie et Marie. Elle a donné une cafetière à sa mère.*

After a reminder that verbs like *donner* have two objects, one could explain that two sets of questions could be asked by outsiders, depending on what information they had and what else they wanted to know. If they knew that Nicole had given a present to her mother but did not know what it was, they would ask:

Qu'est-ce que Nicole a donné à sa mère?

to which the answer would be:

Elle lui a donné une cafetière.

Some pupils might not need an explanation why *mère* has been replaced by a pronoun, particularly as English behaves in the same way. But others might welcome an explanation. Since the question explicitly names the mother as receiving a present, she does not need to be named again in the answer and a pronoun can be used instead. Between *donner* and *sa mère* there is *à*, therefore an indirect pronoun is needed . On the other hand, the nature of the present has to be made explicit. (In linguistic terms, given information is expressed here through a pronoun, which comes early in the sentence, near the noun in the previous sentence to which it refers. New information is expressed through a noun, the cafetière, and receives end focus.)

Questions would follow about the other seven presents.

If, however, it was known that one of the presents was the cafetière and one wanted to know to whom it was given, one would ask:

A qui Nicole a-t-elle donné la cafetière? (or some other less formal question form)

and the answer would be:

Elle l'a donnée à sa mère.

Although the model answer might be written up, explanation of the past participle agreement could be postponed, and the emphasis for this and the other sentences would be on the choice of pronoun.

Box 9.11 A drawing through which to practise ditransitive verbs (E.A.L. Bird, distributed at a conference in Leicester, 1993, and reproduced with his permission)

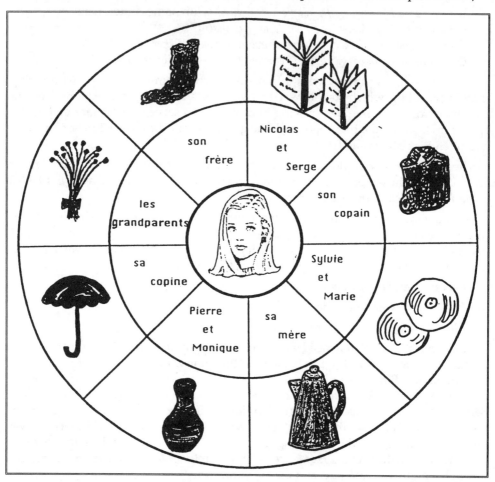

Either at the end of the exercise, or, preferably, a few days after, understanding could be tested by mixing questions on the two patterns. Question and answer practice would be mainly oral, and could soon become more demanding, so that a full answer was really needed:

Est-ce que Nicole a donné des disques à sa mère? Est-ce que Nicole a jeté (gardé) la cafetière?

For written practice, pairs of sentences are obviously the minimum necessary to allow the use of pronouns; longer texts of at least a paragraph with a few gaps for the insertion of pronouns enable the pupils to understand the context better and make more reasoned decisions.

A long time can be allowed to elapse before sentences with two pronouns are introduced; indeed weaker pupils might perhaps not be required to produce them at all.

Word Order in German

Reference was made in Chapter 6 to the difficulties experienced by English learners in getting the German word order right, and an account of the main rules and tendencies was given there.

The two-pillar framework

The rules relating to the two-pillar framework of the main clause are normally learnt fairly successfully within the first two years of study. They are clear and can be practised through a variety of communicative activities.

The detachment to the end of the clause of the prefix (or elements treated as a prefix) in separable verbs can be introduced without analysis through teachers' instructions, such as *paßt auf, nehmt euer Deutschheft heraus, schlagt euer Buch auf Seite 00 auf, fangt an*. The topic of travel almost necessarily involves the use of verbs like *abfahren, abfliegen, ankommen* and various compounds of *steigen*. Daily routines (*aufwachen, aufstehen*), leisure activities (*fernsehen, radfahren*) and compounds of *gehen, kommen, sehen, hören* offer further opportunities for practice.

The position of the past participle at the end of the clause is rehearsed with any account of past activities, that of the infinitive when modal verbs and verbs followed by *zu* are learnt. Different persons of *können, müssen, dürfen* are used in explaining German traffic signs, comparing school rules in Germany and Britain, discussing what pupils are allowed or forbidden to do at home and playing a Snakes and Ladders game like the *Verkehrsspiel* shown in Box 9.12, but in each of them the position of the infinitive is practised. The same is true when plans for a holiday or career are discussed with *wollen* and *werden*, and help in the home is offered with *sollen*.

The rules just described need to be revised as new verbs are encountered, but their unambiguous application and the limitation to one grammatical element only, the verb, may account for the relative ease with which practice normally leads to success.

Word-order rules which deal with more general concepts and can be realised in several different ways cause greater difficulties.

The position of the verb in a main clause

By far the most important is the rule that the verb always comes second (see Chapter 6 for a full statement of the rule and examples). Yet this formulation, though accurate and often remembered by pupils, is not, in my view, very helpful in practice. When the German sentence begins with the subject, as it often does, the rule is self-evident. In questions, as Weinert's study (1990) showed, initial hesitation is followed fairly soon

Box 9.12   A snakes and ladders game with which to practise German modal verbs (and have fun) (Neuner *et al.*, 1988: 90–91)

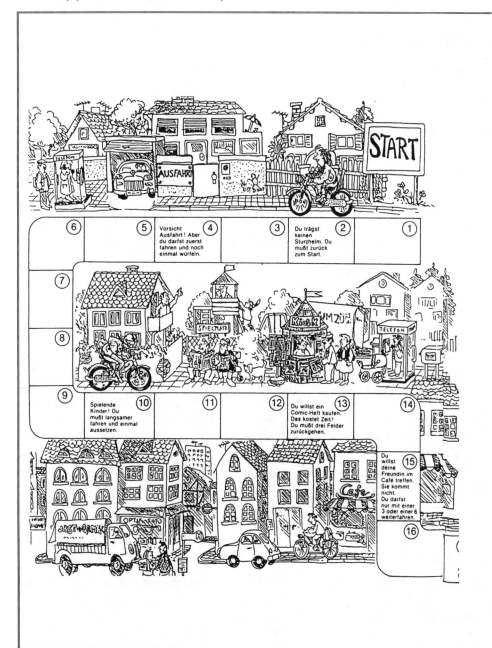

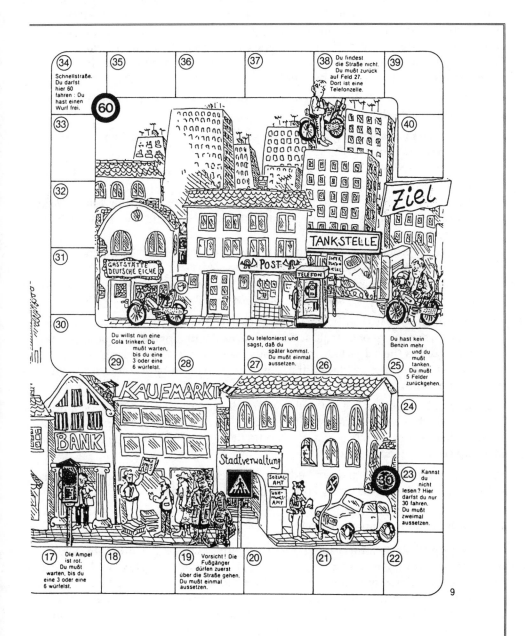

by success. Most problems are caused by the inversion of subject and verb in main clauses, since this conflicts with the deeply ingrained English order of subject–verb–object. Practice should therefore aim at enabling learners to deal with the occasions when other elements are placed at the head of the clause. Such elements, as was discussed in Chapter 6, may be segments of information which are placed in relief in relation to others or attitudinal comments on what is going to follow.

Normal topic work in the first two years of study offers many opportunities for practice. These include:

- the school timetable: *am Montag (montags) haben wir . . .* (contrast with other school days understood);
- description of a holiday postcard or other visual material: *oben rechts liegt das Schwimmbad;*
- description of pupils' bedroom: *vor dem Fenster steht ein Tisch, über dem Bett hängen Poster von . . .* (this is a good opportunity to insist on location verbs instead of the 'existential' *es gibt*);
- comparisons between what pupils do or wear on school days and at the weekend, in summer and in winter;
- sequence of activities during the day, using temporal adverbials, such as *nach dem Frühstück, in der Pause, von . . . bis, dann, manchmal.*

When pupils have had sufficient experience in framing sentences with the German word order, a statement of the rule and a comparison with English may be appropriate. In both languages the subject normally heads the sentence, in both languages another element may sometimes be placed first, but in English the subject comes next, whereas in German it follows the verb.

Attitudinal comments are not tied to particular topics, but there will be a number of occasions when pupils may wish to start a sentence with *hoffentlich, zum Glück* or *leider*, and short oral practice sessions can be fitted in where they are encouraged to make up such sentences.

Practice such as has been described here, or after short clauses with *wenn* and later with *als*, can be conducted orally and also by writing simple texts.

Word order in coordinate sentences

Once pupils start composing texts, they often wish to coordinate sentences, particularly through *und* and *aber*. They will thus need practice with these two conjunctions, and perhaps later with *oder, denn* and *sondern*. There can be considerable confusion here, to which the rule about the verb coming second may actually have contributed. The aim of the practice must be to show that these coordinating conjunctions are in Position 0 and do not affect the word order.

A possible sequence of steps is suggested here, with each step being explained (see Chapter 6) and practised separately:

(1) Two clauses with the same subject joined by *und*:
   Ich gehe nach Hause und sehe ein wenig fern.
(2) Two clauses with the same subject, joined by *und* and inversion in the first:
   Nach der Schule gehe ich nach Hause und sehe ein wenig fern.
(3) Two clauses with the same subject, joined by *und* and inversion in the second:
   Ich sehe ein wenig fern, und dann mache ich meine Hausaufgaben.
(4) Two clauses joined by (a) *aber* and the same subject, or (b) *und* or *aber* and a different subject.
   (a) *Sie war müde, aber sie konnte nicht einschlafen.*
   (b) *Ich bin 13 Jahre alt, und meine Schwester ist 11.*
      Ich lerne Deutsch, aber meine Schwester lernt Französisch.

As their study progresses, pupils have to realise that a number of adverbs and modal particles, like *aber, eigentlich, doch, auch* can occupy more than one position. At the same time, they need to appreciate the limits of this flexibility. *Auch,* for example, is often wrongly placed by English learners in all the positions that the English 'also, too, as well' can occupy.

The time–manner–place sequence

A rule which is sometimes introduced orally, but is more commonly required in writing, is that relating to the order of adverbials, often summarised as time–manner–place. The sequence is often practised in connection with departure and arrival times (*Der Zug kommt um 19.04 in Köln an*), or with ways of coming to school (*Ich komme zu Fuß in die Schule.* In *Deutsch Heute* Bk 1 (Sidwell & Capoore, 1983) pupils are asked to listen to a number of short recordings entitled '*Was hast du/was haben sie gemacht?*', and fill in a grid under the headings *Wer Wann Wo Wohin Was.* Pupils then ask each other how they spent their holidays, using those interrogative adverbs and answering with the aid of cue cards. Some teachers add cards for adverbials of manner, to be elicited by *Wie,* others colour code the cards, so that the completed sentence acts as a visual reminder of the word order. Personal accounts, without cues, can follow, and perhaps be summarised in group reports or a class survey.

Temporal expressions are particularly numerous, and pupils need to integrate them gradually into their feeling for the rule. Substitution tables on the order of adverbials, like those in Box 9.13, can act as visual reference, to be extended as new expressions are met, and as stimulus for practice. New interrogative adverbs can gradually be added to the pupils' repertoire.

Word order in subordinate sentences

The final rule to be considered is that regarding the clause final position of the finite verb in subordinate clauses. This too is an unambiguous rule, without exceptions, yet it causes more errors than the two-pillar rule. There are probably many reasons for this. One may be that, if speech planning proceeds by constituents, as Clark and Clark

Box 9.13 Substitution tables on the order of adverbials in German

Wann, wie oft, wie lang, seit wann, bis wann?				
Ich	gehe	jeden Samstag manchmal, oft selten, nie	ins Kino	
Frau Schmidt	fährt	regelmäßig	mit dem Auto	nach Köln
Unsere Katze	liegt	im Winter	am liebsten	vorm Feuer
Müllers	wohnen	seit einem Jahr		in Berlin
Mein Vater	arbeitet	von 8 bis 4 Uhr		im Büro
Wir sind	um 8 Uhr		zu Hause	angekommen
	spät in der Nacht		bei unseren Freunden	"
	nach einer langen Überfahrt		in Hamburg	"
	pünktlich um 5 Uhr			"
Ich bin	voriges Jahr, nur einmal		in Deutschland	gewesen
	schon oft, noch nie		in einem Konzert	"
	schon lange nicht		im Kino	"

(1977) maintain (see Chapter 8), an English speaker would naturally tend to keep subject and verb together in one constituent. Another reason, connected with the previous one, is the strain felt by the speaker or writer in communicating a complete message while keeping in mind the verb, sometimes in the rather empty form of an auxiliary. The range of subordinate clauses and the fact that some may precede as well as follow the main clause, thus forcing the pupil to observe two different sets of rules, must add to the difficulty.

I am sure that the timing, order and method of teaching subordinate clauses can differ, without affecting success. I want to single out only two aspects of my own approach.

The first is to distinguish between informal speech and written language. Native usage readily accepts no subordination in sentences such as *Sie sagt, es ist zu teuer* or *Ich glaube, er ist krank* after common verbs like *sagen, wissen, glauben, meinen* in the affirmative. Also, questions with *warum* are often answered simply with a declarative statement, so that *weil* can be left until it is required for written or more complex explanations.

The second is to follow one of Slobin's (1973) operating principles of not interrupting the normal word order. That means starting with a subordinate clause placed after rather than before the main clause. One possibility is to start with indirect questions, closely linked to *fragen*, provided pupils are thoroughly familiar with interrogative adverbs. Reporting to a third party questions asked by a correspondent in a letter can be one way of introducing *ob* and other indirect questions, reporting the content of a telephone message is another. Polite questioning in a department store would need *Können Sie mir bitte sagen + ob, was, wo, wann. Weißt du?* can be the opening gambit in a friendly test of knowledge between partners. In revision, the contrast between direct and indirect questions can be brought out, with one pupil encouraging another to ask questions of a third. Clauses with *daß* can follow in due course, when considered judgements have to be given, especially after negative expressions, such as *ich glaube nicht, ich finde es nicht richtig, daß* . . .

Certain subordinate clauses, such as the *wenn* clause, would normally precede the main clause, because they convey the 'topic', about which further information is given later. One can start with short clauses, for example about what one wears or how one gets to school in different weathers, until the position of the verb, both in the subordinate and in the inverted main clause, becomes familiar.

Semantic Rules: Choosing Between the Imperfect and an Action Tense in French

Most of the rules discussed so far have been concerned with grammatical relations: between a noun and one of its determiners, the subject of a sentence and the appropriate verb form, the verb and its complement. In order to apply these rules successfully, the learner has to become familiar with grammatical concepts and perhaps terms, and assign words to word classes. With practice, effecting the relation between words becomes increasingly manageable and even at times automatic. With semantic rules, learners have to go behind the words to the situation and grasp how elements in that situation relate to each other. Presenting and practising semantic rules therefore means helping learners to recognise how these relationships work in different situations, and helping them to develop and refine their understanding of the concepts involved.

The semantic rule, or, more accurately, rules, to be discussed later are those needed to choose between the imperfect and an action tense in French. (The choice between the perfect and the *passé simple* is a matter of convention and will not be discussed; the references will be mainly to the perfect.) It can be argued that in a minimalist syllabus, receptive understanding rather than productive use of a descriptive tense like the imperfect is sufficient. This is indeed the position held by some GCSE examination boards in Britain. On the other hand many learners will want to amplify their account of past actions through descriptions of the background and of their feelings, and at a later stage be able to envisage possible eventualities and report what was said.

One approach to the teaching of the imperfect has been outlined in general terms already: proceed slowly, teach one function at the time, start with one which is easily understood, so that the forms can be learnt without additional conceptual difficulties, and then present further functions at intervals, each clearly represented in one or more texts. The aim is to build up gradually in learners, through the study and discussion of texts and their own writing, a perception of how the imperfect is used, on its own and in relation to other tenses.

The imperfect as the tense for habitual actions in the past

The easiest function to illustrate is probably that of habitual action in the past. *Échanges* 2 (Grunwald *et al.*, 1981) contains a chapter in which life in a Dordogne village today is compared with peasant life in the Middle Ages. After questions on the text, two exercises practise the imperfect. The first brings out how the imperfect is derived from the stem of the first person plural of the present by contrasts such as the following:

Aujourd'hui ...	*Autrefois, au Moyen Age ...*
nous travaillons pour nous	*les paysans ... pour leur seigneur*
nous finissons assez tard	*ils ... encore plus tard*

There are nine pairs in all, including one with *sommes* and one with *il faut*. The nine sentences are then repeated in the *nous* form.

The second exercise contains 15 gapped sentences in which the imperfect of 24 verbs, not all used in the text, is practised in the 3rd person singular and plural. Here are two:

> *Au Moyen Age le seigneur (vivre) dans un château. Le plus souvent, le château (être) sombre et il y (faire) froid.*

Descriptions contrasted with time bound events or actions

In the next section of the chapter a farmer from the village relates to a visiting journalist how he happened to pass by the castle on a night of full moon and saw through the window people in medieval dress eating and drinking. He saw one of them drink a toast to the lord of the manor, and realised that it was the devil! He tells the incredulous journalist that, according to a legend, the knight sold his soul to the devil and returns to the castle from time to time.

The account of the visit is set within a frame: normal print and the perfect are used for the farmer's time bound actions, but italics and the imperfect for (a) descriptions of the setting -late at night, full moon, the great hall lit up, (b) identification of people, (c) accounts of what they were doing at the time. The reasons for the different tenses would probably be discussed in class and the underlying concepts elucidated. These concepts are then applied in four exercises.

In the first, six witnesses of a car accident explain what they were doing when the accident occurred. The rubric for the exercise enjoins:

Demandez-vous:
*Quelle était la **situation**?*   IMPARFAIT
*Qu'est-ce qui **s'est passé alors**?*   PASSÉ COMPOSÉ

The second practises the use of the imperfect to describe *'états d'âme'*: intentions, reasons, feelings. Two clauses have to be linked to form a sentence, first by stating intention through the use of *comme* and the imperfect, leading to action and the perfect, then by starting with the action and giving a reason for it through the use of *parce que* and the imperfect. For example, the following two clauses:

> *M. Rioux et les garçons veulent ouvrir un chemin. Alors, ils prennent des machettes.*

have to be transformed into :

> *Comme M. Rioux et les garçons voulaient ouvrir un chemin, ils ont pris des machettes.*

and later

> *M. Rioux et les garçons ont pris des machettes, parce qu'ils voulaient ouvrir un chemin.*

Eight sentences, all dealing with a topic treated in an earlier chapter, have to be formed in each way. The text is written in such a way as to force the pupils to consider the situation each time, and not to operate mechanically.

A third exercise, again based on known material, deals with incidents during a car drive. Pupils have to decide whether a certain action was in progress or occurred at a point in time.

A fourth exercise, in the form of a story about a holiday incident from an earlier chapter, brings together all the functions of the imperfect introduced so far: habitual action, description of setting and of how people felt at the time, interspersed with events.

Finally, with the aid of an open-ended cartoon strip, pupils are asked to imagine what happened to the journalist, as he went to the castle to investigate whether the legend of the devil was true.

I have quoted the chapter from *Échanges* (Grunwald *et al.*, 1981) at length because, in my view, it uses the right approach with regard to rules which demand sensitive understanding of how one event relates to another. It guides learners towards that understanding through typographical devices, explicit reminders of key concepts and varied practice.

Of course, different topics could have been chosen. The subject matter of the first section could have been brought nearer to the lives of the pupils by getting them to ask older people about living conditions 50 years ago, comparing clothes, means of transport, cost of essential commodities, leisure activities. The well known format of an interrogation to discover a crime can be used to practise background activities interrupted by sudden events.

The descriptive function of the imperfect is the most difficult for pupils to spot. The image quoted earlier of a film set and the action that begins to take place can be exploited through a video, a strip cartoon or the analysis of a text. Pointers can be given to pupils to the kind of information that would often be used to describe the film set: the weather, the location, the people present, how they looked, what they were doing; similarly pointers can be given to the markers that indicate the limits within which an action occurred, its beginning, end or duration. But care must be taken lest pupils regard these pointers as absolute. In the end, observation by pupils themselves, the collection of their own examples as well as analysis of class texts, are the best means to develop a feeling for the subtleties of French tense use.

Conclusions on the Teaching of Grammar

In the preceding pages I have not tried to advocate one simple method, applicable to all circumstances. The principles which I outlined in the introduction to the teaching of morphological rules can be generalised to the teaching of all rules and summarised in the following advice to young teachers:

(1) Try to be clear in your mind what the rule is about, which elements are brought into relation with each other, what concepts are involved, what, in other words, pupils have to understand in order to apply the rule and what they can do through the rule.

(2) If the introductory text is interesting and the new forms and the rule that governs them are clearly exemplified, if the exercises provide enough varied practice, if at the end of the unit the pupils are able to perform some interesting task, count yourself fortunate.

(3) If you need to provide additional or alternative material, think first about the topic on which to base it, whether it should come from the new chapter, earlier chapters, or new material altogether, and whether the relevant vocabulary is already known or has to be taught.

(4) Next, decide on which of the different exercises illustrated in the preceding pages are most suitable for your purpose: questions and answers, oral drills, working from grids, structured or open, cued and open dialogues, sentence completion, gapped sentences, dictation.

(5) Within and between exercises check on the balance between teaching and testing; try to move from structured to freer work.

(6) Try to finish with the creation, or the understanding by pupils of a text, oral or written, or the performance of a task, made possible or enhanced by the learning of the new forms and rules and containing, if possible, some personal element. If you cannot think of such a conclusion, ask yourself: should the new forms just be explained briefly, and the rule be taught later or not at all?

(7) Finally, do not forget the importance of revision.

10 Learning Pronunciation

Introduction

The learning of pronunciation differs in several respects from the learning of vocabulary and grammar. The outstanding difference is that, as well as involving memory or cognitive processes, it brings into play our motor-sensory capabilities, requiring the training of our auditory perception and the control of our vocal organs.

The total number of vowels and consonants in any one language is much smaller than even the most basic stock of vocabulary or grammatical rules (typically between 30 and 50), yet, between them, these vowels and consonants make up every word that pupils learn. This has two consequences. The first is that serious weaknesses in pronunciation can significantly impair one's ability to communicate. Second, whereas vocabulary and grammatical knowledge are built up slowly and incrementally over several years, the whole of the sound system is encountered quite early. Teaching pupils to discriminate between sounds, pronounce words acceptably and connect sounds with letters must therefore also begin early.

The approach to such teaching has changed considerably over the century (for details, see Hawkins, 1981). The early years were strongly influenced by the emergent discipline of phonetics. In 1912, schemes of work in a sample of eight schools showed that the first texts in French (and sometimes German) were all printed in phonetic transcription, that is, used the International Phonetic Alphabet (IPA), whereby every speech sound has the same precise notation, whatever the spelling conventions of different languages.

Inadequate training in phonetics of young teachers and confusion among pupils during the transition from phonetic to conventional spelling gradually dimmed the enthusiasm for phonetics in schools. Nevertheless a handbook on the teaching of Modern Languages published in the mid–1950s showed a majority of teachers still using the phonetic alphabet in the first few weeks to distinguish and practise new sounds (Incorporated Association of Assistant Masters, 1956). By the publication of the handbook's next edition 11 years later (Incorporated Assocation of Assistant Masters, 1967), the use of phonetic symbols had been generally discarded, although early and systematic practice of unfamiliar vowel sounds, whether individually or within words and sense groups, was still common.

It is difficult to establish how much of such practice still occurs in British schools in the mid–1990s. A careful search through the Teacher's Books that accompany published courses and through teaching journals reveals hardly any reference to the teaching of pronunciation. This is not because the spoken word has lost prestige. On the contrary, cassette recordings are an integral element of all new language courses, bringing into the classroom native voices and accents to serve as sources and models for new language. Teachers are expected to conduct all their teaching in the target language, pupils get constant practice in listening and speaking, and proficiency in both skills is well rewarded in public examinations. It is fair to say that much more of the target language is heard and spoken in the classroom than in the past.

So why is there so little mention of pronunciation and pronunciation teaching? The explanation must lie in the belief by course writers that this rich exposure can by itself enable learners to hear accurately and adjust their speech habits so as to produce the sounds of the foreign language correctly. In other words, they hold that natural imitation works.

Is this belief justified? It is not shared everywhere. For example, I have seen teachers in Eastern European countries writing up English words in phonetic transcription to correct a pupil's mistake. In a school course published in Germany in 1981 for the teaching of French (*Échanges*, Grunwald *et al.*, 1981) the end vocabulary gives a phonetic transcription of every word, while word and sentence stress are practised in a school course published in France in 1988 for the teaching of German (*Deutsch mit Spaß*, Neuner *et al.*, 1988).

Perhaps these aids are used to compensate for the absence of native models, but expert opinion seems to be that untutored imitation cannot by itself achieve a good pronunciation.

Here are some quotations from teacher trainers in Germany and the United States (Pohl *et al.*, Rivers) and British linguists and university teachers (Hall, MacCarthy, Nott, Price):

> Pupils' first concern in listening to a spoken message is to understand its meaning. This global understanding is not sufficient for speech sounds to be recognised and imitated appropriately. The pupils' attention has to be consciously directed to relevant phonetic features (translated and summarised from Pohl *et al.*, 1978: 177–8).

> Unless they are gifted with exceptionally well-developed powers of mimicry, learners will almost certainly not be able to imitate as well as they otherwise might even a native speaker who is physically present, much less so a disembodied recorded voice. They need to know what to listen for, what it is they are trying to imitate. Otherwise they may not even realise that what they are saying is by no means a close, let alone a perfect, imitation of what they hear (Price, 1991: 3).

> In the normal foreign language learning situation, with schoolchildren or adults, the pronunciation habits of the mother tongue are well established and are

automatically transferred to the foreign language unless countermeasures are taken. (Hall, 1992: 1–2)

Such countermeasures require knowledge by the teacher.

Slight distinctions in sound which can hinder comprehension of a message are made by movements of the tongue and other organs in the teacher's mouth and throat which the students cannot normally see. Consequently, merely making French sounds which are different from English sounds and urging students to imitate these, without giving some indication as to how they can be produced, may not be sufficient to ensure accurate pronunciation by the students (Rivers 1975: 145).

It is best not to wait too long.

It is worth making the point that whereas command of a foreign language — like the command of one's first language — is something that should go on improving throughout life, habits of speech soon become fixed and do not go on improving. (MacCarthy, 1975b: 4)

Empirical evidence confirms the strengths of speech habits.

The widespread and persistent inability (as many as one in three, or at least one in four, of all students?) [on a French degree course] to form a clear, confident and authentic French *u* [y], even in Year 4, is a clear indication that, in themselves, time, study and exposure are not sufficient to bring about certain changes in speech habits. (Nott, 1994)

Such views cannot be brushed aside. On the other hand teachers have to decide between competing priorities. They seek above all to promote their pupils' confidence, to encourage them to speak. Undue insistence on forcing them to make strange noises can make pupils self-conscious, untimely corrections can inhibit the flow of speech. The guidelines laid down by the French Ministry of Education for the first year of the 11–15 *collège* stress that 'l'acquisition d'une prononciation convenable est en première année une préoccupation importante', but also warn against 'les excès d'un perfection-nisme un peu vain' (Ministère de l'Éducation Nationale, 1985). As listener at language festivals and oral examiner at Advanced and even university level, I have sometimes had to strain to understand what was being said, particularly on prepared pieces. On the other hand, inability to pronounce [y] as in *vu* or [ç] as in *ich* can be isolated faults in otherwise successful communication.

The *Modern Foreign Languages Report* (DES, 1990) tries to strike a balance. Though warning against inhibiting spontaneity, it states:

it is important to pay close attention in the early stages to the quality of pronunciation . . . Some learners may develop a good accent simply by imitating what they hear, but a good number would benefit from deliberate training of the ear and the voice. (9.5) . . . Teachers need to be sensitive to the best ways of helping pupils to get their mouths round unfamiliar sounds (9.7).

These views are unexceptionable, but is sensitivity enough? Helping pupils to make unfamiliar sounds probably means giving them simple instructions in regard to the degree of mouth opening, the position of the lips and the tip of the tongue. This implies knowledge by the teacher of how the relevant speech sounds are produced.

The conclusion seems to be this: the importance of oral communication makes it essential that pupils should try to achieve a reasonable pronunciation. Uninformed imitation followed by practice may lead to fluency, but result at best in non-native sounds, and at worst in a loss of intelligibility. There is evidence that informed and judicious guidance at an early stage can produce satisfactory results.

My aim in the following pages is to help teachers to offer this guidance. Two considerations are uppermost in my mind. First, there must be many teachers who, though possessing a good accent themselves, are not aware of how they are producing it, because, like myself, they entered teaching without having received any notions of phonetics or phonology. (Phonetics deals with the production, transmission and reception of speech sounds, phonology with the organisation of sounds in a particular language.) It will therefore be necessary to go into a little detail in both spheres. There will have to be references to lips and tongue and mouth. Phonetic symbols may have to be used for the sake of precision, though normally together with conventional spelling. (Teachers unfamiliar with the phonetic alphabet will find it reproduced in any medium-sized dictionary and will soon get used to it.) And in the domain of phonology, some knowledge of general principles will enable teachers to present with greater confidence apparently arbitrary features of pronunciation, such as, for instance, the different pronunciation of the middle *e* in *samedi* and *vendredi* or of the initial *i* in French *immobile* and *impossible*.

Second, I shall try to be practical. The aim will not be to present theory for its own sake or to strive after 'un perfectionnisme un peu vain', but to give enough information, so that pupils can be guided, particularly in the early stages, towards 'approximations to correct pronunciation' (Rivers, 1975: 156) within the normal teaching sequence. (For those who want to know more, a few bibliographical references will be offered for each language.)

Bearing in mind these two considerations, I shall first sketch out very briefly what is involved in learning the pronunciation of a language. I shall then describe in outline the pronunciation of French and make suggestions on how to teach it, and go on to do the same with the pronunciation of German.

Learning Pronunciation

For adults the mechanism of speech production has become so automatic that they are not aware of its complexity. Observation of a small child on the way to acquiring speech or of someone with a speech disability may show up some of this complexity, but much of the process is only revealed through instrumental analysis.

The basic facts are these. Air expelled from the lungs travels up past the vocal cords and into the mouth (and sometimes into the nose). Precisely which sound is formed depends on the shape of the mouth cavity and the relative position of three movable organs in it: the lips, the tongue and the soft palate. The *lips* may be neutral, pushed forward (rounded) or spread (as if smiling broadly). The *tongue* has various movable parts: the tip, which can be placed almost between the teeth, raised to different parts of the teeth ridge and curled back to touch the hard palate; the front, which can be raised from an almost flat position to a number of higher positions towards the hard palate, and the back, which can similarly be raised to various heights. The *soft palate* or *velum* is either raised, so that the air stream passes through the mouth only, or lowered, so that there is movement through the nose or the mouth and nose. According to how they are articulated and their carrying power, speech sounds are divided into vowels and consonants. With vowels, air escapes in a relatively unimpeded way through the mouth or nose; with consonants, the air passage is either blocked or so narrowed that air cannot escape without producing audible friction. Another important distinction refers to the auditory result of the vibration of the vocal cords. Sounds produced while the vocal cords are vibrating are called *voiced*: they include all vowels and many consonants, e.g. [b, z]. Those produced without this vibration are called *unvoiced*, e.g. [p,s]. The vibration can be felt by placing the forefinger and thumb on either side of the Adam's apple, and comparing the effect of saying [zzz] and [sss] loudly.

With over a hundred sets of muscles involved in the production of speech, and each change of position of the speech organs affecting the sound made, it is not surprising that the number of speech sounds found in the world's 4000 languages is great. Actually, each language uses only a relatively small number. English, for example, uses around 20 vowels and 24 consonants; French around 16 vowels (15 according to Tranel, 1987) and 20 consonants, and German around 19 vowels and 21 consonants.

The same vowel or consonant may appear in lists of speech sounds in the target language and in the source language, yet its pronunciation can be different. The differences may relate to the amount of muscular tension required, or be determined by the position of the vowel in a word, or its proximity to other sounds. Learning the target sound system means both learning completely new sounds and changing the pronunciation of familiar ones.

Getting these two tasks right involves the development of auditory discrimination and the breaking of long-established habits, and therefore requires much practice. While imperfections and approximations may be excused by sympathetic listeners, special care is needed to avoid mispronunciations that lead to confusions of meaning, whether between lexical items such as *ville* and *vie*, or between grammatical forms such as *il vient* and *ils viennent*, *konnte* and *könnte*.

The influence of one sound on a neighbouring sound has already been mentioned. Sometimes a sound may be omitted altogether (elision), for example [d] in *grandmother*, or [t] in *Hauptmann*, or [ə] in *tout le monde*. Sometimes a sound becomes similar or even identical to its neighbour (assimilation). Examples are *does she?* [dʌʒ ʃi], *das Stück* [daʃ ʃtʏk] and *tout de suite* [tut sɥit]. In French, the relationship between two words is sometimes felt to be so close that the last consonant of the first becomes the first consonant of the second (liaison). One result of these processes is that it becomes harder to recognise words in connected speech.

The unit immediately above a single speech sound is the syllable, containing either a vowel on its own or a vowel surrounded by a certain number of consonants. It is through the distribution of stress between syllables that the relative prominence of one part of the word or of a longer utterance is marked, and knowing where to place the stress is thus another aspect of the learning task.

If the rhythm of a language is constituted by its pattern of stressed and unstressed syllables, then the melody of a language is created by the rise and fall of the voice, the pattern of pitch or tone. Speakers of all languages vary the pitch of their voice as they talk: the faster the vocal cords vibrate, the higher the pitch. In European languages the most important function of intonation is as a signal of grammatical structure, distinguishing, for example, between a statement and a question, or indicating whether an utterance is complete or not. (Compare, for instance the intonation of *sat down* in 'She sat down' and 'After she sat down, loud applause broke out'.)

A final aspect of learning pronunciation is to understand the relation between the sounds and the letters of the alphabet. At first the interval betwen hearing and reading a new word, or vice versa, is normally short, so that the acoustic and visual impression are recollected together, but increasingly learners must become confident in connecting sounds and letters according to new conventions and resisting the influence of familiar ones. It is that influence, rather than any difficulty of articulation, which explains, for instance, why the letter z in German, which is pronounced [ts] in all positions, is managed correctly by English speakers in final position *(schwarz)*, but is often confused with [z], under the influence of English, when in initial position, so that the z of *Zimmer* is pronounced like the z of *zero*.

Learning pronunciation has thus been shown to be a complex task. Some aspects are more important or troublesome in one language than in another, and in the following pages the main features and difficulties for English learners of French and German pronunciation will be considered and suggestions offered on how they can be dealt with.

11 The Pronunciation of French

Bibliographical notes: There does not seem to be one single book in print which is both scholarly and practical. Armstrong, *The Phonetics of French* (Bell, 1932) filled the need admirably, but is out of print, as is the useful MacCarthy, *The Pronunciation of French* (OUP, 1975). The student's book from Martineau and McGivney, *French Pronunciation* (OUP, 1973), a language laboratory course for university students, offers succinct descriptions and hints for corrections. Tranel, *The Sounds of French* (CUP, 1987) and Price, *An Introduction to French Pronunciation* (Blackwell, 1991) are full, but more theoretical than pedagogic.

The Pronunciation of Vowels

The two most important features of French pronunciation are, in my view, the pronunciation of vowels and the role of the syllable.

Even in a summary treatment such as the present, a classification of the French vowel system is necessary. It is given in Box 11.1.

The distinction between front and back vowels refers to the position of the tongue, that between unrounded and rounded vowels to the position of the lips, that between

Box 11.1 The French vowel system (Tranel, 1987: 36). *Note:* In this box [ø] subsumes the vowel associated with the so-called 'mute e'. This is more usually represented separately by the symbol [ə]. The symbol [ɔ̃] is also frequently used instead of [õ]

		Front		Back	
		Unrounded	*Rounded*	*Unrounded*	*Rounded*
Oral vowels	closed	i	y		u
	half-closed	e	ø		o
	half-open	ɛ	œ		ɔ
	open	a		ɑ	
Nasal vowels		ɛ̃	œ̃	ɑ̃	õ

Box 11.2 Examples of the French vowel system (Tranel, 1987: 36)

Front		Back	
Unrounded	*Rounded*	*Unrounded*	*Rounded*
[i] dit, livre	[y] du, une		[u] sous, jour
[e] parler, pied	[ø] deux, monsieur		[o] beau, faute
[ɛ] fait, cette	[œ] neuf, heure		[ɔ] homme, vole
[a] table, soir		[ɑ] bas, Jacques	
[ɛ̃] bien, vingt	[œ̃] un, parfum	[ɑ̃] dans, temps	[õ] bon, Londres

oral and and nasal vowels to the position of the soft palate, that between closed, half-closed, half-open and open vowels to the aperture of the mouth.

The gradual widening of the mouth aperture can be felt by saying in succession the words *lit, les, lait, la*; the difference between unrounded and rounded vowels appears clearly when the lip position is observed in a mirror as one pronounces *lit* and *lu*.

The sounds in Tranel's table are exemplified further in Box 11.2.

In pronouncing French vowels, the following should be noted:

(1) Greater muscular tension and effort are required for French vowels (and consonants too, see below) than for English ones. Compare for example the articulation of the last word in *Elle a reçu une bonne note* with that in *She sang a high note*.

(2) The quality of the vowel remains constant to the end. That means that both the tongue and the jaws maintain their position, whereas in English there is a tendency to glide from one vowel sound to another with a movement of the lower jaw, resulting in a diphthong. This is especially noticeable with open vowels, that is vowels not followed by a consonant, when they are in final position and stressed. In French such vowels are short, whereas in English they are long and frequently diphthongised. (Compare *Elle viendra bientôt* and *She wanted to go*).

(3) Lips play an important part in the articulation of French vowels. For the unrounded vowels the lips are stretched wide, for rounded ones they are rounded and pushed forward. In the numerous syllables formed by a consonant and a vowel, the lips are put into the appropriate position for the vowel even before the consonant is articulated. (Compare the lip position in *les* and *long, dit* and *du*.)

It is worth insisting on lip position, not only because of its intrinsic importance, but also because learners, using a hand mirror, can see as well as hear what happens when they spread or round their lips. They are thus not only helped to produce the right sound, but made to feel in control.

(4) Some French vowels have no counterpart in English and therefore need special attention. They are the front rounded vowels [y] [ø] [œ] as in *du, deux, heure* and

Box 11.3 Lip position in the pronunciation of French vowels

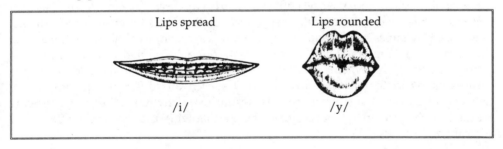

Lips spread

Lips rounded

/i/

/y/

the four nasal vowels [ɛ̃] [œ̃] [ɑ̃] [ɔ̃] as in *vingt, un, dans, mon* (the distinction between [œ̃] and [ɛ̃] seems to be waning (Tranel, 1987: 66; Price, 1991: 72).

French as a Syllable-timed Language

An outstanding difference between English and French is that English is a stress-timed and French a syllable-timed language.

An example will make it easier to understand what these terms mean. In the English and French counting-out rhymes, such as children recite in their games to decide who is 'it', the child that recites the English rhyme emphasises the stressed syllable on four words in each line, pointing to another child on each of the four heavy beats. The unstressed syllables are said more quickly and less distinctly; they are ignored, as it were, in the counting.

Eeny, meeny, miny, mo
Catch a tiger by his toe;
If he hollers, let him go,
Eeny, meeny, miny, mo.

The French child utters every single syllable evenly and distinctly, pointing with each syllable and maintaining the same rate of delivery throughout, only slightly emphasising the last syllable on each line.

Un petit cochon
Pendu au plafond.
Tirez-lui la queue,
Il pondra des oeufs.
Tirez-lui plus fort,
Il pondra de l'or.
L'or ou l'argent, qu'est-ce que tu aimes le mieux?
– L'argent.
– Va-t'en dedans.
– L'or.
– Va-t'en dehors.

The explanation is this. In English, each word is stressed on one syllable, though the place of the syllable may vary between words. In three related words *diplomat, diplomacy, diplomatic*, the stress falls respectively on the first, second and third syllable. Unstressed syllables are pronounced more rapidly and weakly, with the vowel sometimes reducing its sound to a neutral sound. (Compare, for example, the pronunciation of the syllable *ham* when it is stressed, as in *hamster*, and when it is unstressed, as in *Birmingham*). In connected speech this difference in prominence between stressed and unstressed syllables results in the rhythm of the utterance being marked by the strongly stressed syllables. The following is an example, with a line indicating the stressed syllable.

She decīded to spēnd her lāst frēe afternōon with her brōther

French contrasts with English in several ways:

(1) In individual words all syllables are pronounced at about the same speed and receive the same amount of stress, except the last, which is produced with a noticeable increase in energy. Note, for example, the stress on the last pronounced syllable in each of the three words that correspond to the English examples given earlier *diplomate, diplomatie, diplomatique*. The difference between stressed and unstressed syllables is not so marked as in English, and the vowel retains its quality in the unstressed syllable.

(2) As was shown in Chapter 8, speakers do not plan their utterances word by word, but by constituents, so that words that are felt to belong together form one sense group. An individual word simply takes its place as a succession of syllables in the sense group, and it is the final syllable in the group that receives any stress.

A short sentence may thus be regarded in respect of stress as one many-syllabled word:

Je vous écoūte Je vous écoute biēn Je vous écoute bien trōp.

A longer sentence is a series of sense groups, with a stress on the final syllable of each:

Il m'a racontē / que sa cousine Bētte / allait venir de la campāgne / jeudi matīn.

Principles of syllable formation

A brief account of the main principles of syllable formation is given below. It also puts the well-known process of 'liaison' into context and throws light on pronunciation in particular cases.

(1) In a French word there are as many syllables as there are vowel sounds. A word like *par*, for example, has only one syllable. Adding a consonant to make it *part* does not change the number of syllables. Adding a vowel produces a new syllable *paru*.

(2) In contrast to English, French has a very high proportion of open syllables, that is ending in a vowel (including nasal vowels). In the first four lines of the rhyme there are 19 open and 1 closed syllables; in the example sentence there are 15 open and 5 closed syllables.

(3) The high proportion of open syllables is partly caused by the fact that a consonant between two vowels is linked to the second vowel, that is, begins a new syllable.

cochon [ko ʃɔ̃], *raconté* [ʀa kɔ̃ te], *imaginer* [i ma ʒi ne]

(4) Most double consonant *letters* sound the same as when they are single. When placed between two vowels, they too therefore form a syllable with the second vowel.

arriver [a ʀi ve], *je m'appelle* [ʒə ma pɛl]

(There are a few exceptions with *m* and *n*, such as *emmène, ennui*.)

(5) This linking process applies also within a sense group when the final consonant sound of one word links up with the initial vowel sound of the next word.

avec eux [a vɛ kø], *il s'appelle Henri* [il sa pɛ lã ʀi]

(6) Linking also occurs in the separate process of 'liaison', when a normally silent final consonant letter of a word is sounded, and linked to the initial vowel of the following word within the sense group. A change in the pronunciation of the consonant may result.

je vous écoute [ʒə vu ze kut] *quand elle arrive* [kã te la ʀiv]

(7) When the last syllable is formed by a single or double consonant letter + a mute *e*, the consonant is sounded strongly.

verte, grande, rose, balle, achète.

(The pronunciation of mute *e* in the middle of a word or sense group will be touched on later.)

(8) The written combination *vowel+n/m* at the end of a syllable produces a nasal vowel. However when a nasal vowel is followed by *e*, it becomes denazalised. Failure to understand this is a notorious source of error.

certain, certaine, certainement [sɛʀtɛ̃] [sɛʀtɛn] [sɛʀtɛnmã]
marin, marine [maʀɛ̃] [maʀin]
brun, brune [bʀœ̃] [bʀyn]
moyen, le Moyen Age [mwajɛ̃] [lə mwajɛn ã ʒ]
bon, un bon enfant [bɔ̃] [œ̃ bɔn ãfã]

(9) When two different consonant letters occur between vowels, the first belongs to the first syllable, the second to the following.

argent [aʀ ʒã]   *impôt* [ɛ̃ po]   *action* [ak sjɔ̃]

(10) However when the second of these two consonants is [ʀ] or [l], the group thus formed is indivisible

appliquer [a pli ke]   *pondra* [pɔ̃ dʀa]

Other Features of French Pronunciation

In addition to these two major characteristics of French pronunciation, there are others, where achieving a satisfactory performance may take some time, and failure to do so may not endanger communication so seriously.

The pronunciation of consonants

(1) The importance of fully sounding pronounced consonants in final position has already been mentioned under (7) in the previous section.
(2) Initial [p, t, k] are pronounced without the aspiration, or puff of breath, with which they are pronounced in English before a stressed vowel. (Compare English *park, take, car* with French *parc, thé, car.*)
(3) Three consonants can cause difficulties, either because their English counterparts are pronounced differently in certain positions or because they do not occur at all in English.
   English [l] is pronounced differently before a vowel (clear [l]) and before a consonant or finally (dark [l]). (Compare *leave* with *golf, pale*. French [l] is clear in all positions: *lit, filtre, file*).
   The letter *r* in English is not sounded at all before a consonant or in word final position (*part, car*). It is sounded before a vowel, being produced towards the front of the oral cavity with the tongue tip active and directed upwards. In French, the letter *r* is pronounced in all positions. Though a front [r] is sometimes heard on the stage, a back [ʀ] is more common, with the tongue tip inactive and resting behind the lower teeth. (Compare English *red, crowd* with French *rouge, craie*)
   The [ɲ] sound as in *Boulogne, magnifique* does not occur in English.

Mute -e

It was stated earlier that French vowels retain their quality. The one exception is the so-called 'mute -*e*' (*e caduc* in French). The commonly used term 'mute -*e*' is confusing, because the vowel is indeed silent at times, but sounded at others. It takes a long time to develop a sure feeling for the right place to elide the -*e*, but the process is so common that a few guidelines are called for.

(1) In the initial syllable of a sound group, an unstressed -*e* is normally sounded:

   tenez, demandez, le monde entier (**petit** is an exception)

(2) In an internal syllable -*e* is elided when only two adjacent consonant sounds would result from the elision:

   ach(e)ter, sam(e)di, souv(e)nir, tout l(e) monde, moins l(e) quart, je n(e) sais pas, elle est v(e)nue.

(3) The -*e* is sounded when a cluster of three consonants would result from the elision:

   vendredi, Angleterre, Arc de Triomphe, elle ouvre la porte.

Liaison

The principle of *liaison*, whereby a sound bridge is established between the final consonant of one word and the initial vowel of the next, syntactically close word is not confined to French. In English [r] is silent in *for me* but sounded in *four apples*. In French the process is complex. A distinction is normally made between obligatory, optional and prohibited cases of *liaison*.

At school, emphasis has to be placed on obligatory cases, both in listening and speaking. The main ones are outlined here, although the principles will probably be absorbed gradually, through a number of individual instances. *Liaison* is compulsory:

(1) in an article or adjective followed by a noun or adjective:

des enfants, nos petits enfants, ces beaux arbres, premier acte

(2) in a pronoun before a verb, a verb before a pronoun, the first of two pronouns:

elles ont, ont-elles?, allez-y, allez-vous-en

(3) in a monosyllabic adverb or preposition followed by an article, adjective or adverb:

très aimable, pas encore, dans une ville

(4) in *est, sont, était, étaient*

c'est à moi, elles sont occupées, ils étaient arrivés

Intonation

It is not easy for the untrained person to analyse the rise and fall of the voice, and imitation may sometimes offer the surest guide. However it is useful for teachers to know the main principles of French intonation, so that they can counteract the influence of English in their pupils, if necessary.

In unemphatic speech there are three main tunes. In each the intonation curve shows a continuous line in short utterances, and a series of ups and downs in longer utterances.

Rising

(1) A yes–no question:

On va au cinéma? Tu comprends?

(2) An unfinished statement:

Quand je l'ai vu, . . . Les enfants ferment leurs livres, (et les posent sur la table)

Falling

(1) Questions beginning with an interrogative word:

Où allez-vous? Pourquoi ton frère ne vient-il pas?

(2) Commands and requests:

—   \   — — —   \   — —   —   — \

    Assieds-toi   Dites à Madame que je l'attends en bas

(3) Statements of not more than two syllables in total length:

—\   — \

    Bien   C'est ça

Rising–falling

    Statements of more than two syllables in total length:

— —   — — —   \

    Le train est en retard

— —   —   — — \

    (Les enfants ferment leurs livres), *et les posent sur la table.*

The influence of spelling on pronunciation

The mistakes in written French so often made by English pupils — and French ones too, as was shown in Box 9.10 — demonstrate the problems caused by the variety of alternative spellings of the same sound and by the number of consonants which at times are written though they are not sounded.

Conversely, spelling is on the whole a reliable guide to pronunciation. Most consonants have one regular corresponding sound and are silent in final position. Among the vowels, most of the difficulties occur in relation to the different groups of letters which are sounded with one nasal vowel. Thus for example the endings *in, im, ain, aim, ein, eim* all sound [ɛ̃].

However the very large number of English/French cognates, so helpful in reading, can interfere powerfully with pronunciation. A survey of errors made by university students in their first, second and final year in 237 oral exposés over seven years (Nott, 1994) confirms what must be the experience of many teachers and examiners at lower levels.

There is first of all the transfer into French of general features of English pronunciation, such as sounding the final consonants, the diphthongation of vowels and English stress patterns (as in *problem* for *problème*). But there are in addition mistakes typically associated with the English pronunciation of certain letters or groups of letters, such as the *a* in *parents, ir* in *une firme, in* in *industrie, tion* in *international* and, most notorious of all, *eu* in *Europe*.

To these mistakes directly due to interference from English must be added mispronunciations of a few words which are in common use, yet are exceptions phonologically, such as *ville, eu, pays*.

Summary

The pronunciation of vowels and the role of the syllable are particularly important for English speakers to learn. Articulating vowels correctly involves forming sounds that do not occur in English, keeping the sound constant without letting it slide into a diphthong, using vigorous muscular action. Special care is required in pronouncing the large number of French/English cognates with their treacherous similarity of spelling.

Attending to syllable-timing not only helps to achieve a regular, French rhythm in one's delivery, but also facilitates smooth linking within a sense group. A feeling for the right time to elide *-e* and for the right intonation is likely to develop gradually.

12 Teaching the Pronunciation of French

In guiding pupils' pronunciation, one needs to distinguish between the first few months, when the new sounds are heard and produced for the first time, and the intermediate stage, when a stock of words and phrases has been acquired and is available for practice, contrast and remedial work.

Pronunciation Teaching as Part of Initial Presentation

In some ways the early stages of language learning do not seem propitious for the teaching of pronunciation. Most course books are planned around topics or functions and without regard to any phonetic progression, and pupils' main concern is to use the new medium.

On the other hand, this is the stage when new words and phrases are presented and modelled by the teacher, when pupils are keenest to listen, imitate and repeat, and when learning how to pronounce the language can clearly be seen as a step towards successful communication. It is also the time, by common consent, when it is important to establish the right speech habits.

Whether new words and phrases are first heard on tape or not, they are often spoken again by the teacher for pupils to imitate, once the meaning is clear. As part of their presentation, teachers can draw attention to features of pronunciation, such as the greater muscular effort, the position of the lips, the even rhythm with a stress on the final pronounced syllable, the link between the final consonant of one word and the initial vowel of the next word.

How much and what they say will depend in part on the response of the pupils as they are asked to repeat in chorus, in groups or individually. The emphasis will be on phrases or short complete utterances, although isolated words may sometimes have to be repeated. Indeed it may sometimes be necessary to go further and break down a word or a difficult combination of sounds and rebuild it from the beginning or the end. Hand gestures or signs on the board or OHP can emphasise the position of stress, a link between two words or an obvious intonation pattern.

If the pupils see the word written, attention can be drawn to the fact that the letters *s, t, d* in final position are not sounded, and that final unaccented *e, es* are also silent, but that any consonant before them is sounded fully.

If some pupils' efforts at imitation are manifestly unsuccessful, it is probably wiser to pass on to another section of the lesson and to return to the troublesome sound in a practice and early correction session.

Pronunciation Practice and Correction in the First Few Months

Regular practice and early correction are required for several reasons: pronunciation, like any other aspect of language learning, needs constant revision; the establishment of new skills in particular calls for regular if short bouts of training; pupils must not be allowed to become self-conscious about their pronunciation and lose confidence.

Five minutes of pronunciation practice towards the beginning of a lesson can be used for repetition of words, phrases and short utterances for their pronunciation, or for reading selected words or phrases written on the board or an OHP. The session should be short, but pupils should be clear that the focus is on good pronunciation.

Alternatively the session can be devoted to detailed instruction on how a specific sound is produced, first in isolation, then in words known to the pupils. Chorus, group and individual practice is recommended. A satisfactory, not necessarily perfect performance is to be hoped for. If a pupil still has difficulties, a friend might be asked to help privately later.

The instructions suggested here have been written for teachers untrained in phonetics and without easy access to reference works. They are very brief and cannot take account of regional differences or individual problems, but they are meant to provide some kind of phonetic first aid when a particular problem arises. Teachers are advised to try them out on themselves before the lesson. They may also find it useful to have available in class a little hand mirror. With this before them, pupils can compare the shape of their mouth with that of the teacher, as they try to follow the instructions and produce the sound. The instructions cover almost all the vowels, grouped according to the classification at the beginning of Chapter 11, and the three difficult consonants.

Front unrounded vowels [i, e, ɛ, a], as in *dit, thé, est, tabac*

If one looks into a mirror as one says these four vowels in turn, one notices that the front of the tongue is clearly visible throughout, the tip of the tongue is placed against the lower teeth and the mouth aperture gradually widens. The instructions to pupils might be as follows:

[i] Put a finger on your throat directly under the chin. Say English *is*. The finger will not move very much. Now spread your lips wide, with the corners well apart, and

say a French [i] or a French word with [i], using extra muscular energy. You should feel the swelling of the throat muscle.

[e] Put the tip of your tongue firmly against the lower teeth and spread your lips energetically. The jaws should be a little more apart than for [i] (check the difference in a hand mirror).

[ɛ] Start from [e] and open your mouth wide, as if you were saying the vowel in English *pat*.

[a] Say English *I*, and isolate the first element, with the corners of the lips drawn apart and the mouth more open than for [ɛ] (check in the mirror).

Back vowels [ɔ, o, u], as in *homme, beau, douze*

[ɔ] The lips should be pushed forward and rounded, the jaws well apart (mirror).

[o] The lips are pushed forward and rounded, leaving an opening just large enough to insert the tip of your little finger (mirror). Muscular effort of tongue and lips needed. Avoid dipthongation.

[u] The lips are pushed forward and strongly rounded, leaving a very small opening. Muscular effort of tongue and lips needed.

Front rounded vowels [y, ø, œ, ə], as in *une, deux, neuf, me*

These vowels resemble front vowels in tongue position and back vowels in lip position.

[y] Below are three approaches to the production of this difficult sound.
    (1) with lips pushed forward and strongly rounded, try hard to say [i].
    (2) Make as if to whistle a high note.
    (3) Start English *you*. Pronounce the whole syllable with strong lip rounding, lengthen the first element.

[ø] Either start from [e] and pronounce it with strongly rounded lips or round your lips as for [o] and try hard to say [e].

[œ] Start with the lips well rounded and forward, as for [ɔ], and the corners of the mouth drawn together, then bring the tongue forward, aiming at [ɛ].

[ə] This is fairly easy. The lips are rounded, as between [ø] and [œ]. One can start from either and modify it towards the other.

Nasal vowels [ã, õ, ɛ̃, œ̃], as in *blanc, bon, vin, un)*

Some pupils are quite successful at imitating nasal vowels, in which the air passes through both the mouth and the nose. Others require help, and need to realise that the nasal quality accompanies the vowel throughout.

[ɑ] Put your fingers lightly on either side of your nostrils and say *n* quite vigorously: you should feel the vibration. Is there any vibration when you say [l] or [z]? Now say [a] while keeping the nasality.

Alternatively make a long AH as in *calm*, then nasalise this.

[ɔ̃] If imitation is unsuccessful, start from [o] and try to make [ɔ̃] with nasal vibration, prefixing [n] if necessary, and keeping the lips rounded.

[ɛ̃] If unsuccessful, start from English [æ] as in *man* and try to make [ɛ̃] with nasal vibration, prefixing [n] if necessary. Lip position is as for [ɛ].

[œ̃] Start from [œ] and try to introduce nasality into it, prefixing [n] if necessary. Keep the open rounded lip position.

The three troublesome consonants [l, ʀ, ɲ], as in *école, craie, espagnol*

[l] To get the feel of where the French [l] is pronounced, start with a French [i], then pronounce [li] several times and move to [l] + other vowels, until you are confident about the position of the tongue. Then go on to practising final [l] following a vowel. Start with [i] + pause + [l], then join up the vowel and [l]; repeat with other vowels and any words that are known or cognates, such as *hôtel, animal, ville, école*.

[ʀ] The important point is to keep the tip of the tongue resting behind the lower teeth. One way is to start with the [a] in the English word *father* and raise the back of the tongue as if clearing one's throat or gargling. Pronounce [a] several times, then [ʀ], then words with [ʀ] in various positions: *arabe, Paris, Europe, rapide, rien, rouge* rounding the lips before a rounded vowel), *pratique, treize, grand, personne, mercredi, pourquoi*.

[ɲ] Starting from English *onion* or *spaniel* and ensuring that the tip of the tongue is placed against the lower teeth should suffice.

Practice after the First Few Months

This sub-heading is deliberately vague. Some teachers may question altogether the need to continue with pronunciation sessions, others, more favourably inclined, may differ for how long into the course they should be held, and the level, performance and lexical knowledge of particular classes will undoubtedly influence form and content of what is done.

In the following a few types of exercise are briefly described that I have seen used by teachers, used myself or read about.

Auditory discrimination exercises

Pupils' inability to produce a sound correctly may sometimes stem from an inability to hear it accurately. They may either consider it simply a variant of a sound in their own language or fail to distinguish it from other sounds in the target language. Whatever the reason, the result can be an unexpressed reluctance to admit to a difficulty and an unwillingness to try and put it right.

Where there is evidence of such auditory confusion, special discrimination exercises can help to make pupils listen more attentively. They can also serve to bring home to them that certain words found in both languages sound different in French. Auditory discrimination exercises thus perform an awareness-raising and preparatory function for subsequent productive exercises.

Exercise 1. Focus on one pair of sounds

Pairs that are sometimes confused are [u] and [y] and nasal vowels like [ã] and [ɛ̃]. Pupils write, say, *ou* and *u* on two cards. The teacher reads out a series of words, containing either vowel. Pupils hold up one card according to what they think they heard. Since this is a teaching rather than a testing exercise, aiming to strengthen pupils' ability to identify a particular sound, several words containing one sound should be read out, and then several with the other, before they are mixed. One can start with words that pupils know, but carry on with unfamiliar ones, to ensure concentration on the sound. The advantage of cards over a tick on a worksheet is that the teacher receives immediate and continuing feedback and therefore can add to or reduce the number of examples. It is probably better to concentrate on one pair of sounds at the time and not to go on too long.

Exercise 2. Same or different?

After a series of exercises on individual pairs, this can act as a periodic, more comprehensive exercise. Pupils prepare two cards: *même – différent*. Teacher reads out pairs of words or phrases; pupils hold up a card to show whether they heard the same or a different vowel sound. Examples of pairs might be *banc/bon, vent/vend, vent/vont, plein/pleine, elles viennent/elle vient, le garçon joue/les garçons jouent, ce train est lent/ce train est long, il est tout vert/il est ouvert, il y a un autre appartement au-dessous/au dessus de nous,*

Exercise 3. French–English cognates

The teacher reads out a list of cognates, some in French, some in English. Pupils put up a card with *Français* or *Anglais*.

As reinforcement, the texts of all these exercises to improve auditory discrimination can be written out in two columns and read as pronunciation exercises in subsequent sessions.

Exercise 4. Discrimination in context

For this first-year exercise the teacher writes across the board or OHP *elles ont, elles sont, elles font, elles vont.* As each sentence of a short text like the one here is read out, a pupil goes up to the front and stands below the appropriate verb.

> *Annick et Caroline sont deux filles. Elles ont douze ans. Pendant la semaine elles ont cours. mais le samedi après-midi et le dimanche elles sont libres. Quelquefois elles vont en ville, quelquefois elles font une promenade avec leurs parents, quelquefois elles vont voir leurs grandsparents.*

The text of an oral exercise like this, indeed of any pronunciation exercise, should be kept and worked into a subsequent exercise or used for a dictation. The more revision and reinforcement there is, the better!

Productive exercises: sounds in individual words

Exercise 5. Individual sounds

Words and phrases familiar to pupils, containing sounds that caused difficulties in previous lessons and/or will occur in a forthcoming one are either spoken by the teacher to be repeated or written up to be read aloud. Repeating involves auditory discrimination as well as pronunciation, reading aloud reinforces awareness of the spelling-sound relationship. An example of the second type might be:

> Lisez les mots suivants correctement: *douzaine, Madeleine, certaine, certainement; nation, national, international.*

Exercise 6. Minimal pairs

Words differentiated in meaning only by one sound are set out in two columns, to be read either downwards (teaching) or across (testing). Six to eight pairs might focus on words containing (a) two nasal vowels, for example *cent, son,* (b) a nasal and an oral vowel, e.g. *parisien, parisienne* or (c) a silent and a voiced consonant, e.g. *grand, grande.* One contrast per session, perhaps repeated, makes a stronger impact than two or three.

Exercise 7. French–English cognates

The syllabic basis of French pronunciation should be stressed with longer words, such as *télévision, différent, infirmière, européen*

Exercise 8, The spelling–sound relationship

Several variants are possible:

Variant A. Jumbled words. Pupils have to group, say, 20 words familiar to them according to sound.

Variant B. *Donnez-moi une liste de mots qui se terminent/commencent par le son . . .*

Variant C. *Trouvez des mots avec un sens différent, mais avec le même son. Par exemple un mot qui se termine avec le même son que **vingt** est **main**.*

Productive exercises: sounds in connected speech

Exercise 9. Linking

This exercise practises *l'enchaînement consonantique,* whereby the final pronounced consonant of a word links up with the initial vowel of the next word. At this level, practice can be limited to links with *il/elle, cet/cette, un/une, notre/votre/quatre, avec, pour.* Examples: *il_a faim, elle_a faim, il_arrive, elle_arrive, cet_hiver, cette_idée, notre_enfant, votre_amie, quatre_oranges, avec_une_amie.*

The groups should be read without a break, and with the consonant starting a new syllable (and double consonants pronounced like single ones). Practice with short groups should be followed by practice with longer groups, such as *elle_arrive_avec_une_amie.*

Exercise 10. Liaison

Cases of obligatory liaison, sometimes with changes in sound, should be opposed to cases where liaison is forbidden. *les femmes/les hommes, nos parents/nos amis, nous partons/nous arrivons, dans dix minutes/elle a dix ans, elle habite au numéro neuf/ je me lève à neuf heures, elles s'appellent/ comment s'appellent-elles? c'est vrai/c'est inutile, ils sont là/ils sont ici* It is probably best to practise one of the three types of liaison at a time (see the section on *liaison* in Chapter 12.) Then practise it inside a sentence, preferably taken from recorded material heard in a previous lesson.

Exercise 11. Mute -e

Pupils tend to pronounce medial *e* at all times. It is probably best to learn common words and phrases where *e* is silent as they occur, but if confusion arises, a list could be drawn up and practised, including, for example, *Mad(e)moiselle, sam(e)di, méd(e)cin, tout l(e) monde, tout d(e) suite, il y a beaucoup d(e) monde, je n(e) sais pas.*

Exercise 12. Stress and intonation patterns

Intonation is probably best learnt by careful imitation of native speakers, but if there has been obvious misunderstanding of listening material or if pupil's own intonation could lead to misunderstanding, some remedial action is needed. Contrast the intonation in short statements with that of yes/no questions, that of short statements with that of longer statements, that of yes/no questions with that of questions beginning with an interrogative word: *je pars/tu viens avec moi?, j'ai faim/quand j'ai faim, je mange un gros sandwich, tu pars?/ qu'est-ce que tu vas faire?*

Stress may require more deliberate and frequent action. This should bear partly on cognates, to counteract the influence of English, but mainly on utterances as a whole. Apart from closely listening to native speakers, simple expansion exercises can remind pupils to put the stress on the final syllable of a sense group. *Elle arrive. Elle va arriver. Elle va arriver bientôt.*

Productive exercises: sounds in context

Exercise 13. Interesting names

Pupils draw up a list of people or places or things connected with France and of interest to them and pronounce them well. The lists might be of first names of French correspondents, of towns, football teams, famous people, and so on.

Exercise 14. Shouted messages

This is an exercise to practise syllable division, rhythm and the position of stress. Pupils imagine that they have to shout a message to someone at some distance. Examples might be *Le | dî | ner | est | prêt | . Je | vien | drai | te | cher | cher | à | si | x heures. |*

Exercise 15. The ad hoc exercise

This is probably the most important exercise of all. Pupils have to aim for a high standard of pronunciation in short exchanges within a known context. If there is still mispronunciation of *un/une*, ordering food and drinks will practise them, asking and giving directions calls for a good pronunciation of *où, rue, tout droit, à droite*. Rehearsing clock times necessitates the pronunciation of both oral and nasal vowels. One would hope that some transfer will occur when pupils practise or make up dialogues of their own!

Finally there should be opportunities when pupils feel sufficiently motivated to record themselves, listen critically and work hard on pronunciation as well as content. Such opportunities might comprise the preparation of a short spoken text for internal assessment or for sending to one's correspondent, the learning of a poem or song or preparing to take part in a public performance.

As with all aspects of language teaching, the teaching of pronunciation will be most effective when it is singled out for special attention at some time and at other times is closely integrated with other language work.

13 The Pronunciation of German

(Bibliographical notes: Hall, *Modern German Pronunciation: an introduction for speakers of English* (Manchester University Press, 1992) is scholarly, practical and accompanied by a cassette. MacCarthy, *The Pronunciation of German* (OUP, 1975), unfortunately out of print, contains clear descriptions and teaching hints.)

The pronunciation of German is often considered to be easier for English speakers than that of French. Many sounds are close to corresponding sounds in English , there are no nasal vowels or silent final consonants, and the relationship between spellings and sounds, though not always the same as in English, is fairly regular.

However German vowels retain their quality without diphthongisation, they are often articulated with stronger muscular tension, lip movement and precision than in English, particularly when in initial position of a stressed syllable, sounds not found in English have to be produced, and the influence of position on the pronunciation of some consonants noted. There is therefore much to be learnt and practised.

The outline here will deal in turn with individual vowels and consonants, features of connected speech, stress and intonation and the relation between spelling and sound. Despite their importance, regional differences will be ignored for the sake of brevity.

Vowels

There are 19 vowels, commonly divided into seven pairs, two unpaired vowels and three diphthongs. They are listed in Box 13.1, with the phonetic symbol and two examples for each.

Several observations are called for about the vowels in the two paired sets. Members of a pair are articulated fairly near to each other, but they differ in two important respects: *the degree of muscular tension* and *length*. Vowels in Set A are tense, those in Set B are lax. The difference is clearly felt when speaking; watching the movement of the lower jaw in a mirror or placing one's fingers under it offers further proof.

In the stressed position there is an even more noticeable difference: the vowels in Set A are longer than those in Set B. (In some books they are printed with a length mark after them.) Keeping them long is particularly important for English speakers: compare

Box 13.1 The German vowels, with examples

The seven pairs			
Set A	Set B	Examples	
[i]	[ɪ]	Miete, viel	Mitte, Tisch
[e]	[ɛ]	beten, Tee	Betten, elf
[ɑ]	[a]	lahm, Tag	Lamm, Wasser
[o]	[ɔ]	Ofen, so	offen, Stock
[u]	[ʊ]	Mus, sucht	muß, Mund
[y]	[Y]	fühlen, kühl	füllen, hübsch
[ø]	[œ]	Höhle, schön	Hölle, können
The single vowels and the diphthongs			
[æ]		Käse, Mädchen	
[ə]		bitte, gesund	
[ai]		sein, weil	
[au]		blau, auch	
[oi]		neun, deutsch	

German *Wien* with English *been*. In the unstressed position the vowels of Set A remain tense, but become short, as in the first syllable of *wieviel*.

How are learners to recognise how a vowel sounds, given that the letter is often the same? Spelling gives some clues: if a vowel is doubled or followed by *h*, it is tense and long; if it is followed by a double consonant or two consonants it is normally lax and short. However the symbol–sound relationship is complicated, as will be shown later.

The vowels in detail

[i] [ɪ] For the long vowel, the lips are spread wide and the tip of the tongue is pressed against the back of the lower teeth with considerable tension. To obtain this close position, say *yeast* vigorously and lengthen the vowel; alternatively say *teeny weeny*. It is particularly important to keep this position before *r*, as in *mir*. For the short vowel, the tongue position is the same, but the muscles are less tense and the mouth is a little more open.

[e] [ɛ] For the long vowel, the tongue is pressed against the lower teeth, but the mouth is a little more open than for [i], with the lips spread and half the row of upper teeth visible. Concentrate on making the sound long, the tongue remaining in the same position until the end, without a glide. For the short vowel, the jaws are a little further apart; the short *e* of English *get* can be used.

[a] [a] The difference between the two sounds is small. The mouth is wide open, the tip of the tongue touches the back of the lower teeth loosely.

[o] [ɔ] For the long vowel, the lips are pushed forward and rounded, leaving an opening large enough for the tip of the little finger. The tongue should be kept quite tense, without a diphthong. For the short vowel, the lips are opened a little further, but still rounded.

[u] [ʊ] The long vowel has strong protrusion and lip rounding, leaving just a small opening. For the short vowel, the lip rounding is less tight.

[y] [ʏ] All English speakers have trouble with these sounds. Hall recommends starting with [i], keeping the tongue tense and still, and adding lip rounding. MacCarthy suggests starting from the other end, with lips pushed out and away from the teeth and strongly rounded, 'like the mouth of a trumpet', and the opening between the lips very small. The mouth should be kept in this position (check in a mirror), as one tries to articulate [i]. Another approach is to shape one's lips as if to whistle on a high note. The shorter vowel is slightly less rounded. MacCarthy (1975b) recommends keeping the lips in this position while saying the whole of the English phrase 'hit or miss'.

[ø] [œ] For the long vowel, either start with [e] and then protrude and round the lips, or start with [y] and lower the jaw a little. For the short vowel, the lips are slightly protruded but well separated, leaving a large opening between them. Start with an English *e* as in *get* and push out the lips.

[æ] The written symbol for this sound is often *ä* as in *Mädchen*. This may lead English speakers to pronounce it as in English *bat*. In fact the articulation of [æ] is almost the same as that of short [ɛ] except that the sound is longer and closer.

[a] The lips are slightly open, the tip of the tongue is against the back of the teeth, but without tension. Its pronunciation in final position is near to a close [e] or even to a short [i]. Thus the final vowel of *bitte* or *Eule* is not far off that of English *bitty, oily*.

The [a] in final *-er*, as in *besser*, is more open, nearing a short [ɛ] or even [a]. The different pronunciation of final *-e* and *-er* should reflect the important grammatical distinction between, say, *gute* and *guter*.

[ai, au, oi] The corresponding English diphthongs are generally acceptable, although stronger lip rounding is needed in German [au] and [oi].

Consonants

According to Hall, 61% of the sounds in German utterances are consonants. He demonstrates their role as the backbone of the German sound system by quoting a children's song, of which one version runs:

Drei Japanesen mit dem Kontrabaß
Saßen auf der Straße und erzählten sich 'was.
Kam die Polizei. "Ja, was ist denn das?"
Drei Japanesen mit dem Kontrabaß.

The song is sung through several times, using one vowel throughout each time, giving, for instance:

Dri Jipinisin mit dim Kintribiß
and so on.

The meaning can easily be recognised. That would not be so, if one consonant only were used.

It is thus fortunate that three-quarters of the 20 German consonants present no major problems to English speakers, except that they have to be articulated forcefully. Five consonants are difficult to pronounce or conflict with English habits, and six others change their quality in a certain environment.

The five troublesome consonants

[ç] (the *ich-Laut* as in *ich, durch, Mädchen*) Common English mistakes are to pronounce this sound as if it were written *k* or *sch*. Yet it can be learnt. One way is to start by pronouncing the English words *human* or *huge* very vigorously, then just say the beginning. Another is to start with the first vowel of *yes* and whisper it. If [ç] causes problems after a consonant, as in *durch* or *Mädchen*, introduce [i] between the consonant and [ç], saying *durrich* and gradually reduce the [i].

[x] (the *ach-Laut* as in *Bach, lachen, doch, Buch*) It is easier to start on this sound when it is articulated towards the back of the soft palate after [ɔ] and [a], as in *Loch, Bach*. Begin by saying [ɔ] and raise the back of the tongue until the friction becomes audible. Do the same with [a]. Once this 'scraping' sound has become familiar, go on to [u] *as in Buch* and [ʊ] as in *Frucht*.

[l] Hall sugests five steps:
(1) Practise [l] followed by a vowel, as in *viele, Felle*.
(2) Say the words again, holding [l] for three or four seconds *vielle, Fellle*, thus getting a feel for the position of [l] in the mouth.
(3) Say the words again, leaving out the final vowel.
(4) Say the words again in the same way, adding a suitable consonant or consonant combination *hielllt, hälllt, willlst*.
(5) Reduce the length of the [l], making sure that the tongue position remains the same.

Another approach is to start with a long [i] and with the lips spread wide, place [l] in front of [i], giving [li] as in *Lied, Lieder*. Get the feel of the consonant and follow steps (2)–(5).

[r] The main point for pupils to remember is to keep the tip of the tongue behind the lower teeth. They should try to make a scrapy noise as if to clear their throat or gargle. Suggestions about the order in which words with [r] might be practised will be given in the next chapter.

[ŋ] This is the sound one hears in *singen, Hunger, Finger, jung, Zeitung* and in *krank, danke*. In English, words derived from verbs like *singer* are pronounced with [ŋ], but others, like *finger*, are pronounced with [g]. In German no such distinction is made, *singe* rhymes with *Dinge*.

Consonants that change quality according to position

Six voiced consonants cannot occur in final position and are replaced by their voiceless counterparts. The following takes place:

[b]>[p] [d]>[t] [g]>[k] [v]>[f] [z]>[s] [ʒ]>[ʃ]

This replacement occurs

- at the end of a word
- at the end of a syllable followed by a suffix
- within a syllable before another voiceless consonant.

The letter may not change, but the pronunciation changes and the voiceless consonant is articulated quite strongly. Box 13.2 shows examples of this dual pronunciation.

Box 13.2 Examples of consonants that change quality according to position

Non-final	Word-final	Before a suffix	Before a consonant
lieben	*lieb*	*lieblich*	*liebst, liebte*
Kinder	*Kind*	*Kindheit*	*Kindskopf*
fliegen	*Flug*	*Flugzeug*	*fliegt*

Another consequence of this feature of German phonology is that there are pairs of words that have different spellings but the same pronunciation, for example *Tod/tot*, *Rad/Rat*, *wird/Wirt*.

Reduction and simplification in connected speech

In connected speech, particularly of an informal register, sounds can lose something of their quality. Sometimes the change extends to the written language, as in the contracted forms *am, ins, zur* or is marked in writing to indicate colloquial style, as in *fürs, hinterm, ich hab's*, but, on the whole, it remains a feature of the spoken language. The middle one of three consonants may be elided, so that *jetzt zahlen* is heard as [j ts saln], or one consonant is assimilated to its neighbour, so that *wenn man* is heard as [v m man].

Pupils would probably first learn to cope with these features of the spoken language receptively rather than productively, but it does not seem unreasonable to expect that by the intermediate stage forms like *ich hab's, sie hat's, wie war's?* would be used in appropriate circumstances.

One further example of assimilation deserves notice. Just as at the end of the English words *happen, bottle* the final vowel is almost swallowed , so in words ending in *-en* and *-el*, such as *Socken, Mantel* the letter *e* is only half sounded.

Other Features of German Pronunciation

The glottal stop

The glottal stop is one of the distinctive features of spoken German. A slight but noticeable break is made before a word beginning with a vowel, so that it is cut off from the preceding word. This contrasts with the strong tendency in English to link words. Compare, for example,

I'm eating an ice with *Ich esse ein Eis*

Yet the glottal stop can be heard in Standard English too before a forcefully articulated vowel, as in *I'm absolutely certain. Are you?*, or between adjacent vowels, as in *co-author*. Making a glottal stop is thus not so much physically difficult for English speakers as contrary to speech habits. The most common occurrences of the glottal stop are:

(1) Initially at the beginning of an utterance and before the initial vowel of a stressed syllable

   Am Abend gehe ich oft aus

(2) Internally in a past participle and a compound word when the second element begins with a vowel

   geöffnet, gearbeitet, Beamter, bergab

However in certain compounds (before *auf, aus, ein* and a few more), there is no glottal stop

   sie geht hinaus

Word stress

All German words have a fixed stress, which pupils learn in the course of memorisation and use. It is therefore unnecessary to go through in detail the numerous rules and exceptions about the place of word stress. Doubts can be resolved by consulting a dictionary. However, the general principles deserve to be stated:

(1) In the great majority of native German words of more than two syllables, the stress falls on the root rather than on any affixes (*gute, gesehen, verkauft*). In nouns and simple infinitives this means in practice that the stress falls on the first syllable.

(2) In compound words too the stress generally falls on the first element, although in longer words a secondary stress may be added (*Eisenbahn, Eisenbahnkarte*).

(3) In words containing a prefix, the general principle is that prefixes which can occur independently are stressed, others are unstressed (*ausgehen, Ausgang; bedeuten, Bedeutung*).

However there are exceptions, particularly with *durch, um, über* and *unter*, where the position of stress sometimes distinguishes between literal and figurative meaning (*durchs Fernrohr durchschauen, einen Trick durchschauen*). The prefix *un-* is usually stressed (*unklar, unnötig*), but the stress may also fall on the root (*unglaublich*).

(4) With foreign words, the principle is different. Stress falls on the final syllable (*Universität, Friseur*), or on the penultimate, if the last syllable contains [ən] (*spazieren*). With words ending in *-ik* there is no absolute rule: *Musik, Politik* but *Grammatik*.

Sentence stress and intonation

Intonation, as was stated in relation to French, is best learnt by careful listening, but, as in other aspects of pronunciation, pupils' imitation can be made more successful if their attention is drawn to significant features of the model. Hence the principles governing sentence stress and intonation in German will be outlined here, with numerous examples.

German, like English, is a stress-timed language. A stretch of speech of any length is a succession of stressed and unstressed syllables, with content words — nouns, verbs, adjectives — being given prominence rather than function words, and groups of words felt to belong together being pronounced together in sense or tone groups. The stressed syllables tend to be spaced out evenly, creating a rhythmical framework for the sentence:

Meine Mutter geht heute abend in die Oper

(A line above a syllable shows that it is stressed, a dot that it is unstressed.) (In a slow delivery, *geht* and *heu* might also be stressed.)

In most utterances, the meaning makes it clear that one stressed syllable (the *nucleus*) stands out as more prominent than the others. The stressed word is often the one that carries new information and is consequently placed towards the end of the sentence (see the section on word order in Chapter 6):

Meine Schwester hat ein neues Kleid gekauft

(The nucleus is marked by a slash above the line.)

Sometimes, however, only the intonation can indicate what the speaker considers to be the nucleus:

Sagen Sie es mir!

Sagen Sie es mir!

At the level of the sentence, intonation fulfils what is both a communicative and a grammatical function in reflecting whether speakers are making a statement, asking a question or giving a command, whether their utterance is finished or still incomplete.

In unemphatic speech three main intonation patterns or tunes can be distinguished, with a marked change of pitch on or immediately after the nucleus.

The first tune

In the first tune, there is a *sharp fall from a relatively high pitch* to a lower one at the nucleus, and any unstressed syllables following the nucleus also remain on a very low pitch. If the nucleus is formed by the very last syllable, the fall occurs within it. The fall tends to be steeper and more abrupt than the corresponding pattern in English. English speakers should keep the nucleus high and then jump down in pitch. This is the 'conclusive' pattern, used in statements, commands and questions beginning with an interrogative word.

The following examples of the first tune are selected from *Grundzüge der hochdeutschen Satzintonation* (von Essen, 1956). They are in seven groups:

(1) Short utterance with an unstressed syllable before and after the nucleus

     Es regnet   Verzeih mir!

(2) The nucleus is on the final syllable

     Ich weiß   Gib acht!

(3) Several unstressed syllables follow the nucleus

     Er arbeitete   Vergleichen Sie bitte

(4) Longer utterances

     Ich muß eine Brille haben   Wir fahren mit der Bahn

(5) Utterances with a further, slightly weaker nucleus

     Heute hab ich gut gegessen   Die Wälder schweigen

(6) Questions beginning with interrogative words

     Wohin geht ihr?   Wieviel Geld hast du bei dir?

(7) Second, conclusive part of an utterance

     Am anderen Morgen kam er wieder   Ich freue mich, daß du gekommen bist

The second tune

In the second tune there is a sharp *rise* from a low point to a high point and then *the voice keeps on rising* until the end of the tone group. If the nucleus is the last syllable, there may be a rise within it. This pattern is characteristic for yes–no questions, and is sometimes heard as a friendly alternative for questions with interrogative words:

   Kommst du ?   Verstehen Sie mich?   Schmeckt's?

The third tune

In the third tune there is also a *rise, but the voice stays at a level pitch* to indicate that the sentence is still incomplete:

   Am anderen Morgen, | *als es noch dunkel war,* | *kam er wieder.*

This tune is also used for greetings and other ritual expressions:

   Danke   (Guten) Morgen

As this has shown, German intonation is not too different in its basic tunes from English intonation. Yet there are variations for the sake of emphasis or contrast that can only be appreciated through extensive listening. English speakers sometimes do not raise their pitch high enough on the second tune or do not maintain the level high pitch on the third. They are also tempted at times to rely only on attitudinal intonation patterns where German also uses lexical and syntactical means, especially modal particles. Here are just a few examples:

It will be all right (reassurance)	*Es wird schon (gut) gehen*
What's going on here? (interrogation)	*Was ist hier denn los?*
Come along! (impatient command)	*Komm doch (mal)!*
I knew it! (triumphant)	*Ich wußte es ja/doch!*
Show me your book (friendly command)	*Zeig mir mal dein Heft!*

The relation between spelling and pronunciation

There are two ways in which the spelling–sound relationship can help the learner of a foreign language: if it is regular and consistent, and if its conventions are similar to those of the native language.

In regard to regularity and consistency, German spelling is on the whole helpful. This applies particularly to stressed syllables, where the spelling can often provide a clue to whether the vowel belongs to the long, closed set or to the open, shorter set.

In a stressed syllable the vowel is pronounced *long*, if it is:

(1) doubled *(Tee)*,
(2) followed by *h* *(Sohn, kühl)*,
(3) a single vowel in an open monosyllable *(so, da)*,
(4) a single vowel (with or without *h*) in a polysyllable followed by a single consonant *(Ofen, beten, fühlen)*,

(5) a single vowel in a monosyllable that can be inflected and is followed by a single consonant (*Tag, gut*),

(6) a verb form whose root vowel in the infinitive is long *(sucht)*.

The vowel is pronounced *short* if it is:

(1) followed by a double consonant or *ck (Mitte, können, Stock)* or

(2) followed by two or more consonants *(elf, hübsch)*. This rule, however, has many exceptions. In the following pairs, for example, the first vowel is pronounced short, the second long *hart, Bart; Frost, Trost; Kuß, Gruß*. For words ending in *ß* only an inflected form can reveal the pronunciation: *ss* short, *ß* long *(Küsse, Grüße)*.

Altogether the relationship between spelling and pronunciation is not always simple. The differing pronunciation of certain consonants in non-final and final position has already been mentioned, the letters *g* and *h* are variously pronounced and the pronunciation of foreign loan words is sometimes unpredictable. Compare, for instance, *Chemie* and *Orchester*, or *Offizier* and *Portier*. Even with native and common German words there are inconsistencies that learners simply have to accept. For example the vowel is pronounced long in *vier, viermal, Viereck* but short in *vierzehn, vierzig, Viertel*. However learners often take these variations in their stride as just one feature of the new words they meet.

In the second respect, the differences between English and German in the spelling–sound conventions, though not huge, are sometimes insidious. The letter *z*, as has already been mentioned, has to be pronounced [ts] in all positions, *w* has to be pronounced like English *v*, while German *v* sounds like English *f*, and German *y* in words like *Physik* or *dynamisch* sounds like *ü*. Common cognates like *Problem, Familie, Europa* have either a different stress or pronunciation. All these are traps for the unwary. At worst, certain letters are pronounced in an English way, so that, for example, *Wurst* is made to rhyme with English *worst*, and even pupils of moderate proficiency may fail to notice the umlaut on a vowel, mix up the pronunciation of *ei* and *ie* in *weiter* and *wieder*.

All these difficulties must be borne in mind when planning a pronunciation teaching programme.

14 Teaching the Pronunciation of German

The same general approach will be recommended for German as that described in relation to French. It is to be hoped therefore that teachers primarily interested in German will be willing to return occasionally to the chapter on French.

During *the initial presentation* new words are modelled by the teacher and imitated by the pupils; during *regular short sessions in the first few months* the pronunciation of selected words and phrases is practised and, where necessary, corrected, with guidance on lip, tongue and jaw movement; finally *revision of pronunciation* after the first few months, based on a larger stock of examples, deals with features of pronunciation that are continuing to give trouble.

The exercises suggested for French can also be adapted to German: they are the standard ones of discrimination between minimal pairs, sorting into groups according to sounds, repeating and reading aloud, and as many contextualised and imaginative exercises, based on the vocabulary known by pupils and on their interests, as can be devised.

The actual content of practice is of course specific to German. Here I go through features of German pronunciation in the order in which they were discussed in the previous chapter, and suggest a few activities for each.

Vowels

Auditory discrimination exercises

These can sharpen pupils' awareness of differences between sounds and provide models for their own production. In the early stages the distinction between singular and plural nouns may be evident from the context, but the difference in sound can provide a further, and sometimes stronger clue. Pupils can be asked to say whether the question relates to one or more items in utterances like the following: *Wieviel kostet dieser Apfel?/Wieviel kosten diese Äpfel? Kennen Sie meinen Bruder?/meine Brüder? meinen Sohn?/meine Söhne? meine Tochter?/meine Töchter?*

Later pupils must develop the ability to recognise which member of the pair is heard in *hatte/hätte, waren/wären, konnte/könnte, wurde/würde, mußte/müßte, wußte/wüßte.* This ability can be trained in two ways. A connected piece is read out, with pupils having to indicate, on the basis of context and sound, which verbal form they heard. Alternatively, if the clues prove insufficent, the attention of the pupils can be specifically directed to the sound, by asking them to show which member of a minimal pair has been used in sentences like the following:

Wenn ich Fieber hatte, mußte ich im Bett bleiben / Wenn ich Fieber hätte,
müßte ich im Bett bleiben
Konnten/ könnten die Schüler ihre Hausaufgaben auch in der Schule machen?
Wenn die Königin da war, kamen viele Leute / Wenn die Königin da wäre, kämen viele
Leute

It is important, however, not to limit oneself to sound recognition, but to bring out the different meanings signalled by the sounds, and to return subsequently to a longer piece, where only one form is used, but where sound and context reinforce each other. The same text can later be used for reading and even writing practice, and as a springboard for speaking activities, so that the connection between pronunciation and grammar, and between the different skills is made plain.

Productive exercises: individual vowels

All vowels need practice, but those that need it most are the front rounded vowels that have no counterpart in English [y Y]. Practice can take different forms: repetition is the most obvious, but contrast with another vowel can make clear to pupils how to place their lips and tongue. Here, for example, are some ways of practising [y]:

(1) repetition of the vowel in isolation;
(2) repetition of words known to the pupil, such as *müde, grün, Brüder, früh, kühl, typisch*;
(3) contrast between [i] and [y] to show the need for lip rounding, for example, *Wiese/Wüste, vier/für, Tier/Tür*;
(4) contrast between [u] and *[y]* to bring out the different positions of the tongue, for example, *Hut/Hüte, Buch/Bücher, Schule/Schüler*;
(5) contrast between [y] and [Y], for example, *Hüte/Hütte, Grüße/Küsse*;
(6) phrases, such as *viel Vergnügen, ein grüner Hut, ein süßer Kuchen, ein gutes Frühstück*.

Similar exercises can be devised for the other vowels.

There is also need sometimes to insert a short exercise to practise sounds where teachers have noticed interference from spelling or English. It may be desirable for example,

(1) to distinguish *ei* from *ie* by contrasting *dein, Wein* with *dien, Wien*;
(2) to show that *ä* is pronounced fairly close by linking *Dänemark, Mädchen* with *Schweden, gehen*;
(3) to practise cognates such as *England, Familie, Europa, Paris, Berlin*;
(4) practise the pronunciation of *y* in loan words such as *Physik, typisch, Psychologie*.

Productive exercises: ad hoc and revision exercises

Ensuring that pupils pronounce Set A vowels in stressed syllables long, clear and tense must be a constant objective of pronunciation practice. From time to time one might put up on the board or an OHP words from past lessons that contain such vowels. Lists of words associated with particular topics can serve as revision for both vocabulary and pronunciation. And songs, old and new, learnt by heart, offer both pleasure and reinforcement.

Consonants

Individual consonants

The consonants singled out in the previous chapter — the *ich- Laut* and the *ach-Laut*, *l* and *r*, will need most practice, but for several others the influence of English or spelling may also have to be combated.

(1) The *ich-Laut*. If pupils still have difficulties after following the instructions given in the previous chapter, start with *ja*, pronounce the initial sound very long and soft, then say the following, with the consonant very long *ich, Michael*.

Practise in three series:

(a) *dich, natürlich, rechts, Milch, München, durch, Kirche;*

(b) with the ending *-chen Mädchen, bißchen, Kätzchen;*

(c) with the ending *-ig richtig, fertig, billig.*

Pupils who pronounce *ch* as if it were written *sch* may benefit by an explicit contrast *dich/Tisch, Kirche/Kirsche*.

A little mental arithmetic on the model of *zwanzig geteilt durch vier, dreißig geteilt durch fünf, zweiundsiebzig geteilt durch acht ist*, conducted first in class, then in pairs or between teams, revises numbers as well as pronunciation, and can be fun.

(2) The *ach-Laut*. If pupils continue to confuse the *ach-Laut* with *k*, ask them to start with *k*, then slowly open their mouth while letting the stream of air come out. Tell them to imitate someone snoring. Keep the snoring, scraping sound long, then utter it with [a] in front.
     Practise all the numbers containing 8 up to 88, then *Nachmittag, gute Nacht, eine kleine Nachtmusik, Johann Sebastian Bach*. Then go on to words with *-och* such as *Loch Lomond, noch, noch einmal, Tochter, Woche*, to *auch, rauchen, Bauch*, to *Buch, Kuchen, suchen* and finally to a few expressions *Tag und Nacht, mit Ach und Krach, Hunger ist der beste Koch*.

(3) [l] Pupils are least likely to have difficulty with initial [l], so one can start with words like *lesen, lang, London, Leute*, followed by the combinations [bl] or [pl] in *blau, Blume, Platz*, then go on to more difficult combinations with consonants produced in the back of the mouth *Glas, glauben, klein, Klasse*. If final [l] proves difficult, in words like *viel, mal, hell, null, vielleicht, Milch*, the alternative approach

described in the previous chapter, in which [i] is sounded after [l], to make *vieli*, then is gradually withdrawn, could be used. A few quick multiplication exercises provide revision both of the [l] in *mal* and of numbers.

(4) [r] It is best to start with a combination of voiceless consonants like [p,t,f,k] and [r] in words such as *Freund, Preis, Kreide* and then go on to initial [r] in *rot, Ring*, to medial [r] before a vowel *hören*, before a consonant after a short vowel *warten* and final [r] after a short vowel *Herr*.

Changes in consonantal value

Pupils sometimes fail to replace voiced by voiceless consonants in word or syllable final position (see the previous chapter), but the result seldom grates or leads to misunderstanding. If remedial action is needed, it can start with an awareness-raising contrast between English and German. Pupils are asked to listen to pairs of similar-sounding words and say whether they can hear a difference in the final consonant. Examples might include (English word first) *land/Land, hand/Hand, lob/Lob, vague/Weg, active/activ*. This can be followed by German–German pairs, such as *Hunde/Hund, Hände/Hand, Liebe/liebt, Tage/Tag*.

Another exercise might be to choose a word family, and ask pupils to say which of two consonants they hear. An example might be *fliegen, ich fliege, ein Flieger, eine Fliege, sie fliegt, der Flug, das Flugzeug*.

These discrimination exercises, in which pupils have listened only, could be followed by the teacher writing out illustrative pairs on the OHP or board and drawing out from pupils in which conditions the different sounds are heard.

In the end one has to go on to the most important exercises of all, to production exercises, reading aloud or repeating, concentrating first on one ending, then on another, and finally mixing them.

Consonantal clusters and sequences

These are often troublesome. Initial [ts] needs constant practice because of the confusion caused by the spelling *z* and interference from English. For the same reason, initial [+ consonant] also needs practice, whether it is spelt *sp, st* or *sch + consonant*. There are so many words with these initial clusters that a quick revision of words recently met is simple and effective. Pupils can themselves be asked to produce lists and see who remembers the greatest number. This exercise can serve for vocabulary revision too, because pupils can be asked to make sentences incorporating their chosen words, demonstrating thereby that they know its meaning and use.

Multiplication exercises with *zwei*, scenes at the railway enquiry office (*Verzeihung, wann fährt der nächste Zug nach . . .*) or café (*Zweimal Tee mit Milch (Zitrone) und Zucker, bitte*) offer opportunities for practice.Problems of pronunciation may also occur when [ts] is in close proximity to the letters *s, sch, z*. McCarthy (1975b) quotes a few examples of sequences calling for quick changes in articulation: *zusammen, inzwischen, diese zwei, das zu sagen.*

Finally compounds often bring several consonants together. Two kinds of problem may arise, each of which requires practice. The first is recognising the boundaries of the two components and, in particular, identifying *z, st, sp* when they start the second word and pronouncing them accordingly. This is needed, for example, in compounds of *Zimmer, Straße, Spiel,* when these come second, as in *Eßzimmer, Bahnhofstraße. Fußballspiel.* (Plans of houses and street maps provide good practice for the first two.)

The second problem is to ensure that the two words do not merge into each other. This means sounding an *s* at the end of the first word, as in *Geburtstag, Weihnachtsbaum, Lieblingsgruppe,* and sounding the consonants on either side of the word boundary, whether they are the same, as in *Handtuch, Radtour,* or different, as in *Eisschrank, Hausschlüssel* (although assimilation often blurs the distinction).

Other Features of German Pronunciation

The glottal stop

I believe that it is worth while teaching pupils to make the glottal stop where necessary. Omission of the stop is not such a noticeable error as mispronouncing *ü* or *ch*, yet overall it can make even fluent speech (or a *Lieder*-recital) sound somehow un-German and at times unintelligible. Pupils can be taught the physical action of holding their breath briefly and then releasing it, when a word or stressed syllable begins with a vowel, without discomfort or embarrassment being caused. It may be best to start when a word receives emphasis, as, for instance, in *Ich komme um acht. Ich habe nur eine Cousine. Möchtest du ein Eis oder einen Saft?*

Words or syllables that are emphasised often occur towards the end of an utterance, whether they are separable prefixes or past participles. Encouraging pupils to notice and imitate the glottal stop there, not only improves listening and speaking, but helps to develop a feeling for the shape and rhythm of the German sentence. Examples can occur in commands: *Steh auf! Dreh dich um! Paß auf! Gib acht!*, in directions: *immer gerade aus,* in reporting past events: *ich habe schwer gearbeitet/gut aufgepaßt/mich gut unterhalten.*

Word stress

For most pupils, learning where to place the stress is an integral and, on the whole, successful part of learning to pronounce a word. If a class or individual pupils seem to be making too many random guesses, the following approach has proved useful. Pupils draw up two lists of words they know, one set with the stress on the first syllable, the other with the stress elsewhere. A number of entries are discussed in class, categories are agreed and their characteristics identified. The teacher writes up a table with examples from each category and pupils copy it into their notebooks, underlining or adding words that have caused them particular trouble. The exercise or a testing variation in the form of jumbled words can be repeated periodically.

Intonation

It is not easy to remedy faulty intonation. Pupils may learn to distinguish betwen individual sounds, but detecting changes of pitch is hard for the untrained ear. On the other hand, unless they can imitate a good model, they may transfer and even exaggerate their own English intonation patterns.

The first step is probably to draw attention to the difference between the rising tune of the yes/no question (the second of the three tunes described in the previous chapter), as in *Kommst du?* and the falling (almost rising–falling) tune of statements and wh-questions, as in *Ich heiße Monika. Wie alt bist du?*. It is arguable whether the two tunes should be contrasted at once, or whether one should demonstrate and practise one tune at the time, and then bring them together, perhaps in a dialogue. Whichever approach one chooses, the following teaching sequence has proved useful:

Choose one or two utterances from a cassette recording in which the intonation curve can be clearly followed (or differentiated if a contrast is intended). Play the extract, write out the text on an OHP and mark the intonation curve on it, either through the system of lines and dots used in the previous chapter or some other signs. Play the extract again, repeat it yourself pointing to the OHP and/or making hand movements. Repeat this several times, and encourage pupils to join in, first in chorus and then individually. The intention is that this combination of repeated and directed listening and visual support through signs and hand movements will lead to a correct imitation of the recording. Here even more than elsewhere praise for success, whether in a simple utterance or a well performed part in a dialogue, can raise confidence and motivate further effort. If pupils then produce the right intonation in utterances of their own devising, teachers can be justifiably pleased!

At some stage pupils may hear variations for the sake of emphasis or contrast on the two basic tunes. For example a questioner who has just asked one pupil *Wie alt bist du?*, using the first tune, might turn to another pupil with *Und du?* or *Und wie alt bist du?* using the rising second tune. In the early stages these fine distinctions need not be pursued.

The third tune, indicating that the utterance is still incomplete, comes into its own when *wenn* and other subordinate clauses are introduced. It is fairly easily recognised and imitated with practice.

Final Remarks

The same conclusions apply to the teaching of German pronunciation as to the teaching of French pronunciation. I have described the difficulties which confront the English learner and which have to be solved. I have also been at pains to bring out the close connection between pronunciation, vocabulary and grammar. There are times during a lesson or series of lessons when these other language elements deserve priority, but there is also a strong case for brief but regular spells in which difficulties of pronunciation are tackled and pupils strive to speak the language well.

15 Understanding Spoken Language: The Listening Skill

The first and major part of this book was devoted to vocabulary, grammar and sounds, because together they form the substance of language, the material used in human communication. Communication involves comprehension and production, of spoken and written language or, in terms of the user's activity, listening and reading, speaking and writing. Each of the four modes or skills of communication has its own distinctive properties, which affect the way language is expressed. In the second part of the book, these properties will be examined and implications for teaching discussed.

I will start with the listening skill, needed for the comprehension of spoken language.

The Aural Comprehension Process

The capacity of even native speakers or advanced learners to understand spoken language, quite apart from familiarity with the subject matter, is affected by three factors: the complex ways in which we process what we hear, the characteristics of spoken language in different circumstances and the level of understanding required.

We do not perceive whole sentences as a sequence of isolated sounds. Normal speech is so rapidly and informally articulated that half the words cannot be recognised in isolation, yet listeners have little difficulty in following it. They even 'hear' words or parts of words that have been drowned by an external noise (Crystal, 1987). What seems to be happening is that listeners take in the raw speech and immediately and unconsciously try to organise it into syntactic groupings or chunks (constituents) that make sense, interpreting what they hear in the light of what they have heard already and what they expect to hear next. In this process they are selective: they concentrate on those elements in the utterance where a number of alternatives would be possible, and which therefore give significant information, and pass over those elements that are entirely predictable and whose information content is small.

One reason why listeners are selective in their attention is that they have only a limited capacity to absorb and process what they hear in the time available. If the speech is too fast, or unclear, or contains too much unknown material, they will try to process what has just gone, and fail to keep up and anticipate what comes next.

While organising what they hear into constituents, listeners hold the phonological representation, the actual words, in their short-term memory for a brief time, normally until they have passed a sentence boundary, and then they forget the exact wording and retain only the meaning.

Listening in Real-Life Situations

The one pre-eminent feature of speech is that it operates in the dimension of time. Spoken utterances are fleeting and immaterial. Once uttered, words and phrases are gone. They can only be retrieved through the cooperation of the speaker, or the use of a recording. Even then, they only strike the ear one after the other, and are not available for inspection, as they would be on the printed page. Even people listening to their own language have to rely on the memory of what they heard, and, as has just been shown, this is not easy.

For foreign language learners this major problem is aggravated further by their limited knowledge of the language. They do not know enough vocabulary and grammar to fill in for the half-heard words confidently and quickly, and to judge which words bring significant information and which ones do not.

The prevalent remedy has been to let learners hear spoken texts two, three or more times. I shall suggest that this approach, though contributing to learning, needs to be complemented by insistence on immediate understanding of familiar material, if it is to take account of the fundamental transience of speech.

There are situations in which this transience presents itself quite starkly; there are others where it is somewhat alleviated. One needs to examine therefore the circumstances in which language is spoken in real life. This is not only because these are the circumstances which learners will face when they go abroad, as they do in growing numbers, and which therefore ought in some way be replicated in the classroom, but also because this replication may call forth relevant abilities that listeners have acquired in their own language.

These situations can be divided into two broad categories. The first can be called *participant or reciprocal situations*, the second *non-participant or non-reciprocal situations*. They share one important feature: the stimulus comes from an exterior source. They differ in as much as in participant situations listeners can exercise a measure of influence over speakers, in relation to the speed of delivery and comprehensibility of the message, whereas in non-participant situations listeners have no such influence.

Participant situations

In participant situations, listening occurs during a verbal exchange to which only two or a few people contribute. The duration of the exchange may vary: it may extend over several utterances, with each participant building on the contribution of the other(s), and taking turns to listen and to speak, or it may consist simply of one utterance and one response. What is important is that immediate proof of successful listening is required. Sometimes a nod or a brief expression of agreement are sufficient, sometimes the response must be an action, sometimes a verbal continuation of the exchange follows.

The most common type of participant situation is that of conversations between people who know each other fairly well. It is also the one where the conditions are the most favourable to successful listening and thus to the foreign language learner. There is normally a background of shared knowledge between the participants; whoever introduces a new topic will seek to link it to what is already known. Language comes in short bursts or chunks, in which the sentence structure is normally fairly loose and free from syntactic complexity. The demands on the listener's memory are consequently not excessive.

Equally importantly, there is a wish to make the conversation succeed. The speakers are keen to convey their message, often rephrasing what they have said, occasionally checking on whether they have been understood. This rephrasing, together with inessential details, redundant to the main point, and 'fillers', like 'weißt du' or 'eh bien', all contribute to giving the listener more time to process the input. The speaker's body language, facial expression, gestures and intonation can also facilitate comprehension.

If the two participants are at different levels of proficiency, as happens between learners and native speakers, the more advanced will normally speak more slowly and distinctly, and be ready to rephrase or explain something that has obviously not been understood.

Even in the most favourable circumstances, however, there is a crucial element of unpredictability. We do not know exactly what our interlocutor will say (there would be no point in listening if we did!), and there is therefore purpose to our listening.

Conversational exchanges sometimes take place over the telephone. The absence of visual support means that explanatory gestures on one side and visual signs of incomprehension on the other cannot be used, but otherwise the favourable circumstances mentioned earlier will apply.

Face-to-face exchanges also occur during the so-called service encounters in public places, such as shops, streets, public transport and eating places. They are also marked by a clear purpose and by an element of unpredictability. A questioner who seeks information or requests a service will have some expectations about the range of possible answers, but the exact reply may be succinct or unexpected. Expressions of incomprehension may bring about repetition, elaboration of meaning or helpful gestures, but this cannot be guaranteed, and comprehension depends on specific language knowledge.

Non-participant situations

The other category of non-participant situations includes in the first place listening to third parties, such as relatives or friends of one's correspondent talking to one another. There is no obligation to respond oneself, but there is also no possibility of intervening.

A second type of non-participant situations are talks and lectures. English learners attending school lessons with their correspondent or following a guided tour can find themselves in the position of having to listen over an extended period of time. It is a very tiring experience!

Finally, within the category of non-participant situations, one must mention speech heard through machines, public address systems, tape recorders, radio and television. Public announcements are, to a certain, extent predictable in content, though sometimes distorted in their sound. Reception is clearer on television and radio, but comprehensibility varies greatly. Speech on radio ranges from quick-fire comic repartee to scripted, condensed and read news items, with spontaneous items somewhere in the middle. On television there are scenes where the visual context powerfully aids the comprehension of speech, while in others the focus is mainly on the words, and considerable linguistic knowledge is required to understand what is happening. This applies equally to films.

The characteristics of spoken language in different circumstances are summarised in Box 15.1, where the + sign indicates presence and the – sign absence.

Box 15.1 The characteristics of spoken language in different circumstances

Circumstance	Immediate response needed	Message adjustable (speed, etc.)	Short bursts of language	Redundancies	Body language	Discourse markers
Friendly interaction	+	+	+	+	+	–
Service encounter	+	+/–	+	–	+/–	–
Others talking	–	–	+	+	+	–
Talks/ Lectures	–	–	–	–	+/–	+
Radio/ TV	–	–	+/–	–	+/–	–

Levels of understanding

Different levels of understanding are required according to situations. Pohl *et al.* (1978) distinguish between two broad categories 'complete understanding' of questions, requests, wishes and commands in participant conversations, and 'gist understanding' of longer texts, for example talks and lectures, in non-participant situations. In Box 15.2 a more detailed categorisation is suggested.

Box 15.2 Levels of understanding spoken language required in different circumstances

Level of understanding	Type of utterance and examples	Frequency of utterance
Exact and complete understanding	1. Message of one or few words (Question, answer, request, command)	Normally once
	2. A sequence of unconnected items (Typically a number — time, money, telephone; also an address)	May be repeated
	3. A series of steps (directions, recipe) or telephone message	May be repeated and amplified
Scanning for detail	4. One or a few items to be picked out, particularly in announcements	Once only
Gist understanding, some detail	5. Extended utterance (anecdote, story, talk, lecture)	Once only, may have redundancies

This categorisation is by no means exact or exhaustive. One could add understanding of the subject, that is, what the utterance is about, or understanding the speaker's attitude or intention. And sometimes gist understanding has to turn into exact and complete understanding.

Listening to the Foreign Language

The description given in the previous section was of listening in its natural use, when listeners who know the language are in situations where they want to listen and understand what is being said to them. The conditions in a classroom with about 30

Box 15.3 Categories of listening tasks, with examples

Categories	Examples
Identification	Drinks ordered by different people
Classification	Sorting hard and soft goods bought at a store
Selection	Matching a text with one of several pictures
Information transfer	Filling in a grid of ages, hobbies
Carrying out instructions	Writing telephone messages, routes, recipes
True–false	Assessing truth of statements about a picture or interview
Grasping gist	of an extended utterance
Summarising	
Evaluation of attitudes	

young adolescents slowly learning the foreign language are very different. How can their capacity to understand the spoken language be developed in such circumstances?

Three developments since the 1970s have provided some of the right conditions.

The first has been the increased importance assigned to the spoken language in public examinations.

The second has been the almost universal inclusion of audio recordings as an integral part of course materials and the use of such recordings to guarantee reliability in public examinations.

The third, closely related to the first two, has been the greater role accorded to listening within the learning process. New language is presented orally, often on tape, with native speakers offering models of what to say in everyday situations. In order to practise and thereby fix the new language, pupils have to listen, often two or three times, to a spoken text to accomplish a given task. Some of the categories into which these tasks fall are given in Box 15.3, with a few examples.

The result of all these developments has been an immeasurable increase in the exposure to the target language and a consequent improvement in pupils' listening skill.

However, something more is required to upgrade listening as a learning activity into listening as an act of communication. First listening to a tape recorder has to be complemented by listening to live interlocutors. For most adolescents going abroad, whether on an exchange or a family holiday, listening will mainly occur in participant situations, in friendly interaction or service encounters. Listening to a cassette is not a participant situation. A tape recorder cannot offer the flexibility of human interlocutors, modify its own speed or rephrase its message as a result of feedback from the listener.

Second, the conditions of listening have gradually to be brought nearer to the conditions of real-life listening. Listening again and again to a tape recorder admirably exploits that machine's role as an aid to *learning*. Listening twice is probably necessary in large-scale national examinations, but these special conditions need not dominate what happens in the classroom. For, as I have insisted previously, in real life words and phrases have to be caught in flight, and do not come again. It is therefore worth playing a text again *at the end* of a lesson, or to play a new text on the same topic. If pupils can understand most of it first time, they will have given tangible and satisfying evidence that they are ready to move on. Playing through *familiar* material once only as revision is an excellent way of measuring pupils' progress.

Teachers therefore retain an important role in developing their pupils' listening skills. They fulfil it by seeking to introduce into the classroom conditions as similar as possible to those of real-life listening, by targeting special features of spoken French and German and practising listening at different levels of understanding.

Creating participant situations

The use of the target language by the teacher is probably the most important way of accustoming pupils to listen to the foreign language. At first the language flow is mainly unidirectional, but from the beginning the pupils are experiencing the language as a real means of communication here and now. They have a real purpose in listening, to find out what they are expected to do, understand what is being said and take part in the experience of the class. As they learn phrases through which they can interact with the teacher, a true participant situation slowly develops.

The language of classroom routine is limited, but it can gradually expand into that of personal relations, incorporate some of the language being learnt through the course book, and go beyond it. Only the teacher knows what pupils may *want* to listen to.

Teachers have to decide when to help and when to prod. Withdrawing support, or more positively, raising expectations is a difficult operation. As Johnstone (1989) demonstrates, what may appear to the teacher to have been a two-way exchange has in fact been built on a scaffolding of questions to which the pupil contributed no more than *Oui, Madame* and *regardé la télé*. He calls for problem-reducing strategies to be turned into problem-creating strategies. Recording one's own lessons may reveal how often one's questions (and the pupils' answers!) are needlessly repeated, thus allowing pupils to listen with one ear.

Demanding first-time understanding and quickening one's speed of delivery on familiar material, and deliberately introducing some unknown material, become increasingly important. If one recalls that in participant situations, particularly service encounters, short messages are normally not repeated and demand immediate response, then this willingness on both sides to move towards first-time understanding can be a significant step towards real listening.

It may be possible to bring other live speakers into the classroom. For example,

Johnstone (1989) suggests that all senior pupils should engage in interaction with younger pupils as an integral part of their curriculum. They would benefit by experimenting with strategies designed to bring out their younger partners, while these would be in unthreatening interaction with more fluent speakers.

Where a school can count on the services of a foreign-language assistant, listening in small groups can turn into genuine participant situations. A visit by a native speaker can provide an unexpected source of interesting information.

Nor should the interaction between pupils be underestimated. The range of language may be limited, and role-play can descend into routinised function-speak, as the dialogue about sporting interests quoted in Chapter 7 shows, but when one partner possesses information in which the other is genuinely interested, the quality of listening is high.

Finally, a recording from another course held in the stock room, that deals with the current topic, but differs slightly in setting or choice of language, can introduce that element of unpredictability that is characteristic of real life situations.

Improving the comprehension of spoken language

It is worth asking the question: is exposure to spoken language sufficient by itself to improve listening comprehension or would some targeted practice help? Certainly as much exposure to connected speech spoken at normal, not necessarily native, speed is important. This applies particularly to French, where, as stated in Chapter 11, words are subordinate to sense groups. Attention to pronunciation and auditory discrimination can prevent mishearings and misunderstandings. Knowledge of syntax will improve listeners' ability to segment what they hear into meaningful chunks. But, in addition, Box 15.2, showing different levels of understanding required in different circumstances, suggests where practice might be useful.

Exact and complete understanding of short messages

This is frequently needed, as the table shows. Close attention to vocabulary is the first requisite. The APU survey of performance in listening after two years of study found that 'a knowledge of vocabulary sufficient to understand key words was often the major factor in determining success, even in the most difficult items' (APU, 1987a: 10). Ignorance of one vocabulary item may make a short text difficult. If a girl phones to ak whether her friend can come over, she may hear her friend's mother say: '*Je regrette, Martine a la grippe.*' There may be a follow up to indicate that Martine is ill or in bed, but the nature of her illness will not be clear unless the word *grippe* is known. To revise vocabulary in context one can easily use appropriate material from the audio recordings included with every course.

In the course of general revision some words need special attention. Numbers above ten are notoriously difficult to catch, yet they are used in so many contexts that practice is both important and easily arranged. Proper names of places and people are sometimes not recognised when spoken, particularly in French.

While every effort should be made to ensure that core vocabulary is known, the willingness to make intelligent guesses and use contextual clues, even in short messages, should be encouraged. Once pupils possess a stock of words, the teacher can show a picture and say a sentence to describe it, coughing or making some noise on one word and inviting the class to suggest what was left out. The following is just one possible example.

Picture of a man in football strip, raising his arms in triumph

Bravo! Eric vient de marquer un (cough).

Other examples might be of a woman looking at a row of numbers on a television screen and realising that she has just won a prize in the National Lottery, or of two 16-year-old students holding up notifications of their examination results. Even if the missing word was not previously known, the context may suggest it. If the whole sentence is then written down, the association with the picture may aid memorisation.

Attention to grammatical words is also important. The APU survey also found, not unsurprisingly, that listeners needed to be able to connect different constituents in a message, and identify key syntactical relations. There are, in particular, some grammatical words whose influence on the meaning of a sentence would be noticed immediately in print, but can easily be missed in speech. In French the negative particle *ne* is often abbreviated or even swallowed in connected speech, and pupils must listen out for the positive *que* or the negative *pas, plus, rien, jamais, aucun(e)*. The *r* that signals the French future or conditional tense can also be overlooked. In German the presence or absence of the Umlaut in *hatte/hätte, konnte/könnte* and other modals must act as an alarm bell to look for other cues.

Question words often occur at the beginning of an utterance, before the listener is really alert. They are often short, they may also be accompanied by equally short prepositions. They can therefore be missed, even at less than normal speed. But it is critical to distinguish *Bis wann bist du in Hamburg?* from *Seit wann bist du in Hamburg?*, or to catch the initial preposition in *D'où viens-tu?* or *Par où tu vas passer?*

Since production sharpens reception, and question forms are essential in interaction, a small number of question forms can be singled out every week for pupils to make up questions to their neighbour, other pupils, even the teacher. At intervals an exercise of jumbled sentences can specifically target understanding and responding to questions. Pupils have before them a worksheet with, say, six statements, possible replies to five questions that the teacher will read out. The time allowed for matching answers with questions can be progressively reduced. Gapped dialogues, set in clearly identified contexts, can also provide practice.

Enabling listeners to understand extended utterances

One of the main results of the APU surveys was that a longer text, for instance a dialogue of four or five utterances, frequently offered more clues than a shorter one. Indeed, when very short listening texts were revised between surveys and made slightly longer, and the same questions were asked, more pupils were successful (APU, 1987b: 6).

The structure of extended utterances may differ. There may be a central idea, or an opinion or attitude simply repeated in different ways, or a narrative, unfolding along a temporal sequence. The aim of practising gist understanding is to help pupils identify the different kinds of clue characteristic of each structure.

It may be easiest to start with discursive texts. In some, clues emerge through repetition of key words or tell-tale adjectives of approval or disapproval. The account of a holiday, the description of a place or a person, can be given by the teacher — perhaps as one side of an imaginary telephone conversation, or in conversation with the assistant, where the key points can be stressed. In either form, the delivery should sound natural, with hesitations and fillers, and opinions elaborated and strongly expressed.

With discursive texts where there is a temporal sequence, such as the account of a shopping expedition or an accident, the structure can be suggested by filling out the different stages and introducing short pauses between them.

In other kinds of text a main idea is stated at the beginning, in the so-called topic sentence, and elaborated subsequently. Here, for example, are the opening sentences in what three people have to say about their town (from *Deutsch Heute 2*, Sidwell & Capoore, 1983):

(1) *Ich wohne hier seit fünf Jahren und ich wohne gern hier.* (List of advantages follows.)
(2) *Ich bin hier in diesem Dorf geboren. Ich würde aber lieber in der Stadt wohnen, weil ich das Leben hier ein bißchen langweilig finde.* (List of disadvantages follows.)
(3) *Ich wohne hier seit vielen Jahren, und die Stadt hat sich in dieser Zeit sehr verändert.* (List of changes follows.)

Pupils can be alerted to devices which speakers use to structure what they are saying. Five girls between 15 and 17 were asked how late they were allowed to stay out *(Deutsch mit Spaß Book 2*, Neuner *et al.*, 1988). All voiced a similar attitude: parents quite reasonable , but still greater freedom wanted. They expressed themselves differently, but two discourse markers clearly signalled the mixture in their views: an initial *eigentlich* in *Eigentlich darf ich viel, . . . , Eigentlich kann ich nicht klagen, . . .* alerting the listener that this was only partially so and that a qualifying *Aber . . .* would soon follow.

Where audio recordings have a clear discourse structure, they could be used to practise gist listening, even if their original purpose was different.

The aim of these and other exercises should be to practise and not to test. Understanding could be checked orally, with suggestions about the central idea requested first and information on detail elicited gradually and tolerantly. If the text is difficult, listeners can be guided in the right direction by a question; if the text is easy, they can be expected to discover the theme for themselves. One test of likely success is for teachers to ask themselves before choosing a text: would my pupils be able to give its gist in one sentence? If there is one key word that may cause difficulty, as for instance *sich verändert* in the third sentence about the home town on the previous page, it can either be explained in advance or worked into a question. The golden rule is always to have a trade-off between the difficulty of the text and the difficulty of the question(s) or task.

And there are also texts which cannot easily be pigeon-holed, but where the class collectively can understand the main points, or which should be allowed to make their own impact.

16 Understanding Written Language: The Reading Skill

The Reading Process

The literature about reading in L1 and in FL is enormous. There are two main reasons for this. One is the great importance of reading: in L1 it is the gateway to literacy, in FL there is a world-wide need to read specialist publications in other languages. The other is the continuing debate about the nature of the reading process. Since the contrasting views in this debate have direct and different implications for practice, an outline of the three main models of the reading process is of more than theoretical interest.

The first is a 'bottom–up' or 'text-driven' model. The reader is thought to start from the text (the bottom), and construct meaning from words, phrases and sentences. Proponents of this view look for ways of grading and simplifying texts, particularly in regard to vocabulary, if they are considered too difficult. They are also concerned with language-specific features.

In the teaching of FL this was the favoured view up to the 1970s, fitting in well with examinations that encouraged careful and total understanding of the text.

The second is a 'top–down' or 'reader-driven' model. The readers' purpose determines how they tackle a text, whether they skim, scan or study it. Their knowledge of the world and of text genres, as well as of language, enables them to make hypotheses and predictions about text content. Advocates of this view argue that to simplify a text is to rob it of its characteristics; authentic texts should be used instead, to be tackled selectively through tasks that give purpose to reading and can be graded in difficulty.

The influence of this model can be seen in many task-based teaching materials published since the 1980s. It also explains the interest in reading strategies and their possible contribution to improving reading proficiency.

The latest, the so-called interactive view, strikes a balance between the other two. The ability to decode language rapidly and accurately, and the capacity to make predictions based on context and text conventions, are both considered important, particularly in FL. Weaknesses in one aspect may be compensated by strengths in another. For instance, scientists may make intelligent guesses when reading publications in their field, despite relatively modest language proficiency.

Another as yet unresolved research question is whether proficiency in FL reading is a function of general proficiency in that language, or is related to reading proficiency in L1. The tentative conclusion is that language proficiency is the determining factor until a certain threshold has been reached, after which students, having gained a wider and surer linguistic base, can use thematic and contextual clues to greater advantage. The practical question is whether language teaching should include the teaching of specific reading strategies. If so, what would these be, and when and how would they be taught? (For a fuller discussion of research into all these issues see Alderson & Urquhart, 1984, Barnett, 1989 and the three articles by Klapper, 1992a, b, 1993.)

Some of the questions raised here will be referred to again later, as the place of reading at different stages of a course is discussed.

Preliminaries: listening and reading compared

Two ways in which reading differs from listening need to be stated at the outset. They are obvious and perhaps for that reason rarely mentioned, yet I believe that their significance is sometimes insufficiently appreciated.

The first is that, in contrast to listeners, readers are in control. They are not reliant on someone else to communicate with them, they can engage with a text directly, go on reading for as long as they wish, go back or jump ahead. Though they need to read fairly fast to become efficient readers, it is they who control their own reading speed. This makes reading the skill in which it is easiest for the learner to achieve autonomy, and easiest for the teacher to promote achievement in pupils with different ability and interests.

The second difference is as important. While the spoken message is transient, and words often seem to run into one another, the whole of the written or printed text remains visible and stable. Each word retains its identity and place in relation to others in a sentence; the eye, assisted by punctuation marks, is able to take in and segment phrases, sentences and paragraphs. One implication of this is that the written form can support the spoken, another that written texts lend themselves better than spoken texts to detailed study, since individual words and sentences can be scrutinised and different parts of a longer text compared.

Two other differences between spoken and written language make themselves felt at different stages in the learning process. Etymological relationships between the foreign language and English may appear clearly in print, but not in speech, so that in the early stages efforts have to be made to exploit the positive and mitigate the negative aspect of these relationships. Secondly, authentic spoken and written texts differ in the amount of redundancy, the length and density of sentences and the complexity of grammatical structure. These difference may be blurred in the first two or three years, when texts are composed or adapted for instruction, but must be confronted at some time.

The Place of Reading at Different Stages of a Course

The initial stages: familiarisation with the printed word

Past fears that early exposure to print could cause interference from L1 have proved exaggerated. On the one hand, it was found that delayed introduction to the printed form did not eliminate the risk of interference and that it brought disadvantages of its own. More positively, when pupils see how phrases like *ich heiße John* or *je suis anglaise*, which they have learnt orally, look in print, they have acquired a visual prop to memory and are using another sense in the learning process.

The printed word is thus normally introduced quite early as a representation of what pupils have already heard. Very soon, as the same words are used in exercises and new combinations, pupils can be said to be reading in the sense of extracting meaning directly from the printed or written text.

Reading and the learning of new language

For the first two or three years of a course, the written form can play an important, sometimes underexploited role within a multi-skill approach to the teaching of new language. At this stage, the speaking and reading parts of a chapter are normally composed without any rigid demarcation of register. Both can serve to introduce the vocabulary and grammar which pupils need for certain topics and which should enter into their long-term memory. While fulfilling this common purpose, the reading parts can preserve the distinctive function of written language. They can introduce and describe, set a scene, outline a situation, sketch in characters. They can thus provide the background in the third person and bring in some of the new language that will be used later in dialogues, in the first and second person. They can perform a similar function in narratives, describing events and situations from outside, before someone gives a spoken, more subjective account. A reading text can also occur later in a unit, perhaps taking up the main theme from a different viewpoint.

Some kinds of practice tasks are the same as those mentioned in connection with listening. Younger pupils can fill in crosswords, put together half sentences, replace sentences in the right order, declare whether statements about the text are true or false, indicate on which line certain information appears, draw a plan according to written instructions. Older pupils who have read a narrative can draw up a list of verbs which take the action forward, transform the story into a strip cartoon, and create, with the teacher's help, dialogues between key characters (Kavanagh & Upton, 1994).

One type of task which can be used with different topics and at different levels involves matching a text with one out of several photographs, drawings or other texts. In one exercise the name plates at the bottom of a block of flats have become mixed up

Box 16.1 Reading for textual clues: What is the man's job? (Kavanagh, 1988: 10)

---

chauffeur de taxi, bibliothécaire, jardinier, caissière
dans un supermarché, militaire, coiffeuse,
professeur, plombier, mécanicien, cosmonaute,
vendeuse de billets de loterie, femme de chambre.

Monsieur Edouard Sannier

Moi, je travaille un peu partout, et j'aime bien ce côté de mon travail. Je n'aimerais pas passer ma vie dans une usine, à voir toujours les mêmes têtes, faire toujours les mêmes choses. Je suis quelquefois dans un hôtel, ou dans une boutique, le plus souvent chez des particuliers.

A l'école, je n'étais pas brillant éleve, mais j'étais bon en travaux manuels. Alors; j'ai fait un CAP, j'ai trouvé un emploi chez un monsieur, et au bout de cinq ans, je me suis établi à mon compte. Je ne prends pas beaucoup de vacances, mais j'ai un bel apartement, et ma femme et moi, on s'entend bien.

Le seul problème avec le métier que j'ai, c'est que les gens me téléphonent chez moi, à n'importe quelle heure, pour me demander d'aller immédiatement chez eux: il y a une fuite, ou bien le chauffage est en panne.

---

and have to be rearranged in accordance with brief descriptions of the tenants and their attitude to the neighbours below, next door and above (Page & Moys, 1982). At a higher level, pupils read four texts in which people describe their job, without actually saying what it is. The pupils' task is to identify which job the four people have, out of a list of 12, with the help of clues in the text. One of the texts and the list are reproduced in Box 16.1.

As pupils read intensively various texts on the same topic, they meet key words again and again in different contexts and encounter different ways of expressing the same idea. All this enriches their language and gives them flexibility when they come to speak or write on a similar topic. For example, the identification exercise illustrated in Box 16.1 is followed by a list of phrases from the four texts giving reasons for liking or disliking a job. Pupils are asked to use this list to say how they would feel about being a shop assistant, miner or bank clerk. Finally they write a portrait of a person, his or her work, attitude and other details. When they advance further, they will be ready to make their own lists from what they read. They will have learnt that other people's words are the raw material with which to express their own opinions and feelings.

Reading texts, permanently available for inspection and comparison, can thus serve to introduce, consolidate and enrich new language, and form the basis for extension to speaking and writing. If the course book does not contain enough reading texts, teachers could find, adapt or compose some themselves. (For advice on how to compose texts see Kavanagh & Upton, 1994; for a collection of ingenious and graded texts see Kavanagh, 1988.)

Towards unaided reading

For the first two or three years of a school course pupils will have concentrated on learning key vocabulary and grammar, with explanations of meaning given by the teacher, in notes and marginal glosses and an end vocabulary. Reading, like the other skills, will have contributed to learning. But if pupils are to benefit fully from their reading skill, and be able to read on their own for pleasure and information, they have to learn to read without the teacher. This requires an extension of their receptive vocabulary and a developing capacity to understand authentic texts.

The first steps in that direction can be taken in the first two years. Carefully set tasks in scanning authentic documents, such as visiting cards, birth announcements, notices, posters, brochures, etc. can demonstrate that information can be gleaned without having to understand every word. It should also be possible to find short texts, such as puzzles, poems or captions to pictures, that can be understood in their entirety and with the minimum of help. At the same time pupils' attention can be drawn to the constant meaning of certain prefixes and suffixes and to ways of unravelling compound nouns.

However, as the research noted earlier shows, there has to be a certain amount of lexical and grammatical knowledge before a programme to extend pupils' reading proficiency can be effective. Developing the ability to infer the meaning of words from context, which must figure in any such programme, cannot succeed if the context is not understood either. Pupils must be able to recognise tense endings and the principal parts of common irregular verbs, distinguish plural and singular forms, know personal pronouns, be alert to negative constructions. In French, pupils should have developed the ability to take in nouns and any following adjective in one glance, in German, separable verbs and the clause final position of the verb in a subordinate clause should no longer hold any terrors.

A programme to improve reading proficiency should contain two parts, each complementing the other: helping pupils to develop strategies with which to approach texts, and providing fairly easy and appealing texts, preferably complete, for pupils to read and enjoy on their own.

Helping pupils to develop reading strategies

American research evidence about the effectivenes of strategy instruction is not conclusive. On the whole, however, it is positive, particularly when several strategies are used in combination; furthermore instruction appears to improve reader morale and confidence (Barnett, 1989). Most teachers will therefore wish to pass on the strategies of successful readers to those who are still struggling.

Put simply, reading strategies should help pupils to make sense of a text as a whole and to deal with unknown vocabulary. I would summarise them as follows:

(1) Read through the text as a whole first to get an idea of what it is about; use the title, any illustrations and subtitles to help you.
(2) If you want to know more about the text, go through it paragraph by paragraph.
(3) If you come across a word that you do not know, decide provisionally whether it seems important or can be ignored.
(4) If the word seems important, see whether the context, that is what you have read before and what comes next, gives any clues about its meaning.
(5) Look for other clues too: is there an English word that looks like it? Is it a noun, verb, adjective or something else? Is it a compound word; has it a prefix or suffix?
(6) If still in doubt, look up the word in a dictionary.
(7) With longer texts, each paragraph often represents a step in the argument or story, with the first sentence acting as signpost to the topic of the paragraph.
(8) Do not give up.

These are broad lines of action, not infallible rules. It may not be easy to decide whether a word is important until most of the text has been understood: low-frequency words are often not amenable to contextual guessing. For example, in the French text about the plumber reproduced earlier, the clue that he is often called away from home does not become significant until the exact meaning of *il y a une fuite* and *le chauffage est en panne* has been ascertained.

For that reason it is more appropriate to talk of a gradual process of strategy training, based on a variety of exercises and texts, rather than of teaching. The aim is to develop a flexible and purposeful approach to reading as part of the normal syllabus.

In order to practise inference from context, a short text can be distributed in which a few unfamiliar words have been underlined. For each word four alternative translations or synonyms are given , two being lexically and one grammatically inappropriate. From there one could progress to a similar exercise without solutions on offer, but with approximate guesses accepted.

An elaborate sequence is proposed by Nuttall (1982) to prove to the timid that not every word needs to be understood:

(a) Supply a text with obvious gaps, and ask questions that can be answered from the incomplete information available.
(b) Supply a text containing some difficult words that are not essential to general understanding, and again ask questions that can be answered from the information available.
(c) Supply a text containing some new words that need to be understood, and ask questions that demand such understanding. The challenge is to answer by looking up as few words as possible.

Box 16.2 A newspaper story, suitable as a reading text (Page & Moys, 1982: 28)

Un python royal dans la cuisine !

Il n'est pas souvent qu'on se trouve nez à nez à quatre heures du matin avec un serpent python dans la cuisine, surtout quand on habite au premier étage d'un immeuble de banlieue. Cette aventure est arrivée dans la nuit de lundi à mardi à Mme Corre demeurant à Mérignac (Gironde). Réveillés par des bruits de vaisselle, Monsieur et Madame Corre ont d'abord pensé à un cambrioleur. Puis, regardant dans la cuisine, ils ont vu que leur visiteur n'avait qu'un mètre de long mais qu'il rampait.

Les pompiers sont venus prendre en charge l'animal après l'avoir endormi avec un gaz soporifique. On réalisa que le serpent, un python royal adulte qui semblait âgé de 7 à 10 ans, était venu de l'étage supérieur par une conduite d'aération. Son maître étant absent, le serpent avait décidé de visiter les appartements de l'immeuble. Le python fut transporté au zoo de Monsieur Verbeke, collectionneur de reptiles. Là, Olivier, le petit-fils de Monsieur Verbeke, s'amusa beaucoup avec l'animal parce que le python royal est complètement inoffensif. Nourri d'une souris de temps en temps, le python attend au zoo que son légitime propriétaire vienne le chercher.

Instead of focusing on specific problems, one can work cumulatively through a series of texts, and see how far the pupils find the suggested procedures helpful. Box 16.2 contains one of such texts. The title and the photograph give an immediate indication of the topic, the subject matter is likely to prove of interest, the incidents in the story are clearly sequenced in time, there are a number of cognates and words likely to be known but also unknown ones, the piece is complete and clearly comes from an authentic source.

One can imagine several ways of treating the text in Box 16.2. An initial perusal of the whole text seems essential. Then there are various possibilities. One is to go through the text in class as a training exercise, inviting suggestions, referring to a list of strategies, discussing with the class whether a particular word needs to be looked up or can be kept on hold. Another is to let pupils work in pairs, another is to let half the class concentrate on the first paragraph, and the other on the second and third. A bargain could be struck with the class whereby the translation was offered of a few unusual words such as *rampait, conduite d'aération* against a promise to look up as few words as possible in a dictionary.

It will be clear from the foregoing that I do not favour looking up words in a dictionary, unless they contribute information that is significant in that context. *Fuite* in the text on the plumber seems to pass that test, *conduite* (or the more common *conduit*) *d'aération* in the article does not. Nuttall (1982: 69) writes: 'One of the first things to be said about a dictionary is *don't use it.*' It breaks concentration, distracts attention from the text and slows down reading. A combination of glosses in the margin for unimportant words and contextual guessing reinforced by a dictionary check seems preferable.

However the ability to use a dictionary effectively is important, and needs training. Points to practise are:

- remembering the order of the alphabet to locate the general area,
- using the guide words for the first and last entry on the top left and top right of a page to locate the right page,
- looking down the column to locate the right entry,
- getting to know the layout of entries.

Training can be both challenging and enjoyable as pupils strive to better their look-up time.

Finally pupils' efforts to understand can be decisively assisted by teachers' choice of text. There is strong evidence from research (Buhlmann, 1984) and also indirectly from readers' feedback that organisation and arrangement outweigh other factors in making a text accessible. By organisation is meant that the information is presented in a logical order, with, for instance, a clear temporal sequence or an explicit relation between cause and effect. By arrangement is meant that the organisation is transparent, internally through the use of discourse connectors, externally through paragraphing and subtitles. A newspaper article may sometimes appeal by its eye-catching title, but then disappoint through its unclear structure and use of jargon. A survey among learners by Yorios (1971) found that only 34% and 26% respectively found newspapers and magazines easy, whereas fiction and textbooks were considered easy by 65% and 63%. These figures confirm the established popularity of fiction as reading material.

Extensive reading

According to Nuttall (1982: 65): 'An extensive reading programme is the single most effective way of improving both vocabulary and reading skills in general.' The experience of reading real books, however short, or complete stories, is motivating in itself, for it creates a sense of achievement. The desire to read on to find out what happens next not only quickens reading speed, but develops in a natural way the capacity to distinguish between what is essential and inessential to the story. Finally, there is good evidence, quoted by Klapper (1992b), that by the repetition of vocabulary and syntax the benefits of fluent reading extend to the whole of language performance.

Details of how to organise extensive reading are given in Nuttall (1982) and Swarbrick (1990). The basic requirement is the availabilty of a large number of books from which to choose. They need to be varied in content, attractive in appearance, preferably short and more accessible on the whole by immediate word recognition than through contextual clues (Klapper, 1993). If they are to be available from at least the second or third year of study up to the fourth and fifth year, they need to be graded, and thereby appropriate for readers at different levels of language proficiency. Fluent reading being the aim, a selective end vocabulary or glosses in the margin should render the time-consuming looking up of words in a dictionary unnecessary.

Some checks on whether the books have actually been read and some feedback from the pupils to gauge the appeal of different books are desirable, but they should be as lightly and informally administered as possible. I used to devote one lesson out of four from the third year onwards to silent extensive reading in class. Pupils would come up to my desk individually when they had read about two pages at their own speed, and I would ask them two or three simple comprehension questions. Pupils in Swarbrick 's school use the school library and fill in simple record sheets (Swarbrick, 1990). There are undoubtedly other organisational arrangements that work well.

17 Producing Language: The Speaking Skill

Speaking in Real Life and Speaking in the Classroom

For many pupils the prime goal of learning a foreign language is to be able to speak it. Teaching should therefore help them to achieve that goal to the best of their ability.

Yet the task is not easy, because conditions in the classroom are very different from those in real life. There speaking normally occurs in a domestic, social or occupational environment. Except for the fairly infrequent occasions of a talk or a lecture, only a small group of people, typically two, are involved. At times people speak to each other simply to demonstrate friendliness or sociability, but much the most frequent case is that one person has a reason to address the other: to request information or service, share experience, suggest action. The other replies, and a dialogue ensues.

In the planning and execution of what they intend to say, speakers follow the process described by Clark and Clark (1977) and outlined in Chapter 8. It will be recalled that this process involves five steps: deciding on the discourse structure (invitation, instruction, report, etc.); planning the global structure of the sentence to convey the message (statement, question); choosing the actual words constituent by constituent (noun phrase, verb phrase, short clause); bringing to mind their pronunciation; speaking. Production is quick, although speakers may hesitate momentarily as they decide which words to choose.

In brief, the common marks of speaking in real life are: situations necessitating speech, a purpose which speakers wish to achieve through speaking, the involvement generally of just two people or slightly more, quick interaction between the interlocutors, unpredictability in what each will say, and of course knowledge of the language.

Conditions in the classroom are very different. There are 20 or more pupils sitting together, who traditionally would only speak in answer to questions from the teacher. They are slowly learning the foreign language and are often reluctant to display any inadequacies, or even run the risk of doing so, before their peers.

Speaking in the classroom thus has two functions: one is to learn the language, the other is to use it as people do in real life. The two functions often overlap: speaking to learn can lead to speaking to communicate, and this in turn consolidates learning. But the precondition for communication is learning, so that pupils are in a position to accomplish the last three steps of the planning and execution process: decide on the constituents, the right words needed in a situation, and produce them with the right pronunciation. When new language is introduced, either by the teacher or on tape, pupils speak to learn, they repeat again and again just as they listen again and again. They speak to practise pronunciation, to associate words with real entities or their visual representations, to become sure of meaning, form and syntactic links. Possible relations between items within a constituent (for example noun and adjective) and between constituents (verb and object) are explored, constituents are varied and recombined, expressions for seeing a doctor are adapted for a visit to the dentist. The aim is to integrate new language into the existing semantic network, so that it is not displaced by subsequent acquisitions, but is instantly available for production.

Speaking to learn can turn into speaking to communicate when the teacher can tap into two of pupils' natural desires: to be sociable with friends through talk and games, and to express themselves. When the class is broken down into pairs or groups of friends, one of the essential features of real-life use, interaction, has been introduced. When situations in the foreign country are simulated that pupils accept as likely or at least possible, a credible purpose is given to their exchanges. Speaking becomes even closer to reality when it is accepted that pupils remain conscious of their normal environment and wish to express their own views or talk about their own experiences.

For a time language may be prescribed in some way — or, from a different viewpoint, linguistic support may be given — so as to build up knowledge; then, as learners grow in confidence, they can vary their utterances, express themselves more freely and hence unpredictably.

Speaking activities in the classroom can thus be at various points in a spectrum from constraint to freedom within the following five parameters.

(1) the extent of variation: no change – limited change – free expression
(2) the extent and nature of constraints: cue cards, symbols, etc. – objective data – free choice
(3) the extent of predictability: formulas – information gap
(4) the extent and nature of interaction: no interaction – pairs, groups – strangers
(5) the extent of realism or personal involvement: role-play – simulations – personal expression.

A few examples of how different activities fit into this framework, mainly at the elementary and low intermediate level, are given here.

(1) A text is distributed to the class giving information about a girl, Amélie Durand — age, address, family, birthday, pets, favourite school subject. Three girls receive cue cards detailing their identity. One corresponds exactly to Amélie, the two others almost. The class questions the three girls to discover the real Amélie. For the three girls, the language is prescribed by the cue cards; for the class the subject

matter of their questions is laid down by the text, but the language is left open. There is interaction and an element of unpredictability and challenge (Kavanagh & Upton, 1994).

(2) Pupils are asked similar personal details by a stranger (other teacher, foreign language assistant, visitor). The language is freely chosen, but may have become overused in role plays with a partner. With a stranger the information gap is real. It can be extended, if pupils can question the stranger too.

(3) Pupils reporting on the day's activities (see Box 9.4). The possible combinations are given, but pupils choose those that apply to them and extend their answers freely later through interaction with others.

(4) The drill *Je me suis lavé la figure ce matin* (see Box 9.6). The variations in the language are limited and prescribed, but the first speaker can choose the noun, and the other two can add attitudinal and therefore personal comments.

(5) The *horoscope* drill (see Box 9.8). This seems a very tightly structured exercise into which a very limited personal element is introduced only in the third run. But one could envisage a follow up activity with, say, five pupils acting as astrologers in different parts of the classroom, each forecasting the future in turn for some of their fellow pupils. Appeals for clarification and evasions or inventions would follow naturally with whatever means the participants can muster.

As in listening, problem-reducing and problem-creating elements are both necessary. The first build up a feeling of control, the second motivate and encourage risk-taking and creativity. Teachers will decide for themselves when and how to move from more supportive and constraining activities to freer ones. They can introduce the element of unpredictability either through the format of the task or by encouraging the pupils themselves to use their imagination. For instance, once the basic expressions for shopping or booking accommodation have been practised, pupils may find out that certain items or facilities are unavailable and have to react suitably, or they may have to decide in small groups on the respective merits of items differing in price or quality. Similarly, a request for directions may be met by a question *Vous êtes à pied ou en voiture?*, forcing both partners to adapt what they say next. The following is a witty variation in an exchange between two pupils (Johnstone, 1989):

Comment vous appelez-vous?
Je m'appelle Bond, Jules Bond.
Bonjour Monsieur Bond.
Appelez-moi Jules.

In setting up the parameters I have not distinguished between activities practising vocabulary and grammar and those practising functions and whole messages. Both can enhance linguistic proficiency, but also produce rigidity in expression, and both can lead to communication, even at an early stage, as the Bond example has shown.

Managing Conversation

The structure of conversation

Several of these examples have dealt with individual sentences and variations within them. Yet sentences normally occur within connected stretches of language, and it is important that pupils should learn to manage these longer stretches in L2, as they do, perhaps unconsciously, in their L1.

In speaking, the main form of discourse at school level is conversation, discussion being reserved for more advanced students. Even longer stretches of talk, as in the description of a house, or the account of an accident, are normally punctuated by interventions from one's interlocutor, so that they can count as conversations.

If one looks at the Jules Bond dialogue, it is evident that the utterances do not follow each other arbitrarily, but form a short but coherent spoken text, the coherence being created by the fact that each participant builds on what the other has said. There is a clear formal structure: the dialogue is made up of two pairs of utterances, and in each pair one can identify an initiating utterance (I) and a response utterance (R). Although discourse has been analysed in different ways and with different terms by scholars, it is widely agreed that I and R together form the minimal unit of interactive discourse, called *exchange* (Stubbs, 1983). (Pohl *et al.*, (1978) aptly call an exchange *ein Replikenpaar, eine Einheit von Rede und Gegenrede*, a unit of talk and countertalk.) Each utterance expresses a speech act or communicative function: in the Jules Bond dialogue, the first I is a request for information about the identity of the interlocutor, and R is a statement, giving that information; the second I is a greeting and R an unpredicted friendly order.

There are a few situations where a single, almost formulaic exchange suffices. Examples are greeting – greeting, leave-taking – leave-taking, congratulations – thanks, apology – acceptance, inform – acknowledge, and the simplest form of service encounters, such as buying a cinema ticket or asking the price of an item. But conventions of politeness often demand a third utterance, an expression of thanks as feedback or follow-up (F). Whoever offers an apology, for instance, may feel it necessary to add an explanation, a statement of self-blame or acceptance of responsibility.

More complex situations, such as seeking advice on accommodation in a tourist office or arrival at a camp site, would normally consist of several exchanges building up to a *transaction*. The transaction from Kavanagh and Upton (1994) shown in Box 17.1 deals with making arrangements to go out together.

The transaction has an almost exemplary structure. It is in two parts, with a break after *d'accord*. Part I consists of two exchanges: I–R, I–R–F; Part II also of two: I–R, I–R.

Below I will discuss how useful this awareness of discourse structure could be in teaching, whether it would be more productive to concentrate on utterances as

Box 17.1 An example of a *transaction*: making arrangements to go out together (Kavanagh & Upton, 1994: 8)

Jacques:	*Si on allait à la piscine?*
Jean:	*Ah, non. Je n'ai pas envie de me baigner.*
Jacques:	*Alors, qu'est-ce que tu veux faire?*
Jean:	*Je voudrais bien aller au cinéma: il y a un bon film à l'Odéon.*
Jacques:	*Ok, d'accord.*
Jean:	*Tu viens chez moi?*
Jacques:	*Non, je n'aurai pas le temps.*
Jean:	*D'accord. Devant le cinéma, alors? A neuf heures moins le quart?*
Jacques:	*Bien. A tout à l'heure.*

expressions of speech acts and what else would improve pupils' ability to sustain a conversation.

Increasing Variety of Expression

Knowing the formulas used in single exchanges must form part of even the smallest survival kit of any learner expecting to use language in face-to-face encounters. Greetings, leave taking expressions and congratulations can easily be incorporated into classroom language, and the inevitable lateness or small misdemeanour can be exploited to teach not only formulas for apology but also some of the most common explanations or excuses. *Ce n'était pas ma faute, Madame* or *Es war nicht meine Schuld* are likely to prove very useful!

But these are minimal requirements. Different routes to increase pupils' linguistic resources will frequently converge. All additions to their stock of vocabulary and grammatical knowledge, when integrated with existing knowledge, widen the range of what pupils can say. If, for instance, expressions of likes and dislikes are known, they can be applied to newly learnt objects, places and activities. If pupils already use *porter* or *tragen* when they say what they are wearing now or what they wear in different weather, they can add *mettre* or *anziehen* for further items of clothing and re-use all this vocabulary in discussing new purchases, together with expressions for trying on, (un)suitability and revision of like and dislike vocabulary.

The same goal is achieved by the exploration and assimilation of different ways to realise individual speech acts.

The dialogue on making arrangements to go out together quoted earlier can serve as an example. One approach is to proceed exchange by exchange, looking first at alternative contexts, while using the same expression, and then at other ways to realise the speech act.

Thus the first step would be to invite suggestions from the class to replace *aller à la piscine* with other leisure time activities that Jean and Jacques might have chosen. Suggestions might include *aller patiner, aller au cinéma, aller au Foyer, faire une partie de tennis, passer chez Robert écouter ses disques, jouer avec son ordinateur.* How would the I-utterance look if one still used the *si + imperfect* phrase, but with different vocabulary? How would the R-utterance look in consequence, still with *je n'ai pas envie*? The various formulations could be put up on the board or on an OHP.

The second step would be to ask for or provide alternative ways of making a suggestion: *Tu veux venir à la piscine/ nager? Ça te dirait d'aller à la piscine? Robert et moi, on veut aller nager cette après-midi, tu nous accompagnes/ tu viens aussi?* Alternatives for the response might be elicited, perhaps some softer ones: *pas tellement, tu sais, je n'aime pas tellement nager*, perhaps more specific: *je suis un peu enrhumé, l'eau est trop froide.* Perhaps it is altogether impossible to go out (friend expected, too much work), and this explanation, together with an expression of regret, would end the dialogue. Once again the material would be written up, and time would be given for the pupils to copy it and try as many formulations in pairs as they wished.

A similar procedure would be followed for the next exchange, probably in a subsequent lesson.

Before the pupils are invited to construct a whole transaction, there might be a discussion on what normally happens when arrangements are made to go out. As a result, a schematic representation of the common discourse structure in such situations might be put up in L2. It is given in English in Box 17.2.

With the help of this discourse schema and the previous linguistic work pupils have considerable freedom to experiment.

Some teachers may wish to start at the complete transaction level and go down to individual exchanges while keeping the whole picture in mind. As is pointed out by Kavanagh and Upton (1994), laying bare the structure of the transaction, or, as they put it, 'presenting a framework with stage directions' can be used with other topics, such as ordering a coffee or arrival at a campsite. It also recalls the more elaborate *canevas pour une négociation* mentioned in Chapter 3 as one of the activities to revise vocabulary at intermediate level.

Discourse structure varies. In reports of events, for example, it is likely to follow a chronological order, in descriptions, several structures are possible. The description of my best friend, for instance, may proceed along three lines: physical characteristics, temperament and character, common interests, or it might be based on one comprehensive idea: Why X is my best friend. The description of a house can be built round a sketch plan or assume that one is taking a visitor round. Whatever the discourse structure chosen, preparation, both on the linguistic and the organisational level will

Box 17.2 The discourse structure of making arrangements to go out together (a simple schematic representation)

First exchange		
	Proposal made	
Proposal accepted	Proposal refused (reason given)	Proposal refused (reason given)
	Alternative solicited/offered	No alternative possible
	Alternative accepted	End
Second exchange		
	Venue/time proposed	
Venue/time accepted End		Venue or time refused (reason given) Alternative proposed Alternative accepted End

be needed. And, although one of the interlocutors may speak more than the other, the latter would still normally intervene with questions and comments.

Improving the ability to initiate and respond

Though pupils may know the vocabulary related to a particular topic, they may sometimes be hesitant in starting up a conversation. They may also be somewhat slow in responding. Practice in asking questions and proficient use of the different interrogatives — adverbs, pronouns, adjectives — is one way to help them in initiating an exchange and in reacting to what has been said.

In general teachers will want to promote interaction between pupils rather than play a dominant role themselves, but they can stimulate greater variety and encourage pupils to bring out all their latent knowledge. One technique, which is not time-consuming and can be frequently employed once most interrogatives have been met, is to make a statement — the more intriguing the better — and challenge the class to ask as many questions about it as possible, without using the same interrogative twice. (Questions can be written up on the board, so as to avoid repetition and add a visual reminder for weaker pupils. This may be discontinued after a while, particularly with abler pupils, since it slows down the pace.) After three or four months, when pupils have proved that they can use the different forms competently, a group activity can be introduced under similar conditions: one member makes a statement about, say, having gone out the previous evening or having seen an interesting programme on the television, and then has to answer questions from the other members up to an agreed number.

In order to speed up reactions one can organise an occasional quiz, where two teams are challenged to answer as many questions as possible in, say, one or two minutes. They can be on a specific field or general, and should be answered as briefly as possible. A by-product of the activity is the revision of vocabulary and the possible increase of general knowledge. Here are a few possible examples: *S'il est neuf heures en Grande Bretagne, quelle heure est-il en France? A quoi sert un couteau? In welchem Land ist Mozart geboren?*

Conversation as a Social Activity

People talk to each other in the main for a purpose, such as requesting and giving information, reporting what they have done, discussing future action. Learners therefore need first and foremost to acquire the vocabulary and grammar serving their purpose in a particular context. But the smooth course of a conversation also depends on other factors.

The first is the willingness of both partners to take some responsibility for the progress of the interchange. They need to make their meaning clear, seek to understand the meaning of the interlocutor and indicate that they have done so; they may also wish to signpost any change of topic. There are a number of words and expressions which, as it were, lubricate the conversational process and would therefore be useful to learners.

Second, by talking to someone, even a stranger, one is engaging in a social relationship. This assumes a measure of cooperation on both sides. In asking passers-by for directions to the station, I am assuming that, provided they have the necessary knowledge and time, they will be willing to tell me. If the wording or tone of my request, however, has in some way caused offence and broken a norm of politeness, the request will probably be ignored. The parameters of politeness and the linguistic means by which politeness is expressed in different cultures have become a major area of research (Brown & Levinson, 1987; Kasper, 1990). The issue is also a practical one, because non-native speakers need to know how to express themselves without giving offence.

Third, it is both as a contribution to the flow of the dialogue and to maintain social relations that expressions of attention and interest are called for from the listener.

It is not be expected that adolescents can manage these three related aspects of conversational skill adroitly in a foreign language. And social situations are too diverse to be rigidly categorised. Yet I believe that it would matter more to anyone about to spend a fortnight with a French- or German-speaking family to receive some guidance on how not to be inadvertently rude to their hostess than, say, listen to a weather forecast on the radio. And even within the classroom the judicious use of a discourse marker or a German modal particle can give a touch of authenticity to role play. The expressions listed below can be introduced gradually, as a particular topic on the syllabus makes it appropriate.

Conversational strategies

The following is a small selection of expressions useful in helping to structure a dialogue. It overlaps in part with the next subsection on the social dimension of conversation: ways of starting a conversation, for example, will differ according to whether the addressee is a boy or girl of the same age or an older person.

French

Conversation openers:	*Dis donc (Marie-Claire)* *Pardon, Madame/Monsieur. Je vous dérange?* *Je ne vous dérange pas?* perhaps followed by: *je voulais vous demander*
Topic change:	*A propos*
Check on partner's attention:	*Tu vois, vous voyez?*
Back channel:	*Oui, je vois, bien sûr, en effet*
Repair strategies:	*J'entends par là*
Asking for help:	*Pardon? Pardon, je n'ai pas (bien) compris:* *pouvez-vous répéter, s'il vous plaît? Que veut dire X/ce* *mot en anglais? Comment dit-on en français Y? Ça* *s'appelle comment?*
Topic closure:	*OK, d'accord, bien, et voilà*

German

Conversation openers:	*Sag' mal (Birgit)* *Darf ich (einen Augenblick) stören (Frau/Herr* *Schmidt)?* perhaps followed by: *ich habe/hätte eine* *Frage, ich würde/möchte Sie gern etwas fragen*
Topic change:	*Übrigens, was ich noch sagen wollte*
Check on partner's attention:	*Siehst/weißt du? Sehen/wissen Sie? nicht?*
Back channel:	*Genau, gewiß, natürlich, das finde ich auch*
Repair strategies:	*Ich möchte/wollte damit sagen*
Asking for help:	*Wie bitte? Entschuldigung Sie bitte/ Verzeihung: ich* *habe nicht (recht/alles) verstanden: könnten Sie das* *wiederholen bitte? Wie heißt das? Wie heißt/sagt man* *X auf deutsch? Was bedeutet Y?*
Topic closure:	*Also, so ist's*

The social dimension

The considerations which influence the way individuals talk to others have been analysed at length in the research literature (Brown & Levinson, 1987; Kasper 1990). There are the variables of age and gender, social variables such as status, power and distance; if a request is made, is it legitimate, urgent, feasible in execution, in short what is its weight or cost to the addressee? We all have a measure of self-esteem, or face, that we do not wish to be threatened.

People become sensitive to what is appropriate in different situations in their own culture as part of the growing up and socialisation process, and they choose their language accordingly. With requests, for example, the greater the perceived weight of the request by the criteria outlined earlier, the more it will be expressed indirectly, and accompanied by 'disarmers' and 'cajolers' that are intended to mitigate the weight of the imposition caused.

How much subtlety can be expected from learners who are neither proficient in L2 nor familiar with other cultures, and may indeed appear *gauche* at times in their own?

A few specifics are certain. The *tu/vous* and *du, ihr/Sie* distinction needs to be practised in every situation where a young person may be meeting someone of the same age or older, and particularly when persons from both categories have to be addressed, as during a meal or an outing with the correspondent's family. This means being able to switch rapidly from one pronoun and verb form to another, and, in French, switching between *s'il te plaît* and *s'il vous plaît*.

The addition of *Monsieur* or *Madame* in addressing an adult, even in greetings, must not be seen as a mark of servility, but as a conventional norm that cannot be ignored.

A striking feature in modern times is the reduced force of *s'il vous plaît* and *bitte* (and *please*) on their own, so that in requests that carry any weight they are accompanied by other phrases. These frequently include modal verbs, with the conditional form considered more polite still than the present. The following is a list of phrases introducing *requests*, first to a coeval and then to an adult, in ascending order of politenes and with the focus now on the speaker, now on the addressee. (See also the list of classroom expressions in the Appendix.)

French

> *Passe-moi ta gomme*
> *Tu me prêtes ta gomme?*
> *Tu peux me prêter ta règle/passer la colle?*

The same expressions followed by *s'il te plaît*

> *Tu pourrais*
> *Je peux/est-ce que je peux/puis-je aller aux toilettes (s'il vous plaît)?*
> *Vous pouvez (s.v.p.)*
> *Est-ce que je pourrais avoir encore une bière s.v.p.*
> *Pourriez-vous me passer ce livre-là. s.v.p?*

With one or two prefacing remarks, including the nomination of the addressee, and followed by the actual request:

> *Pardon Madame/Monsieur, je voulais vous demander*
> *Pardon Monsieur, excusez-moi de vous déranger*
> *Ca vous dérangerait, gênerait de*

German

> *Gib' mir (mal) ein Brot*
> *Kann ich (mal) ein Stück Brot haben (bitte)?*
> *Kannst du mir (mal) ein St. Br. geben?*
> *Sei so gut/lieb/nett und gib mir (mal, bitte) ein St. Br.*
> *Könnte/dürfte ich (noch) um ein St. Br. bitten?*
> *Können/Könnten Sie mir bitte ein St. Br. geben?*
> *Würden Sie bitte so freundlich/nett sein und mir ein St. Br. geben?*

The affective dimension

In any conversation that goes beyond a short service encounter or a brief factual exchange, it matters for the maintenance of friendly personal relations that the addressees should demonstrate their interest in what is being said. At its lowest a simple back channel phrase will show that one is listening; one can go further and ask for details. But one may also wish to show closer involvement and express one's agreement, approval, surprise, commiseration. The appropriate use of the right phrase may sometimes make up for gaps in one's vocabulary. The following are just a few:

In French: *Tiens, c'est vrai?, c'est pas vrai!* (surprise); *Oui, bien sûr, absolument* (approval); *tu trouves?, quand même* (doubt); *dommage* (disappointment).

In German: *Tatsächlich!, wirklich?, das wundert mich (aber)* (surprise); *das ist (aber) schade!* (disappointment); *das geht ja (doch) nicht* (disapproval), *das ist gut/schön* (satisfaction); *das war richtig, da hast du recht gehabt* (agreement, approval).

One way of practising these phrases would be for the teacher to make statements and ask for attitudinal reactions from the pupils.

In the German phrases the frequency of modal particles such as *aber, ja, doch* will have been noted. Modal particles are a characteristic feature of German colloquial speech. 'By using them one may alter the tone of what is being said and, for example, appeal for agreement, express surprise or annoyance, soften a blunt question or statement or sound reassuring' (Hammer, 1991: 174). Several of these particles have different shades of meaning, but from the intermediate stage onwards, learners could be introduced to the main ones, listen out for particles in authentic recordings and be encouraged to use them when they feel confident.

The learning of the phrases mentioned in this section on talk as a social activity must take its place beside the learning of other parts of the language. When they are introduced appropriately into pupils' conversation, they can make it sound more natural and less like function speak or a dialogue based on cue-cards. The section as a whole is also a reminder that communication between people serves emotional as well as transactional needs.

18 Producing Language: The Writing Skill

Writing fulfils more than one role in the learning of foreign languages. First, it consolidates and reinforces language learnt orally. The very act of writing down something heard helps to fix it in the mind. The written image can serve not only as an aid to memory, but also as a prompt for speech. Second, writing is needed in another important mode of communication, correspondence of all kinds, notes, messages, forms, reports, summaries, essays, etc., and is useful too on occasions where the spoken mode is inappropriate. Third, it offers even to learners with limited proficiency a means of individual and sometimes quite personal expression, which can be changed, revised, refined and kept as a record. The introduction of computers into schools and homes has made writing less error-prone, and its presentation more attractive, while the growing use of FAX machines and of the Internet has accentuated the importance of written communication.

What is involved in learning to write in the foreign language? In the elementary stage, particularly in a mainly oral course, it is first a question of learning the written representation, the spelling of words and phrases one has heard and spoken. This means noting and remembering the choice of letters, especially unfamiliar ones, and their sequence. It means grasping the relation between speech sounds and graphic symbols, including instances, above all in French, when the written form conveys important information not signalled in speech. Then, since in most courses, pupils are encouraged to communicate from the start, and this involves producing sentences, however short, rather than single words, learning to write also means learning to express meaning in simply structured sentences, even if not always accurately.

It is not possible to be specific about the length of the elementary stage — or indeed of any other, because pupils differ in ability and because their performance is also affected by their familiarity with a topic or a particular aspect of it. Yet the APU survey of the written performance after two years of study of about 8000 pupils in French, German and Spanish (APU, 1987c: 40–1) showed that about 60% were able to express themselves in simple sentences when giving personal information, though only about 25% could do so when describing and reporting. (See Chapter 8 for examples from the APU survey of writing.)

In the intermediate stage, writing may still serve to practise linguistic control in relation to topics on the syllabus, but the structure and sequence of sentences receive more attention. Temporal relations, cause and effect, the important and the secondary have to be clearly marked, grammatical cohesion and logical coherence maintained.

At the advanced stage the characteristics of writing as an independent mode of communication receive prominence. The emphasis is on the text as a whole, its suitability for purpose and audience, the balance between its parts, the appropriateness of individual expressions.

Two other ways of viewing the development of the writing skill are by Rivers (1981) and Kavanagh and Upton (1994).

Rivers proposes four stages:

(1) notation or writing down: learning the conventions of the code;
(2) Writing practice: manipulation, recombination and extension of learnt material;
(3) Production under supervision: guided practice in producing fluent and varied expression;
(4) Expressive writing or composition for practical or personal purposes.

Kavanagh and Upton envisage a three-stage sequence:

(1) writing to learn: copy writing, note-taking, gap-filling;
(2) writing to a model: adapting a model text, working from one text type to another;
(3) learning to write: creating one's own texts suited to purpose and audience.

Overall the similarities between the three viewpoints are greater than the differences. Clearly the development of the writing skill is gradual, with complex tasks requiring greater linguistic proficiency and organisational capacity. But at all stages there are possibilities for learners to write something of their own.

The review of writing activities here will follow the stages of development.

Writing in the Elementary Stage: The First Steps

Anyone who has tried to learn a language with an unfamiliar alphabet, for instance Russian or Greek, will remember the intense concentration needed to form the letters and the repeated checks to get the sequence right. French and German in that respect present fewer problems. Yet it is easy for teachers to underestimate the effort and attention required by absolute beginners to learn the spelling of the new language, to remember an accent or an unusual combination like ß or sch. However it is equally easy to underestimate the eagerness with which most beginners are willing to learn to write correctly during the first few weeks of their course.

How can teachers capitalise on that eagerness? I would suggest five guiding principles for this first stage:

(1) Link the spoken and written. Most of what is written, whether it is single words, phrases or sentences, should have been heard and spoken already by the pupils, so that writing is seen as a reinforcement of the spoken and an aid to remembering.

(2) Teach the alphabet fairly early, use it in explaining how words are spelt and encourage pupils to use it too.

(3) Allow for the fact that beginners write slowly. Do not rush writing, anticipate and draw attention to possible pitfalls, be patient with mistakes, but insist on fair copies being correct.

(4) Concentrate on meaning, but also get pupils themselves to discover regular relationships between speech sounds and graphic symbols and instances of unsounded letters.

(5) Use a variety of activities.

Early writing activities

Activities can be copying, listing, labelling, matching, dictation, simple gap-filling, puzzles. Often several activities are combined.

Copying is common in real life to aid retention or have a record of useful information. The challenge to the teacher is to provide a clear purpose for copying in class. Without this, as when pupils are asked to copy a whole sentence in order to insert just one word, slipshod work may result.

The most useful task in the initial stages is to copy conversational exchanges as consolidation of early practice and as a prompt for further practice. Examples are questions and answers about name, age, habitation, family. Weaker pupils may be helped by seeing first the model sentence fully written out, then the sentence partly completed, with an indication of how many letters are required.

Ich heiße Sabine
Ic- h---- Sabine
= . . . .
Wie heißt du?
W-- h---t du?
= . . . .
Ich heiße Matthias
= . . . .
Wie heißt du?
= . . . .

Purpose of a different kind is introduced when copying is combined with listing as means of organising data. For example, most pupils will know the names of some French or German cities and be able to say them. The teacher writes them on the board or OHP as they are proposed, and then writes the population of each next to it. Pupils make a list in order of size, copying both the name and the figure.

The names of famous persons, living or dead, known to the class, or of products made in France or Germany, may be similarly written up, placed into different categories by the teacher (perhaps with the involvement of the class) under an appropriate heading and copied in alphabetical order.

Tasks of this kind not only teach how the names of well-known people or products are spelt, but add to pupils' knowledge about the country. An invitation to pupils to put the lists they have written on a wall display provides yet another purpose for careful and accurate copying.

One last exercise in which copying has a visible purpose inside the learning process is the appropriate matching of captions, whether of single words or of sentences, with visual material.

Labelling of drawings or magazine pictures showing parts of the body, produce, means of transport, clothes etc. is a popular writing activity with young learners. The amount of time expended on drawing must be weighed against the involvement and feeling of ownership generated.

Dictation is a much undervalued exercise. Some teachers point out, rightly, that for most people its use in real life is probably limited to writing down telephone messages, names and addresses or directions, others remember dictation as a component of examinations in the past, apparently designed to trap the unwary, particularly in French. Imaginative ways of using dictation to stimulate learning and discussion among advanced students have been persuasively described by Davis and Rinvolucri (1988), and throughout my own teaching I have found dictation useful from the very beginning.

Short but frequent dictations of a few words or one or two sentences allow the teacher to revise previous acquisitions, to target points that have caused difficulties or are known to need special practice, and highlight particular relationships between sound and symbol or spelling problems. For a few minutes the whole class is quiet, yet active, concentrating on listening and writing. Correction by the pupils themselves or their neighbour can follow immediately, and a quick round of questioning shows the teacher what is known and what needs further practice. Conducted in this way, dictation is a teaching and not a testing exercise.

The following are just some of the phrases and sentences that might be dictated in the initial weeks:

> *Je m'appelle* (Is the spelling of the verb right?)
> *J'ai une soeur et deux frères* (Is there an *e* in *une*? Is *soeur* spelt correctly? Is there a *t* in *et*? a grave accent and a final *s* in *frères*?)
> *Ich habe eine Schwester und zwei Brüder* (Do the two nouns start with a capital letter? Has everyone written *schw*? Is the /ai/ sound written as *ei*? Is there an Umlaut? An initial *z* for the /ts/ sound?)
> *Wo wohnst du?* (Is there confusion between *v* and *w*? Has the *h* been included?)

and so on, according to whatever has been taught so far.

Box 18.1 A gap-filling exercise in the form of a letter at beginners' level (Neuner, 1989: 29)

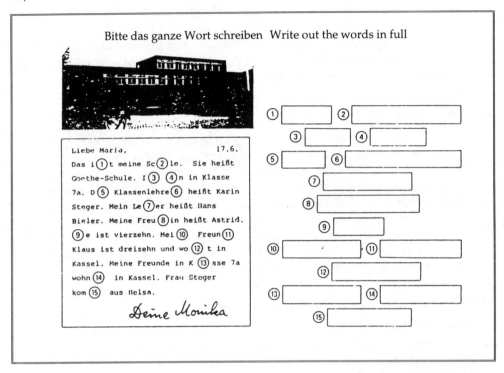

Bitte das ganze Wort schreiben Write out the words in full

All these sentences may have been copied before in an earlier lesson. Dictation does not replace careful writing of new language; it acts as revision and check, because learners forget.

Crosswords and other puzzles that relate meaning and spelling are fun to do, simple *gap-filling* can either focus on letters or on whole words. The example in Box 18.1 reworks the first chapter of a textbook in a spelling exercise that combines gap-filling with copying. Yet it is also within the communicative framework of a letter to a friend and thus looks ahead to a recognised and personal use of writing. (Another format could have been just to fill the gap, but that would have given less practice in writing out whole words.)

Writing in the Rest of the Elementary Stage

Writing still mainly consolidates oral skills, but can begin to emerge as an independent mode of communication. More precisely, writing

- allows time to reflect on elements in conversational exchanges, particularly on common question patterns;
- allows time to decide between grammatical forms and to reflect on the spelling implications of the decision;
- practises manipulation and re-presentation of learnt material in a new form;
- offers opportunities to pupils to use what they have learnt to create their own sentences and express their own meanings.

Writing as support for oral interaction

In courses based predominantly on dialogues in certain settings, there has to be a progression of activities before pupils can communicate flexibly in similar situations. Normally the introductory dialogue is followed by variations, in which key patterns are repeated, but other lexical items are changed. After the pupils have heard, read and spoken these dialogues, writing down the key patterns of the exchange on paper gives them a visible prompt. They can thus take the initiative in further dialogues, and gain the confidence to dispense with written support in the end. *Ça fait combien? Wie weit ist es nach . . . ?* are just two of many possible examples. In longer transactions a written note also serves as a reminder of what comes next.

Writing as a means to consolidate grammar and vocabulary

During the elementary stage fundamental features of French and German grammar are introduced, such as the separate forms for the different persons of the verb, the separate forms for number in the noun group, the rules of agreement. Much of the necessary practice should be oral, and I have suggested some suitable activities in the chapter on grammar, but written practice is essential too, especially in French, because its conservative writing system has retained distinctions shed orally.

Gap-filling is an established and valid exercise to practise grammar and vocabulary. Whether the gap is to be filled with a verb form or an adjective, it is part of a sentence, and thus within a context. An element of testing is inevitable, because of the need to choose, but it can be reduced to a minimum at the beginning by naming the alternatives, limiting them to two, providing several examples of one form before moving on to another and going through the exercise orally before having it written. Some of this scaffolding can be withdrawn for a further exercise, when a definite choice is required.

In the end one can provide a connected text of, say, five or six lines, with a small number of gaps. Such a piece can be a reworking of the lesson text or contain vocabulary from earlier lessons: the essential is that most pupils should be able to work out from the context what kind of word might fill the gap. There could first be a discussion of the suggestions made by pupils, then the teacher would read the whole text aloud, including the missing word. This exercise brings in reading, listening and

Box 18.2 An exercise to practise the use of capital and small letters in German, by correcting a child's letter (Häussermann *et al.*, 1989: 126)

Eight-year old Sabine is writing to her Daddy from a stay in Switzerland:

lieber papa,
kennst du die schweiz? mama und ich sind in der schweiz in einem kleinen hotel und essen
jeden morgen viele semmeln mit butter und honig. das beste in der schweiz ist die schokolade.
es gibt 20 sorten, wenn ich einmal viel geld habe, kaufe ich mir 20 schokoladetafeln.
viele grüße
            deine sabine

---

writing. It also practises the skill of prediction, required both for listening and reading, for semantic as well as syntactical judgements.

Dictation has a definite place in the practice of grammatical forms, particularly in French. It could be only slightly longer than during the early stage, perhaps going over troublesome forms with a touch of humour, perhaps even repeating today what was written yesterday, until the teacher can confidently challenge the class that all of them will get it right.

One of the conventions of written German is that nouns should start with a capital letter. Dictation can be used as a reminder of this, perhaps with an initial emphasis on the connection between an article and a following noun. An occasional alternative, suitable as a pair or group activity, is the correction of a child's letter, as in the example reproduced in Box 18.2.

Writing to recombine learnt material

In dictation the words are read by the teacher, in gap-filling exercises only single words or phrases are inserted by the pupils, with the rest of sentence already printed. The next step is for pupils to write whole sentences or short texts themselves. At the start such writing will not only be closely based on previous oral work, but the actual content of what is to be written will be guided and choice limited. Guidance can be given through (a) symbols, (b) notes from an oral source and (c) written models. Each will be briefly described:

Symbols of different kinds play a considerable role in real life in communicating information. Initial letters or stylised little drawings indicate gender on doors, the site and function of public buidings on maps, facilities in tourist resorts, hotels and camp sites, activities allowed or forbidden. Figures show times of arrival and departure, opening and closing, and the cost of goods. The message conveyed by such symbols is well understood by pupils, and they are quick to accept new symbols introduced in a textbook or by a teacher. They have learnt, in their own language, that the information thus conveyed has to be expanded into a full sentence, when it is transmitted to a third party. The symbols provide the visual props through which they can, for instance, write in the foreign language about the identity of people, leisure activities being performed, the location of a station or a church, ordering an ice cream or a sausage.

Oral information is sometimes recorded by pupils through entries in a table under different headings, as an economical means of indicating variables in a common setting. The compressed information can be expanded into oral and then written statements, say, about the cost of stamps to different destinations, the amount of pocket money received by members of a group and how they spend it, means of transport to get to school, time spent on watching television, nationality of guests in a hotel and length of stay, games played, won and lost.

Written models may sometimes be needed. Some information is conventionally only communicated in writing, and pupils need to have before them appropriate models. These might be models of a form to be filled in, of holiday postcards, birthday cards, invitations to a party, a letter of enquiry to a tourist office on behalf of the family, mini-descriptions of a famous person or a locality. More than one example is needed, so as to provide choice — the holiday postcard might, for instance, offer a number of stock phrases to choose from to describe the weather, the accommodation, the food, the people met. A structure would thus be provided in which the content could be adapted to express personal meanings.

Writing to create independent texts

Are pupils at the elementary stage capable of using writing as an independent mode of communication in its own right and create their own texts? The APU survey confirms that they are (see Chapter 8).

What matters is that one should be clear about the meaning of the phrase 'creating a text'. It is not a question of inventing something, for pupils will be using words and phrases learnt during their course, sequencing them according to the established patterns and rules of the language, perhaps just adapting models, as was shown earlier. Nor is it a question of using language in a novel or unusual way, let alone producing a poem or a literary text, although examples of such texts, produced at the intermediate level, will be quoted later. It is simply a question of making a personal choice about what to write, and trying to ensure that whatever is written, however commonplace, makes sense.

The spread of group work, the introduction of information technology into schools and a greater willingness by teachers to view errors as part of the learning process can all make independent writing less hazardous. Responsibility for the production of a text can be shared in the group, the disk can be easily and tidily altered before the final print out is required, the teacher can see errors in the making on the screen, offer advice and be available for consultation (Hewer, 1989).

Obviously pupils will be most familiar with the topics they have covered so far and the vocabulary and grammar associated with them, although it must be one aim of revision constantly to extend learnt language to new contexts. The challenge to teachers is to think of how to stimulate and enable pupils to write with what they know.

Writing that is more than practice presumes readers. It might be addressed to a specific person or persons, as in letters, to a general readership, as in notices or instructions, or it might be a personal statement or comment by the writer, made available to be read.

This categorisation could help teachers to look in more than one direction for possible writing tasks. For example, giving personal information — about age, physical features, hobbies, family — is a topic which occurs prominently in the early stages of most school courses. It would therefore form the obvious core of a letter to a pen friend. (It is also the topic where the highest mean score was achieved in the APU survey of writing.) However, a number of teachers, while appreciating the motivating effect of a regular correspondence scheme, may wish to delay its introduction until after the elementary stage. But quite interesting texts can be written on the same topic. Pupils can fill in details about themselves in an official-looking form, write a brief description of a member of their family, their best friend, a well-known personality or the inhabitant of another planet. A group of pupils can compose a written portrait of someone in the class (or outside) and challenge another group to discover his or her identity.

If a space can be reserved on a notice board in the classroom for foreign languages, groups of four can take turns every week to fill the space. The following are just a few of possible items:

- a list of important events in school or in town that week
- any birthdays of fellow pupils during the week
- the weather forecast for the week
- the results of any class survey
- favourites: food, drink, music, etc.
- jokes and puzzles.

Once the idea catches on, and the result is pleasingly presented, it is surprising how imaginative and resourceful pupils can be!

Writing in the Intermediate Stage

It is not easy to define the term 'intermediate stage'. It certainly cannot be said to begin or end after a given number of years, since pupils progress at different rates. It may be easier to define it in terms of what has been 'covered', and what still needs to be 'covered'. Though textbooks vary, some degree of uniformity is often imposed by nationally prescribed syllabuses. One can therefore assume that in the intermediate stage pupils will have to encompass the future and the past as well as the present, action and reports as well as description. In terms of writing skill, pupils will be expected to write longer sentences, involving coordination and subordination, and short connected texts.

The intermediate stage can be difficult for both teachers and pupils. Both are aware that much remains to be learnt before meaning can be expressed satisfactorily. To adolescents in a critical phase of personal development the gap between aspiration and capability may be frustrating, to teachers the challenge is even more than usual to teach the new without endangering the old, induce a feeling of progress rather than confusion.

Writing as an aid to learning topic content

When a new situation is introduced in a textbook, perhaps with attendant new vocabulary and grammar, teachers will ask themselves: is the situation such that it would naturally only be played out through dialogue? If so, would pupils be helped to learn the appropriate language by composing a dialogue in pairs, first under guidance, as in the elementary stage, then on their own? Would the situation naturally also involve some writing, for example a letter to a youth hostel, a tourist office, one's pen friend regarding a proposed visit, a hotel about an item left behind? If so, does the textbook offer enough models, or is some additional material needed? In all these cases, writing can contribute to the learning of topic content.

But there are also three other kinds of writing that are appropriate at the intermediate stage. The first focuses on consolidating grammatical forms, the second on extending flexibility of expression and sentence construction, the third on the creation of personal texts.

Writing to consolidate grammar

(Several tasks under this heading have already been mentioned in Chapter 9 on the teaching of grammar, and will therefore receive only summary mention here.) When new verb forms are introduced that contain distinctions specific to the written mode, these need attention. In French, for example, pupils need practice in recognising which to choose among -ais, -ait, -aient; -ons, -ont; é, er, ez. Gap-filling and dictation, or the combined exercise described earlier, are useful for this purpose. Since the right decision depends on awareness of context, longer texts are preferable to single sentences. The aim is to practise rather than to test, therefore the exercises are best done in class, perhaps preceded by advice on what to look for and checked immediately for feedback to learner and teacher.

Written practice is also helpful in German to keep members of the following pairs apart and to link each to an appropriate context: *hatte/hätte; konnte/könnte; mußte/müßte; wurde/würde.*

The difficulty of making the right choice between an action tense and the imperfect in French has been mentioned several times already. This is clearly a case where pupils need to view actions in their context, and see how one is related to the others. The analysis of printed stretches of text must be followed by written production. (For a detailed description of possible exercises see Chapter 9.)

Written exercises have a role to play in the teaching of German word order. Initial practice can be carried out orally and on simple sentences, by putting expressions of time or place at the head of a clause, but this needs to be extended to longer written texts. Above all, different types of coordination need carefully graded practice on the lines suggested in Chapter 9.

Writing to extend flexibility of expression and sentence structure

In the elementary stage most sentences, whether spoken or written, contain only one proposition — a statement or question, an invitation or request. In conversational exchanges in particular, the immediate succession of Initiation and Response ensures a connection between them even without an explicit link.

Why didn't you come last night?
I was ill.

In writing, the relation between cause and effect, or between two events in time, has to be expressed explicitly. Pupils need to be shown various ways of doing this, and be given an opportunity to experiment with them. As their vocabulary and grammatical knowledge expand, they themselves often want to qualify and amplify their statements and go beyond the single sentence. A gradual but planned expansion of their discourse repertoire gives them a feeling of control.

Much can already be done through the present tense, perhaps as part of deliberate recycling of earlier acquisitions. For instance, *expressions of time* can be categorised and experimented with, as pupils are asked to keep a precise record of how they spend the time between waking and leaving for school in relation to what other members of the family do. They may wish to express some or all of the following concepts:

- point in time *à, vers, entre . . . et, encore, déjà*
- posteriority *puis, une fois habillé(e), une demi-heure après, enfin*
- anteriority *avant (de)*
- simultaneity *pendant ce temps-là, pendant que . . .*
- duration and frequency.

A more exciting but more difficult task requiring the use of past tenses would be to ask pupils to write a story ending with a sentence like: *Das ganze Abenteuer hatte nur 30 Minuten gedauert.*

Some *expressions of place* will occur if pupils draw a sketch of their bedroom and comment on it in a letter to their pen friend. Others will be used if the letter describes a tour of the house, different ones will be needed if their correspondent's family is arriving by car from a given port and require directions to the house.

Expressions indicating *alternatives* might figure in this last letter, together with evaluation of *advantages and disadvantages*. There may be other, equally realistic occasions when pupils are asked to give advice and opinions: where best to spend a youth hostelling or camping holiday in Britain, or which of two English language summer schools to recommend. A simpler version of this task is to ask for advice or opinion on the basis of data relating to the foreign country.

Comparisons, contrasts, exemplification constantly recur in both speech and writing, when we give an opinion about someone or something and want to justify it. A portrait of two people, whether they be admired or detested, named or anonymous, allows scope for interesting comparisons. This is not a question of using the comparative or superlative but of making a point by giving an example or invoking a comparison and showing pupils simple ways of doing so.

In writing, one often has to *give reasons or explanations* and link *causes and results.* How often one's letters begin with an explanation why there has been a delay in writing! The following is the first paragraph of an authentic letter from an 18-year-old Swiss girl interested in attending a summer course in England.

> *Ganz herzlichen Dank für die Sommerkurs-Prospekte. Ich melde mich erst jetzt, da bei uns sehr viel passiert ist. Nun geht es aber schnell dem Sommer entgegen. Deshalb hier meine Vorstellungen: . . .*

Though simple in vocabulary and sentence structure, the paragraph is a good example of cohesion, with every sentence explicitly or implicitly linked to the previous one. The first sentence refers to a past event known to both writer and addressee. The reason why that event is only now (*erst jetzt*) followed up is introduced by a clause starting with *da.* The third sentence implies the need for action, and in consequence (*deshalb*) she will set out how she sees the next steps.

For French, various expressions for giving reasons are clearly differentiated by Bérard and Lavenne (1991: 189): *parce que* is used in answer to a request for an explanation, whether this has been explicitly made through *pourquoi,* or is understood:

> *Je ne suis pas venu parce que j'avais un travail urgent à terminer.*

On the other hand,

> *Alors, comme* servent à exposer les raisons, les circonstances, les conditions dans lesquels un événement a pu avoir lieu. Il s'agit plutôt d'un complément d'information donné à votre interlocuteur que d'une réponse à une demande d'explication.

> *Comme il était occupé* (cause), *je n'ai pas osé le déranger.*
> *Il était occupé, alors* (consequence) *je n'ai pas osé le déranger.*

The explanation or cause of an event is often found in the past, as in the examples quoted earlier; practice might therefore be delayed until the forms and use of past tenses are established. Writing a story is also often set in the past. A framework and a model for such writing, with some of the time markers that might be used, are suggested by Kavanagh and Upton (1994).

Finally, pupils will appreciate learning other ways of *reporting speech* than the frequently clumsy construction with *Il a dit que . . . Er hat gesagt, daß . . .*

A concluding remark is perhaps called for. Expressions to extend flexibility are often found in texts used at the intermediate stage but they seldom appear among specific teaching objectives or receive specific practice. I believe that they deserve to do so, since they serve important communicative functions, particularly in writing, as pupils strive to express their ideas. They are not tied to a particular topic, and can therefore be introduced and practised wherever the teacher considers it appropriate.

Personal writing

Correspondence with an individual or a class in a French- or German-speaking school is the clearest example of writing that is addressed to a specific person or group of persons and arises out of a personally felt desire. It not only has an authentic purpose but can also have a motivating effect on learning.

There is much to be said for a guided class-to-class correspondence in the beginning, so as to prevent the early failure of individual pairings through unsuitable matching or dilatoriness by one partner. In one school I know, a class letter is sent in the first and again in the second term, and individual correspondence begins in the third. The class letter is almost a brochure on one theme, determined collectively, and with different aspects prepared by different groups. The school and the town are favourite themes; the group organisation allows pupils of different abilities to contribute, and the common purpose justifies drafting and re-drafting, with the teacher acting as consultant. Both the class brochure and the reply can be displayed on the class notice board and perhaps be on show for an open day or a parents' evening. Together with the personal details likely to occur in individual letters, most of the topics normally covered in the elementary stage are thus revised to good purpose. Very often too, contacts made by letter develop into visits or exchanges, giving rise not only to further correspondence, but to contacts that can turn into life-long friendships.

Correspondence is not the only kind of independent writing that is within the competence of pupils in the intermediate stage. There are three areas of experience which can provide stimuli for writing. The first is pupils' immediate environment. School, for example, still plays a large role in their lives. The two sets of school rules reproduced in Box 18.3, one from the past, the other a humorous spoof, can be the starting point for pupils to work out a set of rules for their own school, whether serious or humorous.

Similarly, the two portraits of the ideal teacher in Box 18.4 can be elaborated through class discussion until pupils are ready to compose their own.

In both examples, pupils can start from a model. But there is also another way to stimulate their imagination. In an issue of *Der Fremdsprachliche Unterricht* wholly devoted to creative writing in French (Vol.3, August 1991), Minuth explains how he had proposed the theme *l'école / l'école à l'envers,* invited the class to suggest expressions that they associated with it and written them on the board. Such a cluster of expressions, whether ordered or not, discussed in groups or not, can serve as a data

Box 18.3 Two sets of school rules (Neuner *et al.*, 1988: 89)

Die Schulordnung des Direktors

§1 Die Schüler müssen pünktlich um 8 Uhr in der Schule sein.

§2 Der Lehrer hat immer recht.

§3 Der Lehrer fragt − die Schüler antworten.
Der Lehrer redet − die Schüler sind ruhig.

§4 In der Pause dürfen die Schüler nicht im Klassenzimmer bleiben.
Im Hof dürfen sie nicht rennen und Fußball spielen.

§5 Die Schüler müssen jeden Tag ihre Hausaufgaben machen und sauber schreiben.

Der Direktor

Die Schulordnung der Schüler

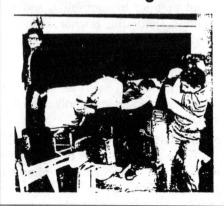

§1 Die Schüler können bis neun Uhr schlafen. Der Unterricht beginnt nicht vor zehn Uhr.

§2 Die Schüler haben immer recht!

§3 Die Schüler reden − der Lehrer ist ruhig!

§4 In der Pause dürfen die Schüler im Klassenzimmer Fußball spielen.

§5 Niemand muß Hausaufgaben machen.

---

bank available to pupils to create their own texts. The class had also read Prévert's *Déjeuner du matin*, which therefore provided a model of a different kind, whose influence is noticeable in the two texts reproduced in Box 18.5.

The second area of experience which can stimulate pupils' writing is the world around them. The contrasting portrait of two people already mentioned earlier can bring into play the vocabulary of physical details and personal qualities commonly acquired in the elementary stage. A striking photograph can evoke a response at different levels, from the purely descriptive to a strongly felt interpretation. A weekly news bulletin can be put up, with small groups submitting two items each, and one

Box 18.4 Two portraits of the ideal teacher (Neuner, 1989: 32)

So wünschen sich Schüler ihren Traumlehrer:

lustig
macht guten Unterricht ✓
verständnisvoll ✓
nicht einigermaßen aus ✓
kameradschaftlich ✓
nett, gutgelaunt ✓
gerecht ✓

Mein "Traumlehrer" sollte den Unterricht interessant machen.
Man sollte auch bei ihm etwas lernen. Außerdem sollten
die Tests nicht sehr schwer sein. Mein Lehrer sollte lustig sein,
jung, groß und schlank. Am liebsten ohne Bart. Mein Wunschlehrer
sollte viel Humor haben und die Fragen so beantworten, daß sie
für jeden klar sind.
Ich wünsche mir einen Lehrer, der viele Spiele und Ausflüge
macht. Ich finde, ein Lehrer sollte öfter Filme zeigen.

Eine Traumlehrerin sollte Zeit haben und mit den Schülern
Probleme besprechen. Aufgaben gibt sie wenig. Gut wäre es,
wenn sie mit uns über Noten und andere Sachen diskutieren
würde. Wichtig ist, daß sie die Schüler versteht. Sie darf
keine Lieblinge in der Klasse haben. Sie sollte Spaß verstehen
und alle Schüler wie normale Menschen behandeln und nicht wie
Babys.

a) Wie soll ein Traumlehrer sein?
Was steht im Text?
Suche 4 Adjektive

_____

b) Was ist auch wichtig (important)?
   Schreibe 5 Alternativen

1. Der Lehrer _____

2. Er _____

3. _____

4. _____

5. _____

c) Was sagt dieser Text von einer
   Traumlehrerin?
   Schreibe so viel wie möglich

Sie soll _____ (1)

   _____ (2)

   _____ (3)

   _____ (4)

   _____ (5)

d) Und *dein* Traumlehrer?

   _____

group in turn taking on the task of editing the items and preparing the final text. We live in a world of advertising: pupils can try their hand at celebrating (or denigrating) their home town on the model of a tourist brochure, or suggest slogans for various products.

Box 18.5 Two poems written by pupils about school (Minuth, 1991: 21)

Le cours

Je suis assise sur la chaise
On sonne
Le cours est fini
Je me suis levée
J'ai ouvert la porte
Je suis sortie de la classe
Je ne me suis pas retournée.

A l'école

Nous sommes arrivés à l'école
et sommes entrés dans la classe
les professeurs ont déjà commencé
mais nous étions encore debout
les professeurs ont parlé, parlé et parlé
et on n'a rien compris

Finally there is the area of pupils' own feelings and preoccupations. Teachers may rightly hesitate before appearing to intrude on their pupils' private world. On the other hand pupils often regret that so little of their thoughts finds expression in the foreign language (Mummert, 1991; Morgan, 1994). The simple juxtaposition on the board of *Je voudrais . . . mais* or *Je rêve de . . . mais* may trigger off a series of expressions through which pupils can describe the gap between aspiration and reality so keenly felt by many in this age group. Even the two poems about school quoted earlier hint at considerable strength of feeling.

There are various ways of encouraging pupils to express their thoughts on paper. Minuth (1991) distributes a notebook to his pupils at the beginning of the year and encourages them to write something in French in it, when they feel like it. He also uses thematic and visual stimuli. Swarbrick (1990) and Morgan (1994) provide simple literary models, Mummert (1991) uses models and also associative clusters on the board. A time limit is important: Morgan allowed a fourth-year French class of girls of average ability two lessons to produce a poem of their own, incorporating some kind of pictorial element. Above all, the pupils must trust their teacher not to be shocked or censorious; advice during the writing process and suggestions for improving the product may be offered, but there must be no compulsion to accept them.

The product is sometimes a poem. As Swarbrick (1990: 23) writes:

> Poetry is a very adaptable creative medium and for this reason is attractive to beginners and intermediate language learners. They soon become aware that the rules that govern poetry are not rigid and that they can trim the language to its simplest form to say what they want to say.

The poem entitled *La pomme* in Box 18.6 was written by a pupil of Morgan (1994), that entitled *Je voudrais* by one of Mummert (1991).

Box 18.6 Two poems written by intermediate language learners (Morgan, 1994: 45 and Mummert, 1991: 9)

La Pomme

La pomme c'est ronde, comme le monde.

Et la pomme c'est vert,

Triste ment le monde ce n'est plus vert.

La pluie coule sur la pomme

Et le monde pleure

Alex

Je voudrais un chien
Je voudrais un cheval
Je voudrais une Porsche
Je voudrais un magnétophone
Je voudrais regarder la télé
Je voudrais une pomme
Je voudrais une bicyclette
Je voudrais un livre
Je voudrais une chambre
Je voudrais des animaux
Je voudrais ...
Je voudrais toi!

Christina

Writing at the Advanced Level

The term 'advanced' in relation to school rather than university normally refers to a self-contained course of two or three years, taken by pupils who have demonstrated proficiency and interest at the intermediate stage.

In line with the greater maturity of the students, the advanced course no longer deals with daily routines or holiday experiences, but with environmental or social issues or works of literature. The approach is still through all four skills, but writing receives greater weight, and a piece of written work often concludes the intensive treatment of a topic or part of a literary work.

The demands made on students are considerable. Instead of dealing with personal matters, they have to deal with ideas and controversial problems; instead of writing informal letters to pen friends, they have to write essays of some length and construct logical arguments.

This requires in the first place the learning of subject-specific language. This is often a more complex task than simply learning vocabulary. In the field of education, for example, it may mean not only learning terms like *Grande École*, *Berufsschule*, *Baccalauréat Technologique*, but understanding how the entities to which these terms refer fit into the national education system. Subtle distinctions have to be made, as between *enseignement* and *éducation*, *Hochschule* and *höhere Schule*, standard ways of expressing certain ideas have to be assimilated: *eine Arbeit schreiben, unter Leistungsdruck stehen, le collège accueille les élèves de 11 à 16 ans, le lycée dispense, assure un enseignement* . . . Writing about literature makes additional demands, for the language of literary criticism cannot be derived from the works themselves.

Second, pupils' discourse repertoire has to be extended, so that they learn, for example, how to state a problem, enumerate, advocate and refute points of view, draw parallels and contrasts, give reasons, summarise and conclude. In other words, whatever their chosen topics, they need to learn the language of argument, including key discourse-markers, usable both in speech and in writing.

Third, and with particular reference to writing, they need to learn how to organise their thoughts into a coherent whole. If they study how many experienced writers do this, they will notice some recurring patterns (McCarthy & Carter, 1994).

One of the most common has at its basis a simple formula: *problem – solution*. Perhaps because of its simplicity, the pattern is frequently used in advertisements. The following is a very short text, advertising a moisturising cream (*Avantages* No. 66, March 1994):

Ma peau est comme moi, il lui arrive d'avoir soif.
Je lui donne Diffusance.

Another common pattern is *basic situation – particular problem or need – solution*. One of many elaborate examples from advertising can be summarised thus: A fresh skin is important to you. You need a cream that is simple, safe and effective. Cream X is what you need (*répond à votre souhait*).

Sometimes this pattern ends with an *evaluation or comment*. The following newspaper report, quoted in an examination paper, is remarkable for its economy:

(1) *'Au vu du rythme d'accroissement du traffic passagers et marchandises sur l'axe Lille / Paris / Lyon / Marseille, on court à la congestion d'ici à l'an 2000.'*

(2) *Cette constatation est de G. Carrère, animateur du débat national sur l'avenir des transports.*

(3) *Pour soulager cet axe prioritaire, vital pour l'économie, un projet est donc à l'étude: une route nationale à quatre voies qui traverserait la France par l'ouest.*

(4) *Ceci permettrait alors de relier Dunkerque à Bordeaux, via le Havre et Rennes, en évitant l'agglomération parisienne.*

(5) *Une telle réalisation, très lourde, ne devrait cependant pas être achevée avant l'an 2020.*

Sentence (1) states the problem, sentence (2) puts it into context, sentence (3) describes a possible solution, sentence (4) offers an evaluation, sentence (5) adds a comment. Pupils could also note with profit how visibly each sentence is related to an earlier one: grammatically through demonstratives *cette, cet, ceci, une telle*, lexically through *constatation*, referring to the quotation, *axe* repeated and *réalisation*, referring to the *projet*, with the conjunctions *donc, alors, cependant* indicating the relationship at discourse level.

Two other organisational patterns, mentioned by McCarthy and Carter, are *hypothetic – real*, in which a proposition is put forward and then dismissed in favour of another, and *general – particular*, in which a generalisation is illustrated by examples, or a single case is quoted as typical of a general trend.

If the argument of a text is developed over several paragraphs, each is likely to deal with one particular aspect. Very often the paragraph will exhibit a clear structure, with the first sentence announcing the topic, and the subsequent ones exploring this in detail.

To recapitulate, writing at the advanced stage, requires pupils to use subject-specific language appropriately, lay out their ideas effectively and create texts coherently.

Writing as part of the exploitation of texts

Much of the advanced course consists of studying texts in the relevant subject area(s). It is through the intensive exploration of texts that students gain knowledge, develop ideas and acquire subject-specific language. Reading, listening, discussion and writing all play a part in this process. (For one systematic approach to the exploitation of a text, see the article by Nott and follow-up examples by teachers with French, German and Spanish texts in DES/Regional Course, (University of Nottingham, 1988.)

Writing comes into its own here in two places: in the course of the targeted assimilation of important words and expressions, and at the end.

Some of the written exercises are:

- *gap-filling*; gaps should not be fixed at random or mechanically or in relation to a to a particular text. The main criteria should be: *coverage*: words that are widely used in the language and should therefore be known; *collocations*: nouns and verbs that commonly go together; *key terms* essential for a particular topic; *discourse-markers* that signal a link or a step in the development of the argument: *ainsi, par conséquent, einerseits, dadurch*;
- *synonyms* set out in jumbled order in two columns, or, preferably, in a sentence where the simpler synomym has to be replaced with a word or phrase taken from the text. The following is an example based on a text on the economy of the Paris region: *Il y a beaucoup d'industries différentes. = La [gamme] des industries est très étendue*;
- *definitions*;
- *translation* of a short number of English phrases for which the L2 equivalents are in the text.

Sometimes grammatical rules need revising, and appropriate exercises can be devised incorporating new vocabulary.

After a period of concentration on language it is important to go back to content. Students can write down, individually or in pairs, under headings and sub-headings, the main ideas in the text; oral opinions may be invited from all, a formal discussion of arguments for and against may be arranged. This last activity may be delayed until further texts are read, perhaps in a different register or from a different point of view, and exploited in less detail.

Finally both teachers and students may feel that a piece of written work would act as a fitting conclusion. A summary or an experiential, personal piece may be appropriate for students who have but recently graduated from the intermediate stage, but in the later parts of the advanced course a clearly laid out piece of expository or argumentative prose can be demanded.

Writing to develop discourse and organisational skills

In preparing for essay writing, students may find it useful to turn away at intervals from the study of texts and focus specifically on certain aspects of presentation.

The first is the ability to perform in writing certain speech acts or functions in a developing argument: enumerate (reasons, advantages), add a further point, illustrate through an example, compare and contrast. (Lists of discourse markers are sometimes found in textbooks; for French see also the section on 'Language in Use' at the end of the *Collins–Robert French Dictionary* and in Vigner, 1975.) However the most satisfactory approach in my experience is to go back to texts already studied, and discuss the role played by selected words, such as *en effet, d'ailleurs, zwar, außerdem* in their context. This can then be followed by a gap-filling exercise as a check on understanding. In the end, students can be asked to write a short text themselves, individually or in pairs, incorporating the particular word.

The second is the ability to switch from direct to indirect speech and vice versa, and to show some awareness of different registers. Reporting statements by others, whether they be politicians or characters in a literary work, will be called for in many essays and has therefore to be practised.

There are several aspects that need attention. In formal German, reported speech has to be put into the Konjunktiv. This is frequently practised by asking students to transpose direct into indirect speech. A more interesting way is to take a newspaper report of a speech, identify which verbs are in the indicative and which in the Konjunktiv and discuss the reasons. The next step is for students to write the speech themselves and compare it to the report. The points to notice are not only the different forms, but the actual verbs used to introduce the reported statements, and the certainty or doubt about their accuracy which they convey (*erklären, zugeben* as against *behaupten, meinen*).

It should also be within the capabilities of students on an advanced course to report an intended speech act explicitly, writing for example *Les Lebrun m'ont invité chez eux* rather than *Les Lebrun m'ont demandé si je voulais aller chez eux.*

A four-step procedure to move from direct to reported speech, as proposed by Wilga Rivers (1975), is set out in Box 18.7.

One could substitute Rivers' dialogue with a more sophisticated text, perhaps drawn from the topic studied, perhaps omit Step 2, and sometimes introduce other speech acts like *promising, reassuring*. To increase flexibility the procedure could also be tried in reverse, from indirect to direct speech.

Even at student level, writing can reflect differences in intended readership and perspective, which can be explored both through discussion and in practice. The account of a school play could be written from the point of view of an actor and that of a reviewer for a local paper; the study of unemployment could yield a personal *témoignage*, an objective report or a political diatribe.

Creating texts

In order to prepare themselves to write fully developed expository or argumentative essays, students might wish to use the problem – solution pattern in easier tasks. After studying a number of advertisements with this structure, they could write some of their own, individually or in pairs. Two partners can work together in a slightly more elaborate task: one pretends to be writing to a magazine for advice on a problem; the other either suggests a solution, adding an evaluative comment, or else discusses various possibilities and then selects one.

Box 18.7 A four-step procedure to move from direct to reported speech (Rivers, 1975: 284–5)

Step 1.	Students are given a short dialogue like the one below as *foundational content*.
	Pierre: *Bonjour, Marie.*
	Marie: *Bonjour, Pierre.*
	Pierre: *Où vas-tu en ce moment?*
	Marie: *Je vais à la plage. Viens avec moi.*
	Pierre: *Mais il va pleuvoir. Regarde ces gros nuages.*
	Marie: *Impossible. Ça ne peut pas recommencer. Ça fait une semaine qu'il pleut tous les jours!*
Step 2.	Students rewrite the dialogue as *direct address in a narrative framework*
	Bonjour, Marie, dit Pierre en la rencontrant dans la rue.
	Bonjour, Pierre, répond-elle.
	Où vas-tu en ce moment? demande-t-il.
	Je vais à la plage. Viens avec moi, suggère-t-elle.
	Mais, proteste Pierre, en montrant le ciel, il va pleuvoir. Regarde ces gros nuages.
	Impossible, s'écrie Marie. Ça ne peut pas recommencer. Ça fait une semaine qu'il pleut tous les jours!
Step 3.	Students write a paraphrase of the above in *narrative form*.
	En rencontrant Marie dans la rue, Pierre la salue et lui demande où elle va. Elle lui dit qu'elle va à la plage et l'invite à l'accompagner. Pierre proteste qu'il va pleuvoir et lui montre les gros nuages qui les menacent. Mais Marie refuse de croire qu'il va faire de la pluie parce qu'il n'a cessé de pleuvoir pendant toute la semaine.
Step 4.	Finally students write a concise *résumé* in one or two sentences.
	Quand Marie a invité Pierre à l'accompagner à la plage, il lui a fait observer qu'il allait pleuvoir, mais elle a refusé de croire que cela pouvait recommencer après une semaine de pluie.

When it comes to writing an essay, its organisation can be discussed in class for the first few occasions, but in the end students will want to have the freedom to create their own texts.

Box 19.2 A poem written by a 15–16-year-old pupil (Swanbrick, 1990: 21)

FRENCH CALLIGRAM

LA GUERRE

LA
GUERRE
MONDIALE,
LA GUERRE
QUI MET
FIN À TOUS
LES GUERRES.
UNE GUERRE POUR
PAIX, POUR SAUVER
LE MONDE
À JAMAIS.
VOICI LES
MOTS QU'ILS
DISAIENT
APRÈS LA
PREMIERE
GUERRE MONDIALE

But learners also try out on others what they have recently acquired. Beginners call out *Bonjour Madame* or *Bonjour Monsieur* with gusto when they meet a teacher, and snippets of the foreign language can be overheard in the corridor or on the playground. In an article that is both realistic and inspirational, a teacher recounts an episode that occurred in her school (Watkin, 1996):

> The boy who accosted me in the playground was the most disaffected pupil in the school. I experienced a twinge before he simply pointed to the sky and confidently said: *'Le sollail miss, in't it.'*

It is legitimate to interpret the boy's remark to the teacher as springing not from a wish to demonstrate his knowledge but as an expression of an important function of language and one aspect of communication: to establish and maintain social rapport, to show friendliness.

The need for social rapport is felt by most of us; activities that encourage interaction, develop sociability in individuals and strengthen group cohesion are educationally valuable. Pair and group work, role-play, simulations and projects, with their mixture of repetition and improvisation (see the James Bond dialogue), not only provide linguistic practice and serve as preparation for future use, but also satisfy the need for social rapport. They are therefore rightly a popular ingredient of classroom practice.

Reading

The conscious wish to fashion a new medium of expression for one's own purposes and the satisfaction derived from successful execution are most in evidence in the early years of learning, although the poems and essays written by older pupils testify to their continuing strength.

As pupils' proficiency increases, other contributions to personal development become possible. One of them is the opportunity to read in the foreign language for enjoyment and information. As Swarbrick (1990) states, reading for pleasure creates a sense of achievement and promotes autonomy. At the advanced stage, as generations of students can testify, it can offer intense affective and aesthetic experiences.

Using the foreign language and reading interesting texts written in it are educational experiences available to all pupils, whether they go abroad or not. This point deserves to be stressed, because classroom activities are sometimes seen as merely a rehearsal for the *real* use of the foreign language abroad. Evidence from countries in Eastern Europe, where few opportunities for foreign travel are open to pupils, or even to teachers, yet high levels of proficiency and enjoyment are often achieved, shows that this view is not justified. The 'rehearsal' view of the classroom cannot fail to weaken one's resolve to provide the many educational experiences possible in it.

Using the foreign language abroad

However, what I have just written in no way casts doubt on the huge motivational and educational benefits available to pupils in Western Europe who can travel to the country whose language they are studying. The mere fact of having a question understood — by a shopkeeper or passer-by, and understanding their reply — can enhance pupils' feeling of self-confidence. Through their knowledge of the language they can understand what is going on around them, act with some independence, establish social relations. The transition from being a visitor to becoming a participant can take time and require the appreciation of different cultural conventions, but the indispensable key is a degree of linguistic proficiency. It is this which opens the door to many new experiences; without it one remains an outsider.

Language Awareness

The second area in which the learning of a foreign language can contribute to pupils' general education is by making them reflect on language. This is less directly related to language use, nor is it teachers' role to introduce 11–16-year-olds to the study of linguistics. On the other hand 'in any natural history of the human species, language would stand out as the preeminent trait' (Pinker, 1994: 16). Young people know that there are other languages besides their own, but when they begin to study a language like French or German, which show both differences and similarities to English, interesting fields of enquiry open up. How are languages related? What does a language tell us about its speakers' way of life, in the present or in the past? By what processes are words formed and the relation between words effected?

The study of vocabulary is particularly suggestive. At the very beginning of their studies English pupils will notice that a number of words in the target language, be it German or French, bear a family resemblance to their counterparts in English/German *Vater, zehn, Apfel,* English *father, ten, apple*; French *école, arriver, maison,* English *school, arrive, mansion.* The presence of these cognates can be just accepted as a fact that facilitates the learning of German or French, but it can also be linked to what pupils know about the early history of England, the Germanic invasions and the Norman conquest.

One could place English, French and German within a wider context still, and look at the mysterious origin and historical spread of Indo-European languages. The explanation can be done systematically or through some striking example, such as the progress of the word for *wine* from the Near East into Europe, illustrated in Box 19.3.

Who can fail to be excited as they follow the route of the plant, the drink and the word for it, carried by seafarers and traders from Asia to Greece and Rome, and from there by Roman legionaries to the Iberian peninsula, the British Isles and Northern Europe? The philosopher A.N.Whitehead distinguished three stages in relation to intellectual progress: the stage of romance, the stage of precision and the stage of generalisation. The stage of romance is 'the stage of first apprehension. The subject matter has the vividness of novelty; it holds within itself unexplored conections with possibilities half-disclosed by glimpses and half-concealed by the wealth of material.' He urges teachers not to overlook this first stage, with the excitement created in learners, as they begin to perceive the import of these unexplored relationships: 'Education must essentially be a setting in order of a ferment already stirring in the mind.' (Whitehead, 1932: 28).

The word for *wine* has long been incorporated into the various European languages, but movement between languages still goes on. English pupils will soon meet in French and German words like *hi-fi, star, test,* and will be able to quote words taken over into English like *garage* (without being aware of its intriguing link with *gare*), *rucksack, croissant, café.* Again these might just be accepted as interesting or amusing facts, but

Box 19.3 The progress of the word for *wine* from the Near East into Europe (Maas, N.D., quoted in Mebus *et al.*, 1987: 213)

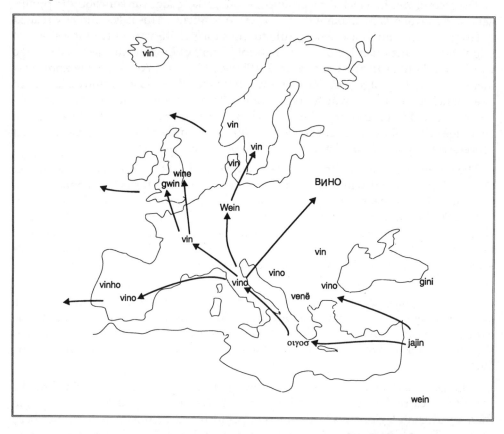

at some stage pupils might like to investigate with what areas of economic activity linguistic exports from each country are associated. The realisation that the vocabulary of a language reflects changes in technology and culture in its widest sense, that such change is a natural feature of every language and that it is sometimes due to influences from abroad should have a broadening effect.

Grammar may have a less general appeal than vocabulary, but quite a number of pupils will be challenged by the idea that a language must have rules or conventions if it is to serve as a communication code. Learning how the relation beween subject and verb or between agent and recipient of an action are expressed, or the distinction is made between continuing and completed actions or realisable and non-realisable conditions can not only satisfy a desire to find out how the particular code works, but lead pupils to compare it to their own, and perhaps stimulate an interest in exploring others.

Cultural Awareness

There is a third educational benefit that pupils can gain from learning a foreign language: an acquaintance with the civilisation and culture of the country or countries where the target language is spoken, and thus a more objective attitude to their own civilisation and culture. (Although the two terms 'civilisation' and 'culture' have much in common, I see civilisation as the topographical and institutional setting in which people live, and culture as defined by the American historian H.S.Commager, (1970) as 'a bundle of patterns of behaviour, habits of conduct, customs, laws, beliefs, and instinctive responses that are displayed by a society'.)

This educational benefit is frequently quoted in official statements. The Statutory Orders for the National Curriculum in the UK (DES, 1991) state under the subheading *Cultural awareness* that pupils should be given opportunities, among others, to:

consider their own culture and compare it with the cultures of the countries and communities where the target language is spoken;

identify with the experiences and perspectives of people in these countries and communities.

The *Programmes et instructions* for *collèges* issued by the Ministère de l'Éducation Nationale (1985) similarly state in relation to the teaching of German:

Le constat par les élèves de la diversité des civilisations et des comportements qui s'y attachent leur permet d'accepter plus facilement les différences dans un esprit pluraliste. L'enseignement de l'allemand contribue ainsi au développement du jugement et du raisonnement.

It is not clear, however, whether enough is being done to bring about such educational benefits.

Modern textbooks certainly contain much that can promote cultural awareness. The syllabus is normally presented in the context of the community in which the target language is spoken. The young French and German people who model the language to be learnt belong to that community and culture, and the external setting is accurately and vividly portrayed through up-to-date photographs and, increasingly, through video and television.

Whether the textbooks show a young English person as an active visitor to that community or not, pupils are quite naturally introduced to aspects of its culture: appropriate greetings, modes of address at different levels of formality, popular dishes and conventions at meals, expected behaviour in school or family, sites, events or historical figures that are significant in the national consciousness.

The language too introduces aspects of culture, whether it be through words specific to it, such as *la rentrée, composter, zweites Frühstück, Stammtisch*, and different pronouns of address, or through words with a specific connotation like *pain* or *Brot* which evoke a different image from the English *bread*.

Critics (Byram, 1989, Byram, Esarte-Sarries & Taylor, 1991, Byram *et al.*, 1994) maintain that pupils only gain a tourist or 'recipe' knowledge, whereas they ought to be introduced 'in an inevitably partial way, to the insider's experience of the "strange" culture as a natural and normal world' (Byram *et al.*, 1994).

In my view such criticism is too harsh. A tourist knowledge is the necessary first step to understanding; if put to the test during a stay in the country, it would enable pupils to operate in the new environment.

Nevertheless more can and should be done. Textbooks tend to focus on one or two localities and families. This is understandable: it allows pupils to become familiar with a particular area and group of people. The result, however, can be that the image conveyed is unrepresentative geographically and socially. Furthermore the concentration on a limited set of activities takes no account of the wider setting in which the young French and German people live and which, as Byram rightly states, forms part of their shared background. Some basic knowledge is desirable both about the framework of society — the major regions, cities, economic activites, even religion and the political system, and about the common stages in the lives of most citizens — recurring events in the year, the course of education, work and holidays. Some teachers may find these suggestions unrealistic at less than advanced level but sources of information are widely available nowadays, and much can be conveyed through visual means, diagrams and tables and also serve for linguistic practice.

The aim of providing this information is first to make plain to pupils the variety that exists within the foreign country — of landscape, climate, economic activity, accent, beliefs — and get them to relate that to the variety with which they are familiar in their own country and society. This may make them less inclined to make generalisations about *Die Deutschen* or *En France*. It may also bring home to them the important fact that some cultural features, or differences between the target culture and their own, have an explanation in geography or history. I have often wished that there could be a short paragraph, either in the pupil's book or the teacher's book, labelled *Un peu d'histoire* as in the Michelin Guides. For example, many textbooks deal with school life in France and Germany, which pupils find rather different from English school life. They might be interested to know that the English concepts of a school as a community and of pastoral care, or the existence of extra-curricular activities and school games can be traced back to the public boarding schools of the 19th century, whereas the secular nature of French state schools and the concept of a uniform and unifying education system go back to the great religious quarrels that culminated in the 1886 Jules Ferry laws. They might not like the French system any more as a result, but perhaps adopt a more rational attitude (. . . *développement du jugement et du raisonnement*).

These are differences at a profound level. Pupils are more likely to notice differences in day-to-day matters. Opinions are divided on how far course writers and teachers should draw attention to them.

On the one hand, it may be argued that highlighting the differences obscures fundamental similarities between Western cultures or human beings generally. Teachers who have organised exchanges have often found that pupils assign more

Box 19.4 Greeting conventions in different countries (Mebus *et al.*, 1987: 87)

importance to the warmth and friendliness of their hosts and how well they get on with their partner than to differences in food or conventions.

On the other hand, Byram *et al.* (1994) argue that even within the European context cultures are, in many ways, unique and they quote anthropologists to show that even superficial differences can lead to negative attitudes. Stereotypes are mainly produced by agencies outside school, such as the media and relatives, and have not been greatly altered in the past by language teaching (Byram, Esarte Sarries & Taylor, 1991).

So can foreign language teaching do more, particularly at the 11 to 16 level, to foster positive attitudes? The task will be made easier if some preconditions are fulfilled: liking for the teacher and subject, successful visits and exchanges, admiration evoked by some sporting personality or historical character, knowledge gained in the course about the target culture.

But one can deal directly with the problem of cultural stereotypes, and within the foreign language syllabus. The main aim should be to get pupils to *relativise* their own culture. They need to accept that:

(1) *Norms are place-specific.* Unless morally reprehensible, they are not inferior or strange. Greetings and behaviour at table are only two of several areas which offer examples. Box 19.4 shows how German exporters are informed pictorially by a bank about greeting conventions in different countries.

Box 19.5 Changing conventions in greetings (Mebus *et al.*, 1987: 86)

Box 19.6 Newspaper extract about changing attitudes to shaking hands (Mebus *et al.*, 1987: 87)

Händeschütteln kommt aus der Mode

Eine Umfrage in der Bundesrepublik Deutschland im Jahre 1984: Nur noch 55 % der Bundesbürger sind für das Händeschütteln bei der Begrüßung, 42 % sind dagegen. 3 % haben keine Meinung. 60 % der Männer begrüßen sich mit der Hand, aber nur 50 % der Frauen. 1973 waren noch 68 % der Bundesbürger für das Händeschütteln. Die Gegner des Händeschüttelns finden diese Begrüßungsform unangenehm, unhygienisch und überflüssig. Die Befürworter finden Händeschütteln menschlich, freundlich und herzlich.

The advertisement can also be used to practise reflexive and reciprocal verbs, with pupils having to match text and photographs:

(a) *Beide verbeugen sich*

(b) *Beide legen die Hände zusammen und verbeugen sich leicht*

(c) *Sie umarmen sich*

(d) *Sie umarmen und küssen sich*

(e) *Einer hebt den Hut, der andere die Hand*

(2) *Norms are time-specific.* Box 19.5 shows past conventions in greeting on the left, current practice on the right.

(a) *Er küsst ihr die Hand. Sie nickt mit dem Kopf.*

(b) *Sie geben sich die Hand, d.h. sie gibt ihm die Hand, und er gibt ihr die Hand.*

The newspaper extract in Box 19.6, which could be used for reading comprehension, shows that attitudes in Germany to shaking hands are changing.

Box 19.7 Comments by French exchange pupils about German life (Neuner *et al.*, 1991: 102–3)

En Allemagne, les parents dépensent beaucoup d'argent pour leurs enfants qui ont tous une chaîne Hi-Fi dans leur chambre. Les jeunes de Forchheim sont pl... que ceux de Bisca... ils peuv... et parf... pour q... chez d...

Die Eltern geben sehr viel Geld für ihre Kinder aus. Zum Beispiel steht in jedem Kinderzimmer eine Stereo-Anlage. Die Jugendlichen in Forchheim haben viel mehr Freiheiten als die in Biscarrosse. Sie dürfen abends sehr lange wegbleiben und dürfen sogar bei Freunden übernachten, wenn sie vorher zu Hause anrufen.

Comment vit une famille allemande

Les Allemands ne vivent pas comme nous. Ils gagnent plus d'argent e n'achètent pas les mêmes choses. Ils dépensent beaucoup pour leur maison et pour des articles de lux Chaque famille est propriétaire de sa maison. Ils ont de grosses voitures et en plus, ils possèdent des vélos ... mobylettes.

Wie eine deutsche Familie lebt

Die Deutschen leben anders als wir. Sie verdienen mehr und kaufen andere Sachen. Sie geben ihr Geld vor allem für ihr Haus und für Luxusartikel aus. Jede Familie hat ihr eigenes Haus. Ihre Autos sind groß, und dazu haben sie auch noch Fahrräder, Mopeds usw. Wir in Frankreich speisen lieber gepflegt, zu festen Tageszeiten, und verreisen in den Ferien. Die Deutschen dagegen haben lieber ein schönes Haus und ein neues Auto und bleiben in den Ferien zu Hause. Die Deutschen essen zu jeder denkbaren Zeit, aber es gibt nur kleine Mahlzeiten.

(3) *One can get used to different norms. Sprachbrücke* prints four fictitious letters home from German tourists abroad. In two countries people eat with their hands, but the food is excellent, in the third, punctuality at meals is not important, in the fourth the writer's previous aversion to rice is overcome by varied and tasty rice dishes. The point being made is that these cultural differences were accepted as facts and did not detract from the tourists' enjoyment.

(4) *One's own norms may appear strange to others.* In a survey of French secondary students' perceptions of foreign cultures, pupils in their fourth year of learning English held the following views:

The English drink tea, have enormous breakfasts, they carry sticks, wear bowler hats, gloves and kilts. They drive on the left in a rainy green country covered with castles, where a monster lives, where you can hear the sound of playing bagpipes all day long and where there is a queen, a king, princes and princesses. The main attraction is Big Ben. (Cain, 1990)

The absurdity of this picture could cause British pupils to reflect that their view of French or German life, gained perhaps from misunderstood items of information in their textbooks or in the media, might be similarly distorted. They might find it instructive to ascertain the perceptions of assistants and exchange partners before and after their stay in Britain.

(5) *How stereotypes are born.* In a French textbook for the teaching of German *Deutsch mit Spaß*, comments by French exchange pupils after a visit to a German town, reproduced in Box 19.7, were translated into German and used, together with other German texts, to practise indirect speech. There is no doubt, however, that they were also intended to show how easy it is to generalise from particular instances.

In conclusion the promotion of cultural awareness raises issues that are not easy to resolve. On the purely pragmatic side there is the question of how to integrate it with the promotion of linguistic proficiency, more fundamentally there is the question about the capacity of young people to accept and respect otherness. It is possible to study a foreign language at school and yet receive a shock on one's first direct experience of a foreign culture. On the other hand, if pupils have been given some knowledge about the historical roots of national cultures, including their own, and led to reflect on how stereotypes are born, their grasp of reality will have extended not only to new means of expresssion and to greater language awareness, but also to a greater and more sympathetic understanding of different cultural norms.

Concluding Remarks

The Language Elements: Separate or Integrated?

As the book nears completion, some questions about its approach and scope may need addressing.

The first concerns the basic decision to deal with the different elements of language separately. Is there not a fundamental interrelatedness between the elements that this decision seems to ignore? Words are pronounced in accordance with phonological rules and sequenced in accordance with grammatical rules. Vocabulary and grammar both express meaning; as Widdowson writes (1990: 87): 'Grammar simply formalizes the most widely applicable concepts, the highest common factors of experience: it provides for communicative economy'. The four modes of communication not only operate on the substance of language but are in close relationship with each other: listening presumes an act of speaking, reading an act of writing. Furthermore, in any teaching unit, at any level, a segment of language is presented as a unified whole, which makes its impact as such.

All this is true. Yet it is equally true that the way words in any one segment can or cannot be substituted, altered or combined with other words, and the way they are pronounced and spelt, is subject to rules or conventions that apply to other segments and to the language as a whole. If it were not so, human beings could not communicate in that language. Moreover, the rules or conventions are not the same for the different elements.

The implications for teachers are threefold. In dealing with any one segment of language, they will want to preserve its unity, so that pupils feel that they are working towards a specific objective, whether it be to achieve a communicative purpose in a given setting, perform a task or understand a text. Second teachers will have to decide which new items in that segment are required for immediate performance and which represent an important investment for the future, and what is involved in learning and teaching them. This is the field covered in my book. Third, and most importantly, they will have to ensure that new knowledge is integrated with old where it matters most, that is, in pupils' minds. And here too the suggestions made in the book about various revision activities may be useful.

Thus in any one lesson or series of lessons the focus may shift between these three objectives, concentrating now on one separate element, now on the segment as a whole, reflecting both the variety and unity of language.

What About the Learners and Classroom Techniques?

The absence of any discussion about learner characteristics may also be open to criticism. After all, the contact with pupils, in a class or as individuals, is at the heart of a teacher's professional life. At the start, one is fearful whether a class of 30 or more will be willing to cooperate; with experience, one sees a class not only as a group with its own dynamic, but as composed of individuals, with distinct personalities, strengths and needs; in retirement, one remembers a few individuals, rather than classes or lessons. As all books and experienced teachers stress, a good relationship between pupils and teacher, rather than any particular method, is the key to successful learning.

Trainee teachers, in particular, should possess some knowledge about the characteristics of pre-adolescent and adolescent pupils, about motivation and the building and maintenance of good working relations. Should this knowledge not have figured among the elements of foreign language teaching treated in the book?

There are several reasons why it was not included. One is that this information is available elsewhere (see, for example, Ur, (1996) and the materials for further reading recommended in it). Another is that these matters are not specific to foreign language teaching and are normally covered in general courses of initial training. The third, and in my view the most important reason, is that learning about children and young people from books is most effectively absorbed when it is combined with learning from seeing and doing, through visits to classes, observation and talking to teachers, and through one's own first attempts at teaching, so that description and experience reinforce each other.

For similar reasons I have not included a chapter on lesson-planning and classroom techniques, which constitute another essential aspect of teaching skill. General advice can be given about the need to decide on the lesson's main objective or core content, about effective questioning or the place of pair, group and class work, about balancing pace and variety with ensuring understanding and adequate practice (see Partington & Luker, 1984; Cajkler & Addelmann, 1992; Ur, 1996). But here too the advice will make most sense to trainee teachers when they see it applied in practice, can discuss with the teachers the reasons for a particular sequence or activity, and can try their own hand at teaching with a class they have observed and whose level they know. In time expertise will develop.

Language — The Fundamental Element

In short, knowing the language and knowing about language is only one aspect of a teacher's professional competence. Yet it is an essential part: the foreign language is after all the subject to be taught, the one constant element compared with the many variables of pupil characteristics, class size or resources that a teacher encounters.

Moreover it is the only aspect where new entrants to the profession do not start at the beginning, but possess knowledge and experience on which they can build. They have linguistic skill, some first-hand acquaintance with the foreign country and its culture, and, in most cases, recollections of their own, not too distant learning. All of these can now be brought into use for a new purpose, directly and without the need of a mentor.

They will probably need guidance in looking at the foreign language from the viewpoint of a beginner or a learner at the intermediate stage; they may also need to examine more closely elements of the foreign language which they have hitherto used unreflectingly. For all these purposes they should have found this book helpful.

As for more experienced members of the profession, I hope that the attempt to bring together the analysis of language, the description of learning and some practical suggestions for teaching will have appeared worth while and convincing, and that some of the details will have proved new and interesting. I also hope that my own enduring fascination with language and my belief in the value of foreign language teaching will have come through.

Appendix: French and German Classroom Expressions

The following is a list of expressions used by French- and German-speaking pupils to each other and to the teacher.

The French list is fuller because a whole class was asked by their English teacher to write down expressions for homework. Most of them have been reproduced here, with figures in brackets to show the frequency of use, but without the spelling mistakes (see Chapter 12). Although the sample is small, it is interesting to note that in speaking to a fellow pupil both the imperative and a more polite form with *pouvoir* are used. In asking the teacher for permission there is a preponderance of the statement form with a rising intonation *je peux?*, but *est-ce que je . . .* and *puis-je . . .* are also frequent.

The German list is an amalgam of lists drawn up by a German teacher, her teacher husband and teacher son and former (primary school) colleagues, and by a Swiss teacher and her three teenage children: it is therefore representative, *exemplarisch*, rather than full.

French

To another pupil

> *Prête-moi ta gomme (2), règle.*
> *Tu me prêtes ta gomme?*
> *Tu peux me prêter ta règle?*
> *Tu n'aurais pas un stylo à me prêter?*
> *Quelqu'un aurait une règle, un crayon, une feuille?*
> *Est-ce que je peux t'emprunter ta règle?*
> *Tu n'as pas des crayons en double?*
> *Tu peux me passer ta colle?*
> *Tiens, passe-moi ton stylo.*
> *Donne-moi ça.*
> *Fais voir ta feuille.*
> *Rends-moi ma règle.*
> *Moi, j'ai réussi mon contrôle et toi?*

To the teacher

Asking for permission

Je peux aller aux toilettes (2), aux WC (2), me laver les mains (2), ouvrir la fenêtre, fermer le store, les volets (2), allumer la lumière, sortir, me déplacer, changer de place, ramasser les copies, effacer le tableau (3)?

Est-ce que je peux aller aux toilettes (2), aux WC, à l'infirmerie, chercher mon crayon, me déplacer, ouvrir/fermer les fenêtres, demander qqch. à ma copine?

Puis-je aller aux toilettes (2), ouvrir la fenêtre/les volets, changer de place, aller au tableau, sortir?

Questions and requests

Vous pouvez répéter? (6), répéter la question/la phrase? vous pouvez vous pousser? fermer la fenêtre (2)/ les volets (2)?

Est-ce qu'on souligne?

Est-ce qu'on a des devoirs?

Qu'est-ce qu'on a pour demain?

Qu'est-ce qu'il y a à faire pour demain?

Quelle est la consigne?

Que veut dire ce mot?

Quel est le sens de cette phrase?

Quelle est la date?

Excuses and general

J'ai oublié mon livre (7), mon cahier (6), mes affaires (5), ma trousse (3), mon classeur, mon compas, mon équerre, mes outils de géometrie, de faire mon exercice (4), de faire signer le contrôle (2).

J'ai perdu ma feuille, mon cahier, mon contrôle, un crayon.

Je me suis trompé d'exercice.

Monsieur, je n'ai pas fait mon exercice (6), mes devoirs, le travail pour aujourd'hui, signer mon contrôle, ma feuille.

Je n'ai pas compris la consigne, l'exercice, la question, ce qu'il fallait faire.

Je n'ai pas (tout) compris.

Excusez-moi, Monsieur, je n'ai rien compris.

Monsieur, j'ai terminé, j'ai fini; moi, je sais; je ne sais pas.

Monsieur, je suis malade, je ne me sens pas bien.

Ma chaise est cassée.

Excusez-moi, Monsieur, le soleil me gêne.

Complaints about other pupils

Il m'embête. Il n'arrête pas de m'embêter (2), de me prendre mes affaires.

Il a pris mon stylo, déchiré ma feuille, m'a mis un coup de pied.

On m'a volé un crayon et mon compas. On a joué avec mon compas.

German

To another pupil

Gib mal deinen Bleistift, ich hab' keinen.

Kannst (du) mir einen Bleistift geben?

Kannst du mir mal eben deinen Bleistift geben, ich hab' meinen vergessen, ich kann meinen nicht finden.

Hast (du) mal einen Bleistift (usw.) (für mich)?

Kann ich deinen Radiergummi ausleihen?

Ich hab' mein Milchgeld vergessen. Kannst du mir was borgen? Bis morgen.

Hast du mal ein Brot für mich? Meine Mutter hat verschlafen und ich hab' solchen Hunger!

Paß auf, das ist mein . . .

He du — gib mir sofort meinen Rechner zurück.

Haben wir was auf?

Hast du das kapiert? ich nicht.

Was hast du denn in der 2 Aufgabe 'raus? Kannst (du) mir mal sagen, was bei (Nr) Aufgabe 'rauskommt?

Zeigst du mir mal schnell deine Hausaufgaben? Kann ich sie abschreiben?

Wie hast du das denn gerechnet? Mein Ergebnis kann nicht stimmen.

Hast du diese Mathe-Aufgabe geschnallt (= hingekriegt)? Ja, ich habe sie gecheckt.

(Am Telefon) Kannst du mir schnell die Deutschaufgabe erklären?

Wie findest du den Herrn M.? — Ganz schön langweilig! Den find'ich echt blöd, nicht gut.

Uff — immer diese vielen Aufgaben!

Find'st du nicht auch, wir sollten (müßten) mal . . . machen, tun?

To the teacher

Asking for permission

Kann ich schnell aufs WC?

Kann ich mal eben aufs Klo?

Frau Meier, ich muß dringend aufs Klo!

Frau R. kann ich den Platz wechseln — ich sehe nicht gut an die Wandtafel.

Questions and requests

Das verstehe ich nicht, hab' ich nicht verstanden.

Ich habe Sie nicht verstanden Frau M. Können/könnten Sie das bitte nochmals erklären?

Ich habe nicht alles gehört — Könnten Sie es nochmals sagen?

Ich bin nicht mitgekommen. Können Sie das (mal) wiederholen?—Frau J. es läutet! Können wir in die Pause?

Kann ich nach Hause gehen? Ich habe Kopfschmerzen. Mir ist schlecht.

Excuses

Ich habe mein Lesebuch, Heft (usw.) vergessen!

Ich kann mein Lesebuch gar nicht finden!

Meine Mutter hat mein Lesebuch nicht eingesteckt!
Ich habe vergessen, die Wörter aufzuschreiben.
Ich habe meine Hausaufgaben nicht gemacht.
Ich habe meine Hausaufgaben vergessen. Ich habe sie zuhaus auf dem Schreibtisch liegen lassen.
Ich habe gar nicht mehr an die Aufgaben gedacht. Hatten wir denn welche auf?
Ich wußte nicht, daß wir 'was aufhatten.
Mein kleiner Bruder hat mein Heft verschmiert/zerrissen.
Meine Oma hatte Geburtstag, da sind wir erst um 9 Uhr abends zu Hause gewesen.
Entschuldigung ich bin zu spät, ich habe vergessen den Wecker zu stellen.
Ich habe verschlafen, den Bus verpaßt.
Ich hatte einen Platten.

Complaints about a fellow pupil

Mein Bleistift ist weg.
Der Michael nervt mich furchtbar.
Der hat mir XXX weggenommen.

References

Alderson, J.C. and Urquhart, A.H. (1984) *Reading in a Foreign Language*. Harlow, Essex: Longman.

Armstrong, L.E. (1932) *The Phonetics of French*. London: Bell.

Assessment of Performance Unit (APU) (1985) *Foreign Language Performance in Schools. Report on 1983 Survey of French, German and Spanish*. London: HMSO.

Assessment of Performance Unit (APU) (1987a) *Foreign Language Performance in Schools. Report on 1985 Survey of French*. London: HMSO.

Assessment of Performance Unit (APU) (1987b) *Listening and Reading*. Windsor: NFER–Nelson.

Assessment of Performance Unit (APU) (1987c) *Writing*. Windsor: NFER–Nelson.

Barnett, M.A. (1989) *More than Meets the Eye*. Englewood Cliffs, NJ: Prentice Hall.

Beck, T. (1993) Du gleichst dem Geist, den du begreifst. *German Teaching* 7, 28–32.

Belyaev, B. (1963) *The Psychology of Teaching Foreign Languages*. Oxford: Pergamon.

Bérard, E. and Lavenne, C. (1991) *Grammaire utile du français*. Paris: Hatier/Didier.

Berman, R.A. (1986) A step-by-step model of language learning. In I. Levin (ed.) *Stage and Structure: Reopening the Debate*. Norwood, NJ: Ablex.

Bialystok, E. (1990) *Communication Strategies*. Oxford: Blackwell.

Blas, A. *et al.* (1990) Combien ça coûte? *Le Français dans le Monde* 235 (août/septembre).

Böll, H. (1953) *Und sagte kein einziges Wort*, quoted here from *Und sagte kein einziges Wort, Haus ohne Hüter, Das Brot der frühen Jahre*, 1973. Köln: Kiepenheuer und Witsch.

Bowerman, M. (1982) Reorganisational processes in lexical and syntactic development. In E. Wanner and L. R. Gleitmann (eds) *Language Acquisition: The State of the Art*. Cambridge: Cambridge University Press.

Bransford, J.D. (1979) *Human Cognition: Learning, Understanding and Remembering*. Belmont: Wadsworth.

Brecht, B. (1964) *Gedichte*. Frankfurt am Main: Suhrkamp.

Brown, P. and Levenson, S.C. (1987) *Politeness*. Cambridge: Cambridge University Press.

Buhlmann, R. (1984) The effects of readability on the understanding of texts in a second language. In H. Martin and A. K. Pugh (eds) *Reading in a Foreign Language* (pp. 18.–38). York: Goethe Institute.

Byram, M. (1989) *Cultural Studies in Foreign Language Education*. Clevedon: Multilingual Matters.

Byram, M., Esarte-Sarries, V. and Taylor, S. (1991) *Cultural Studies and Language Learning: A Research Report*. Clevedon: Multilingual Matters.

Byram, M., Morgan, C. and colleagues (1994) *Teaching-and-Learning Language-and-Culture*. Clevedon: Multilingual Matters.

Cain, A. (1990) French secondary school students' perceptions of foreign cultures. *Language Learning Journal* 2, 48–52.

Cajkler, W. and Addelmann, R. (1992) *The Practice of Foreign Language Teaching*. London: David Fulton.

Camus, A. (1947) *La Peste*, quoted here from *Théâtre, Récits, Nouvelles* 1962. Paris: Editions Gallimard.

Carter, R. (1987) *Vocabulary*. London: Allen and Unwin.

Ceppi, M. (1935) *Notes on the Teaching of French*. London: Bell.

Chaudron, C. (1988) *Second Language Classrooms*. Cambridge: Cambridge University Press.

Clark, H.H. and Clark, E.V. (1977) *Psychology and Language*. New York: Harcourt Brace Jovanovich.

Commager, H.S. (1970) *Meet the USA*. New York: Institute of International Relations.

→Cook, V. (1991) *Second Language Learning and Teaching*. London: Edward Arnold.

Corder, S.P. (1967) The significance of learners' errors. *International Review of Applied Linguistics* 5, 161–9.

Cronbach, L.J. (1954) *Educational Psychology*. New York: Harcourt, Brace.

Crystal, D. (1986) *Listen to Your Child*. Harmondsworth, Middlesex: Penguin.

Crystal, D. (1987) *The Cambridge Encyclopedia of Language*. Cambridge: Cambridge University Press.

Davies, A., Criper, C. and Howatt, A.P.R. (eds) (1984) *Interlanguage*. Edinburgh: Edinburgh University Press.

Davis, P. and Rinvolucri, M. (1988) *Dictation: New Methods, New Possibilities*. Cambridge: Cambridge University Press.

DES (1990) *Modern Foreign Languages for Ages 11 to 16*. London: HMSO.

DES (1991) *Modern Foreign Languages in the National Curriculum* (Statutory Orders). London: HMSO.

Deutscher Volkshochschul-Verband (1980) *Grundbausteine zum Zertifikat Dänisch, Englisch, Französisch, Italienisch, usw.* Bonn: Deutscher Volkshochschul-Verband.

Dreyer, H. and Schmitt, R. (1985) *Lehr- und Übungsbuch der deutschen Grammatik*. Ismaning/München: Verlag für Deutsch.

Dulay, H. and Burt, M. (1974) Natural sequences in child second language acquisition. *Language Learning* 24, 37–53.

Ellis, R. (1987) *Second Language Acquisition in Context*. Englewood Cliffs, NJ: Prentice Hall.

Ellis, R. (1990) *Instructed Second Language Acquisition*. Oxford: Blackwell.

Faerch, C. (1985) Meta talk in FL classroom discourse. *Studies in Second Language Acquisition* 7, 184–99.

Felix, S. (1982) *Psycholinguistische Aspekte des Zweitsprachenerwerbs*. Tübingen: Günter Narr.

Frisch, M. (1961) *Andorra*. Frankfurt am Main: Suhrkamp.

Gagné, M. (1985) *The Conditions of Learning* (4th edn) New York: Holt, Rinehart and Winston.

Gairns, R. and Redman, S. (1986) *Working with Words*. Cambridge: Cambridge University Press.

Gougenheim, G., Michéa, R., Rivenc, P. and Sauvageot, A. (1956) *L'Élaboration du français élémentaire*. Paris: Didier.

Grauberg, W. (1971) An error analysis in German of first-year university students. In G.E. Perren and J.L.M. Trim (eds) *Applications of Linguistics. Selected Papers of the Second International Congress of Applied Linguistics, Cambridge 1969* (pp. 257–63). Cambridge: Cambridge University Press.

Green, P. and Hecht, K. (1992) Implicit and explicit grammar: an empirical study. *Applied Linguistics*, 13, 169–84.

Greenberg, J.H. (1966) *Language Universals: With Special Reference to Feature Hierarchies*. The Hague: Mouton.

Grunwald, B., Lamp, M. and R. and Rolinger, H. (1981) *Échanges* Bks 1–3. Stuttgart: Klett.

Hall, C. (1992) *Modern German Pronunciation*. Manchester: Manchester University Press.

Hammer, A.E. (1991) *German Grammar and Usage* (2nd edn) revised by Martin Durrell. London: Edward Arnold.

Harley, B. and Swain, M. (1984) The interlanguage of immersion students and its implications for second language teaching. In A. Davies, C. Criper, and A.P.R. Howatt, (eds) *Interlanguage* (pp. 291–311). Edinburgh: Edinburgh University Press.

⌐⟩ Harley, B., Allen, P., Cummins, J. and Swain M. (1990) *The Development of Second Language Proficiency*. Cambridge: Cambridge University Press.

Häussermann, U., Dietrich,G., Günther, C.C., Woods U. and Zenkner, H. (1989) *Sprachkurs Deutsch* Bks 1–4. Frankfurt am Main: Moritz Diesterweg.

Hawkins, E. (1981) *Modern Languages in the Curriculum*. Cambridge: Cambridge University Press.

Hawkins, J.A. (1986) *A Comparative Typology of English and German*. London: Croom Helm.

⌐⟩ Hawkins, R. and Towell, R. (1992) Second language acquisition research and the second language acquisition of French. *French Language Studies* 2, 97–121.

Hecht, K. and Green, P.S. (1993) Englischunterricht im Gymnasium: Wie wachsen Wissen und Können? Eine empirische Untersuchung zur Entwicklung der Lernersprache. *Die Neueren Sprachen* 92, 196–214.

Hewer, S. (1989) *Making the Most of IT skills*. London: CILT.

Hudson, R. (1992) *Teaching Grammar*. Oxford: Blackwell.

Incorporated Association of Assistant Masters (1956) *The Teaching of Modern Languages* (3rd edn) London: University of London Press.

Incorporated Association of Assistant Masters 1967: *The Teaching of Modern Languages* (4th edn) London: University of London Press.

Johnstone, R. (1989) *Communicative Interaction: A Guide for Language Teachers*. London: CILT.

Karmiloff-Smith, A. (1986) From meta-processes to conscious access: evidence from children' metalinguistic and repair data. *Cognition* 23, 95–147.

Kasper, G. (1990) Linguistic Politeness: Current Research Issues. *Journal of Pragmatics* 14 (2), 193–218.

Kavanagh, B. (1988) *Pigé* Bks 1–4. Walton-on-Thames: Nelson.

Kavanagh, B. and Upton, L. (1994) *Creative Use of Texts*. London: CILT.

King, L. and Boaks, P. (eds) (1994) *Grammar! A Conference Report*. London: CILT.

Klapper, J. (1992a) Reading in a foreign language: theoretical issues. *Language Learning Journal* 5, 27–30.

Klapper, J. (1992b) Preliminary considerations for the teaching of FL reading. *Language Learning Journal* 6, 53–6.

Klapper, J. (1993) Practicable skills and practical constraints in FL reading. *Language Learning Journal*, 7, 50–4.

Krashen, S.D. (1985) *The Input Hypothesis: Issues and Implications*. Harlow, Essex: Longman.

Lightbown, P.M. (1990) Process–product research on second language learning in classrooms. In B. Harley, P. Allen, J. Cummins and M. Swain (eds): *The Development of Second Language Proficiency* (pp. 82–92). Cambridge: Cambridge University Press.

⌐⟩ Lightbown, P.M. and Spada N. (1993) *How Languages are Learned*. Oxford: Oxford University Press.

Littlewood, W.T. (1981) *Communicative Language Teaching*. Cambridge: Cambridge University Press.

Maas, H. (N.D.) *Wörter erzählen Geschichten*. München: Deutscher Taschenbuch Verlag.

Maddox, H. (19XX) *How to Study*. London: Pan Books. Quoted in Child, D. (1993) Psychology and the Teacher (5th edn) (p. 140), London: Cassell.

McCarthy, M. and Carter, R. (1994) *Language as Discourse: Perspectives for Language Teaching*. Harlow, Essex: Longman.

MacCarthy P. (1975a) *The Pronunciation of French*. London: Oxford University Press.

MacCarthy P. (1975b) *The Pronunciation of German*. London: Oxford University Press.

Martineau, R. and McGivney, J. (1973) *French Pronunciation*. Oxford: Oxford University Press.

⌐⟩ McLaughlin, B. (1987) *Theories of Second Language Acquisition*. London: Edward Arnold.

McNab U. (1969) *Ealing Course in German*. Harlow, Essex: Longman.

Meara, P.M. (1980) Vocabulary acquisition: a neglected aspect of language learning. *Language Teaching and Linguistics Abstracts* 13 (4), 221–46.

Mebus, G., Pauldrach, A., Rall, M. and Rösler, D. (1987) *Sprachbrücke* Bks. 1,2. Stuttgart: Ernst Klett.

Miller, G.A. (1956) The magical number seven, plus or minus two. *Psychological Review* 63, 81–97.

Ministère de l'Éducation Nationale (1985) *COLLÈGES: Programmes et Instructions*. Paris: Centre National de Documentation Pédagogique.

Minuth, C. (1991) Freie Texte im Anfangsunterricht Französisch. *Der Fremdsprachliche Unterricht* 3, 18–23.

Morgan, C. (1994) Creative writing in foreign language teaching. *Language Learning Journal* 10, 44–7.

Muckle, J. (1981) The foreign language lesson in the Soviet Union: Observing teachers at work. *Modern Languages* LXII, 153–63.

Mummert, I. (1991) Kreatives Schreiben im Fremdsprachenunterricht. *Der Fremdsprachliche Unterricht* 3, 4–11.

Nation, I.S.P. (1982) Beginning to learn foreign vocabulary: A review of the research. *RELC Journal* (Singapore) 13 (1), 14–36.

Nation, I.S.P. 1990: *Teaching and Learning Vocabulary*. Rowley, MA: Newbury House.

Neuner, G. (1989) Spielend schreiben lernen. *Fremdsprache Deutsch* 1, 32.

Neuner, G. *et al.* (1988) *Deutsch mit Spaß 4e, 3e*. Paris: Belin.

Nott, D. (1988) A topic based, integrated approach. In DES/Regional Course *Modern Languages for the 16–18 Age Group* (pp. 23–30). Nottingham: In-service Unit, School of Education, University of Nottingham.

Nott, D. (1992) Qui a peur du subjonctif? *Francophonie* 6, 2–13.

Nott, D. (1994) Pronunciation: Does it matter? *Francophonie* 9, 2–17.

Nunan, D. (1989) *Designing Tasks for the Communicative Classroom*. Cambridge: Cambridge University Press.

Nuttall C. (1982) *Teaching Reading Skills in a Foreign Language*. London: Heinemann Educational.

Page, B. (1990) *What Do You Mean . . . It's Wrong?*. London: CILT.

Page, B. and Moys, A. (1982) *Lire*. Cambridge: Cambridge University Press.

Palmer, H.E. (1917) *The Scientific Study and Teaching of Languages*. London: Harrap. (Reissued 1968 Oxford University Press.)

Partington, J. and Luker, P. (1984) *Teaching Modern Languages*. Basingstoke: Macmillan.

Pearson, J.A. (1992) Reflections of a teacher turned pupil. *Language Learning Journal* 5, 38–9.

Peck, A.J. (1988) *Language Teachers at Work*. Hemel Hempstead: Prentice Hall.

Piepho, H.-E. (1980) *Deutsch als Fremdsprache in Unterrichtsskizzen*. Wiesbaden: Quelle und Meyer.

Pinker, S. 1994: *The Language Instinct*. London: Penguin.

Pohl, L., Schlecht, G. and Uthess, S. (1978) *Methodik. Englisch — und Französischunterricht*. Berlin: Volk und Wissen.

Price, G. (1991) *An Introduction to French Pronunciation*. Oxford: Blackwell.

Quirk, R. and Greenbaum S. (1973) *A University Grammar of English*. Harlow, Essex: Longman.

Rivers, W.M. (1975) *A Practical Guide to the Teaching of French*. New York: Oxford University Press.

Rivers, W.M. (1981) *Teaching Foreign-Language Skills* (2nd edn). Chicago: University of Chicago Press.

Roberts, J.T. (1986) Linguistics in the teaching of German. In *German in the United Kingdom* (pp. 100–9). London: CILT.

Sanderson, A. (1982) *Modern Language Teachers In Action*. York: Language Materials Development Unit of the University of York.

Saragi, T., Nation, I.S.P. and Meister, G.F. (1978) Vocabulary learning and reading. *System* 6 (2), 72–8.

Selinker, L. (1972) Interlanguage. *International Review of Applied Linguistics* 10, 209-30.

Shiffrin, R.M. and Schneider, W. (1977) Controlled and automatic human information processing. II: Perceptual learning, automatic attending and a general theory. *Psychological Review* 84, 127–90.

Sidwell, D. and Capoore, P. (1983) *Deutsch Heute* Bks. 1–3. Walton-on-Thames: Nelson.

Slobin, D.I. (1973) Cognitive pre-requisites for the development of grammar. In C.A. Ferguson and D.I. Slobin (eds) *Studies of Child Language Development* (pp. 175–208). New York: Holt, Rinehart and Winston.

Southern Examining Group (1992) *Chief Examiners' Reports Summer 1992 Examinations: French.* Guildford: SEG.

Stevick, E.W. (1976) *Memory, Meaning and Method.* Rowley, MA: Newbury House.

Stubbs, M. (1983) *Discourse Analysis.* Oxford: Blackwell.

Stubbs, M. (1986) *Educational Linguistics.* Oxford: Blackwell.

Swarbrick, A. (1990) *Reading for Pleasure in a Foreign Language.* London: CILT.

Sweet, H. (1899) *The Practical Study of Languages.* London: Dent. (Reissued 1964 Oxford University Press).

Towell, R. (1987) Variability and progress in the language development of advanced learners of a foreign language. In R. Ellis, *Second Language Acquisition in Context* (pp. 113–27) London: Prentice Hall.

Tranel, R. (1987) *The Sounds of French.* Cambridge: Cambridge University Press.

University of Nottingham (1988) *Modern Languages for the 16–18 Age Group.* Nottingham: In-Service Unit, School of Education.

University of Oxford Delegacy of Local Examinations (1991) *Advanced Level Summer Examination 1992 Chief Examiners Reports: Modern Languages.* Oxford: UODLE.

Ur, P. (1996) *A Course in Language Teaching.* Cambridge: Cambridge University Press.

Van Ek, J.A. (1976) *The Threshold Level for Modern Language Learning in Schools.* Strasbourg: Council of Europe (Extended edition, 1977 Longman).

von Essen, O. (1956) *Grundzüge der hochdeutschen Satzintonation.* Ratingen/Düsseldorf: A.Henn.

Vigner, G. (1975) *Écrire et convaincre.* Paris: Hachette.

Vinay, J.P. and Darbelnet, J.L. (1958) *Stylistique comparée du français et de l'anglais: méthode de traduction.* Paris: Didier.

Watkin, K. (1996) Put a sock in the garlic and Chanel No 5. *Times Educational Supplement* 26 April.

Weinert, R. (1987) Processes in classroom second language development: The acquisition of negation in German. In R. Ellis (ed.), *Second Language Acquisition in Context* (pp. 83–9). London: Prentice Hall.

Weinert, R. (1990) A study of classroom second language development. Unpublished PhD Thesis, University of Edinburgh.

Whitehead, A.N. (1932) *The Aims of Education.* London: Benn.

Widdowson, H.G. (1989) Knowledge of language and ability for use. *Applied Linguistics* 10, 128–37.

Widdowson, H.G. (1990) *Aspects of Language Teaching.* Oxford: Oxford University Press.

Wilkins, D.A. (1972) *Linguistics in Language Teaching.* London: Edward Arnold.

Willis, D. (1990) *The Lexical Syllabus.* London: Collins.

Yorios, C. (1971) Some sources of reading problems for foreign language learners. *Language Learning* 21, 107–15.

Index